WRITTEN IN THE STARS

FOOTBALL, AN ARMCHAIR AND THE SEARCH FOR A HAPPY ENDING

RICHARD STOKOE

ISBN 978-1-909122-98-7

I_AM SELF-PUBLISHING

🐦@iamselfpub
www.iamselfpublishing.com

With thanks to my family and friends, who have all contributed to this, whether they realise it or not; to Chelsea Football Club, without whom this book might never have ended; and a special thank you to Vanessa for her unending support and supreme levels of tolerance.

In memory of

John Reginald Stokoe, 1930 - 1997

and

Imelda 'Mel' Holmes, 1958 - 2014

Contents

Part Three: Where The Grass Is Greener

Part Four: Something Pretty Miraculous

Part Five: The Impossible Dream

Introduction

There are a lot of us out there. For every one of the loyal and dedicated fans who regularly part with their hard-earned cash to go and support their team, there might be 10, maybe even 100 who don't, but who are still adversely affected by the outcome of a game that they've chosen to avoid. We are effectively hiding under stones; busying ourselves with other aspects of our lives, but always with an eye on what's happening at Stamford Bridge, Old Trafford, Kingsmeadow, or wherever it may be. The nature of football fandom has changed since the days when the only way to follow your club was to join the tens of thousands who would line the terraces of football grounds every Saturday afternoon or on a midweek evening to cheer on, or shout abuse at, their team. The advent of Sky TV in the UK has offered the game to the masses, and now, anyone who is willing to pay for the privilege can watch two or three games a week in the comfort of their own home. If you're a supporter of one of the bigger clubs, then you'll be lucky enough to catch your team on TV once or twice a month. If not, you can listen to a commentary or watch a transcribed version unfold via the Internet. This plays into the hands of someone like me perfectly. I call myself a football fan because I suffer the way that other fans do, but my own relationship with the game is more like that of a bad pen pal. Every week, often twice, I receive news of how my team is getting on via the radio, Internet or TV, and in return, I offer nothing; I just display varying degrees of happiness or misery.

I'm not proud of having let an away defeat at West Bromwich Albion or a 4-4 draw with Aston Villa threaten to spoil what would otherwise have been perfectly enjoyable evenings spent with family or friends. I have often been proud of my team's achievements though, to the extent that a large part of me feels that I can actually claim them as my own. In that respect, I'm no different to other supporters. Other books have been written about football that explore what it is to be a fan, and in essence, *Written in the Stars* is no different in that I started writing it to try to get my head around exactly why the game has affected me the way that it has. I'm sure there are a lot of people who'll relate to many of my experiences, but I'm also fully aware that those same people, and plenty of others, might be totally bemused by some of the ways that football has affected my thinking. As a form of therapy, it's helped, but nothing could have helped more than the improbable story that developed whilst I was writing it, and all thanks to one remarkable football club.

And for any Manchester United fans out there, I apologise, but then every story needs a villain...

Part One

From Genesis to Relegation

Moscow

In a world where a man can become immortal with one kick of a ball, a whole season's worth of sweat and endeavour has led us to a rain-sodden patch of grass in Moscow. There is no separating the teams. After 90 minutes of normal time and an extra 30 added, the deadlock cannot be broken. There is only one way to settle this epic contest: now is the time that, from a band of weary footballers, a hero will emerge. Forward they stride – Tevez, Ballack, Carrick, Belletti – each holding their nerve to score a penalty for their people. And then, to the shock of some and the joy of others, up steps one of the planet's most gifted athletes; and he misses. You can see it in his eyes. Cristiano Ronaldo knows that he, and he alone, has cost Manchester United their third European Cup. The shoot-out labours on, each penalty converted, until the moment arrives. Destiny sits proudly on the broad shoulders of John Terry as he walks forth and prepares to declare Chelsea the winners of Europe's top prize for the first time in the club's history. Chelsea's captain, England's captain; it's written in the stars. Roman Abramovich, the club's owner, a face in the crowd, in his home country and about to see his dreams realised.

Silence descends. In the distance, a crow caws.

Terry looks assured, he takes two steps back. Edwin Van der Sar looks nervous, and could be forgiven for walking away, but he is a professional. He stands his ground. The kick is taken; he dives to his left and turns his head to the right to see the ball soar past him. The net bulges.

Pandemonium.

A once still sea of blue erupts in crashing waves. Roman staggers onto the pitch and drops to his knees, hands held high, reaching for the sky in victory, the dream made real.

There is a mist around the edges of this picture, and a string section soars to a yearning crescendo, reminiscent of the famous death scene in *Platoon*, before launching into a thunderous rendition of *1812 Overture*.

*

That's how it should have ended. All football should be played out like a film. In the case of the European Champions League Final of 2008, the director would have taken care to choose the best ending of the two he'd shot to be included in the cinematic version. After much painstaking deliberation, he would dismiss the notion that the unexpected makes for better art, succumbing instead to the demands of economics and some men in suits, thus giving the public the ending they want. After all, he could always throw the alternative ending onto the DVD as a bonus.

Someone hadn't read the script properly on that night in Moscow. There's little else that could explain the sudden and unfathomable inclusion of a moment of tragedy in a film in which it clearly had no place. Ronaldo had already missed and nobody had paid to see a farce: to add not one but two twists was just unnecessary. John Terry had to score, for the sake of a good story, but someone decided to throw in a banana skin moment and the captain was the unfortunate victim. Football is a form of entertainment, but the game's history is peppered with bad endings like this, errors of judgement that squeeze the last ounce of romance out of the sport: Wembley 1983, Ashton Gate 2001, Stamford Bridge 2009; the list goes on.

As it was, Chelsea lost, and I was devastated. If it hadn't been for the events of 15th September 1984, I'd have been ecstatic.

For Every Bobby, There'll Be A Jimmy — 1976/77

Of all the thoughts running through his mind as a football lands at his feet and he finds himself free on the edge of the Manchester United penalty box at Wembley Stadium one sunny afternoon in 1976, it's probable that Bobby Stokes is thinking little about the effect his next decision might have on the welfare of a six-year-old boy in a small town in East Sussex. As he fires the ball beyond the despairing dive of Alex Stepney, that six-year-old boy is about to learn a valuable lesson. Southampton's 1-0 FA Cup Final win over United in May 1976 has taught me that there are some things in life that can cause us to be miserable, despite being beyond our control. I am used to being told off by grown-ups when I've done something wrong, but as far as I'm aware, I've never done anything to Bobby Stokes, and nor have I done anything today to constitute the goal being arranged as a punishment for bad behaviour. I'd assumed football to be an entertainment just like any other. Television to me means an escape, and I watch cartoons and films, safe in the knowledge that the result won't affect my life in a negative way. The game was on TV and, consequently, I have no proof that the events were real, so there is no reason for me to feel anything other than the same mild disappointment that a flawed episode of *Hector's House* might cause. And yet, somehow, I know that this is different. Without having watched a second of the game, I already know who the goodies and baddies are, as that had already been determined by a decision I'd made two years earlier. My team have lost a football match and there is absolutely nothing that I could have done to prevent it. Isn't every movie supposed to have a happy ending, one that'll make everyone, without exception, glad that they sat through it? It seems clear to me that, to most people, on this day, and in this particular story, Southampton are the heroes and this is the fairy-tale outcome they all wanted. I feel helpless, and I feel alone.

I learned another important lesson from the same match: sometimes, those people you look up to, and seek guidance and reassurance from, don't tell the truth. At the beginning of the long, hot summer of 1976, there had been more than a passing mention of Manchester United on the television and radio. In the week leading up to the FA Cup Final, the talk that met my ears was of exactly how easily United would beat lowly Southampton, then of the Second Division. I was excited and, as these words were coming from adult mouths, I believed them all. There was no way United could lose. I'd been too young to appreciate the significance of the FA Cup before, but it was special now. My team were being talked about, so now it really meant something. But they lost, and when the game was over, somebody in my family mentioned that, "It's not all bad, at least Bobby Stokes scored the goal, and his name sounds a bit like yours". This was a crumb of comfort thrown at me in a desperate attempt at consolation, and it was a crumb that I gratefully accepted, despite its rotten taste. At least the scorer of the goal that beat my team in the Cup Final had a similar surname to my own. Similar to, but not the same as. It was the slenderest of silver linings amid the darkest of clouds.

*

I could have chosen anyone. It was 1974 and I was five-years-old. We lived in Didcot, Oxfordshire, which is near both Reading and Oxford, so I could have opted for either Reading FC or Oxford United. My Dad supported West Ham at the time and my Mum, Wolverhampton Wanderers (because of the handsome gold shirts I believe), so I could have followed in either of their footsteps. My eldest brother, Ian, supported Chelsea and my not quite as old but still 10 years older brother, Andrew, supported Manchester United, so they too were always an option. But I had never been pushed in either direction; Ian had already left home and Andrew's interest in football was on the wane. It was initially suggested that I should support Stoke City. In what would become a recurring theme, the reason for this was simply that choosing a team whose name sounded a little like my own was as good a reason as any to pledge lifelong allegiance. But I'd first developed an interest in football as a result of a newfound enthusiasm for the game of Subbuteo and the need to embrace the sport that it represented, and that's why Stoke City were never a realistic option. I didn't have the Stoke City Subbuteo team, whereas I did have the Manchester United one. And so it all began.

*

It's now one year on from the Southampton horror show, and I am once again sat in front of the television, about to watch my team playing in the FA Cup Final. Whereas a year ago, I'd been certain that United would win because I'd been told as much, I'm seven-years-old now, and this time, I will not be fooled. I knew nothing about the way football worked last year, but now I know a bit more. I've taken an interest in my team's results, and I've learned that United don't always win when I expect them to: they are just as likely to get hammered by West Bromwich Albion or Queens Park Rangers as they are of knocking four past Everton, and as such, football isn't an easy thing to predict. I've also learned that if Manchester United lose, the abuse I will receive from school-friends will be merciless. The fact that I had a football team had helped me to settle in at my new school, when we'd moved to Bexhill-on-Sea in 1975. Football had helped to break the ice with my new classmates. Within a year, however, following defeat to Southampton and Bobby Stokes, I'd learned that football can also be a curse, and thinking about what might happen if we lose today makes me all the more nervous. But I know that United are the underdogs in '77, and this gives me hope. They'd been the favourites in '76 and they'd lost. Liverpool have just become League champions for the second successive season, and the general consensus is that they will win the final, thus completing the hallowed League and Cup double for the first time in their history. The people saying these things know nothing; they've forgotten how wrong they'd been last year.

As Liverpool, the League champions, get the game started, I am quietly confident that they needn't bother because United – the underdogs, and therefore the heroes by default – will win the Cup. Within minutes, with Keegan bearing down on the United goal, all confidence is lost. United are playing okay, Coppell and McIlroy look lively, and Pearson and Hill both come close to scoring, but in the meantime, Liverpool, and in particular Case, Kennedy and Johnson, are looking dangerous themselves and it's beginning to look as though, if this really is all pre-planned in some way, then Liverpool, the League champions, the team who haven't lost to Manchester United for five years, aren't following the script. Either team could win. As this realisation slowly takes hold, my hopes wobble and my nerves jangle. Ray Kennedy's header is saved by Alex Stepney at point-blank range, and Liverpool continue to pile on the pressure before half-time. Deep down, I know that United need a miracle; or Bobby Stokes.

The second half gets under way and Liverpool seem to have things under control now. Having soaked up the pressure from United early in the game, they're playing like a team who've suddenly remembered that it is they who are the favourites, and that if they win this game, they will make history. But then, following a punt up field from goalkeeper Stepney and a misplaced header by Kevin Keegan, the ball finds its way to Jimmy Greenhoff, 25 yards out. He nods it forward and, all of a sudden, Stuart Pearson is through on goal. He juggles the ball neatly with his head, setting himself up for the shot, and he hits it early, catching it cleanly with his right boot and firing past Ray Clemence at his near post. *Goal!*

The United players jump on Pearson in celebration, and I share their joy. This is the first time that I've seen my team score, and I have never before experienced an explosion of happiness quite like it. I'd been right all along: United, the underdogs, have to win because that's what happens with these things. Two minutes later, as the ball falls to Jimmy Case on the edge of the United penalty area, I'm not worried because Liverpool aren't allowed to score now. He turns smartly, strikes the ball sweetly on the half-volley and sends it straight into the top corner. What? I'm confused. Dejected. Betrayed. Liverpool are level, so what happens now?

What happens is that United push forward again, looking determined to regain their hard-fought lead. The ball is lumped forward, Lou Macari flicks it on with his head, and it finds its way to Jimmy Greenhoff, just inside the Liverpool box. He tussles with Tommy Smith and the ball breaks loose to the onrushing Macari. He pokes it goal-wards, miscuing his shot, but en-route to the advertising hoardings behind the goal, it strikes the chest of Greenhoff and spins apologetically, beyond the helpless Clemence. *And the ball's in the net!*

Now I'm not sure what to do. It's all happened so quickly. How do I know that Liverpool won't score again straight from the re-start? There's still over half an hour to play and I lapse into a state of anxiety, unable to watch for long periods, and I beat a hasty exit from the room whenever Liverpool get close to my goal. The remainder of the game passes me by in a blur of red and white shirts, green grass, patterned wallpaper and disembodied voices. Occasionally, these voices attempt to reassure me that everything's going to be alright, United will win. But I don't trust them. How can I after what happened last year? They can't know how this will end.

Then it ends. A whistle blows. Manchester United have won. The players, my heroes, throw their arms around each other, forming little huddles in celebration. I'm in their midst, in spirit, looking for Jimmy Greenhoff. This is more like it. I understand football again, and I love the way that it works: Manchester United, my team, get to the Cup Final every year and, as long as they're not the favourites to do so, they will win. They'll tease me along the way but, if I pay attention, if I know the form, I'll know what to expect. I love this game.

*

Four days later, with the image of Martin Buchan climbing the Wembley steps to lift the FA Cup still fresh in my mind – a trophy that seemed huge in comparison to anything I'd previously heard referred to as a cup – I'm now watching Emlyn Hughes, Liverpool's captain, lifting a trophy that appears to be at least three times its size. It glimmers and sparkles in the glare of the floodlights and flash bulbs. Liverpool have just beaten Borussia Mönchengladbach 3-1 in Rome to win their first European Cup. I know that I've just witnessed something momentous, partly because Dad has let me stay up late to watch it, but also because the whole event seemed so otherworldly. The game was being played after dark and under floodlights. Liverpool were playing a team with a peculiar name, and the commentary sounded as though it was broadcast via short wave radio, all of which made it seem as though it was describing an Apollo moon landing, rather than a football match. It clearly was football, but the occasion just seemed more magical; to be presented with the Cup, Hughes and his teammates even had to walk across a bridge over what appeared to be a moat. Liverpool's historic triumph hasn't affected my continuing enjoyment of United's win at Wembley, but from this moment on, I realise that, contrary to what I had previously believed, the FA Cup isn't the ultimate prize after all.

The Wrong Ending: Part 1 — 1979

"There's a minute left on the clock. Brady for Arsenal... right across... Sunderland! It's there!" – John Motson, Wembley, 12th May 1979

Had the '77 Final ended differently, I now wonder what might have become of me. On the one hand, I might have lost all interest in football completely and quickly moved onto another all-consuming interest. Another possibility is that I might have buckled under the pressure of yet more ridicule being heaped upon me, cried "Man United are rubbish!" at the top of my voice, and chosen to support Liverpool instead – although at that stage, I hadn't realised that that might be an option. Since the team's victory at Wembley, I had immersed myself in all things United. Every accessory I owned bore the Manchester United name; bags, scarves, pencil cases, sweatbands and pin badges. I learned everything I could about the players, studying Topps football cards, Panini sticker albums, Top Trumps and copies of *Shoot* magazine at length in order to do so. My interest wasn't consigned just to United either; I was well versed in the form and players of the other top-flight clubs too. I admired players from other teams, and would have loved Andy Gray or Paul Mariner to have played alongside Jimmy Greenhoff at Old Trafford. I'd come to believe that my decision to choose to support Manchester United at the age of five had been a good one, but I'd also learned that my team playing in the FA Cup Final each and every year wasn't a given. United had only made it as far as the fourth round in 1978, so I had found myself in the unfamiliar situation of watching the Final as a neutral. I'd been comparatively nonchalant when United won in '77, but by the time they were drawn to face Liverpool again in the FA Cup Semi-Final in March 1979, two years' worth of hard knocks, disappointments, ruthless taunting, shock departures and close squeaks had turned that innocent and naïve seven-year-old into a melancholic and wizened old man of nine.

I've been allowed to stay up to watch the highlights of the midweek game and neither my Dad nor myself know the result. Liverpool are again the favourites and my burgeoning pessimism doesn't give United one ounce of hope. But it's late in the game and it's still all-square. And then the ball falls to Mickey Thomas. He fizzes the it across the box from the left, it bounces once, Jimmy ghosts in behind the Liverpool defence, stooping on the run, and heads past Clemence and into the corner. *Jimmy Greenhoff!*

I'm forced out of my seat with sheer elation. United hold out, and after an epic contest, United are 1-0 winners. However, once the joy has abated, I realise that they've won nothing yet; the happy ending is actually nothing of the sort: there is still the small matter of the Final itself to look forward to.

*

I will always find this difficult to watch. It's the final minute of the Cup Final and Liam Brady lumbers wearily toward the Manchester United box and lays the ball wide on the left for Graham Rix. The Arsenal man gets to it just before two United players can get a tackle in and he crosses to the far post. Whenever I see this goal, I will always think that somehow Alan Sunderland won't get there. He has no right to. It's the last minute of the game and extra-time is looming. When replayed to my mind's eye, the goal will forever be in slow motion – as if by some cruel form of masochistic mental torture – and the ball loops high and hangs for what seems like an age, but it's fine because Gary Bailey will gracefully and effortlessly pluck it from the air, the referee will blow the final whistle, and the teams will regroup for the first period of extra-time. Sammy McIlroy's equalising goal for United had completed a remarkable comeback, from having been 2-0 down with only five minutes left to play. Goals from Brian Talbot and Frank Stapleton had put Arsenal two up at half-time, and they looked comfortable. When Gordon McQueen stuck out a boot to divert a hopeful cross from Joe Jordan past Pat Jennings in the 86th minute, it was still a mere consolation. But when Steve Coppell played the ball to McIlroy two minutes later, the Arsenal defence just seemed to melt. With tired legs wading through air as thick as treacle, Sammy still had enough left in him to knock the ball past two Arsenal players and swing at it with his left foot to send it trickling goal-wards. *"Sammy McIlroy is through, McIlroy is through, and McIlroy... has done it!"* United could win in extra-time – for the first time this afternoon, I had a real sense of hope.

That improbable equalising goal had reawakened my previously held belief that the underdogs win the Cup by default. After Ipswich Town beat Arsenal in 1978, that had been the case for every Final I had experienced thus far. Arsenal had finished above United in the League this season, had beaten them 2-0 the last time the teams met, and therefore, they were the favourites. We all know how it goes, in nearly every fictional football story it happens just like it had in this game. The underdogs, the team that everyone wants to win, play like headless chickens for three-quarters of the game and find themselves a couple of goals behind. And then something changes. Whether it be as a result of Roy Race scoring a late and heroic hat-trick or Billy Dane's boots suddenly rediscovering their magic touch, the heroes come back, and they win. For Billy Dane read Sammy McIlroy. But this story had an appalling script. As I was still thinking about Sammy's goal – a goal that was scored barely 60 seconds earlier – Rix's cross is still floating, evading Gary Bailey completely, and is then sucked toward Alan Sunderland's right boot. He prods the ball into an empty net, and it's all over. So where was the happy ending? The extra-time winner that would fill the viewers' hearts with gladness and send them home with the knowledge that everything was right with the world? Just imagine the reaction had the evil Empire destroyed the Rebel Alliance and Darth Vader killed Luke Skywalker. The audience would have shuffled out of the cinema feeling hollow and unfulfilled.

But there it was: Darth Sunderland scored the winner for the bad guys in the last minute and it is the bitterest pill I've ever had to swallow, whereas Arsenal fans everywhere have been treated to their very own bespoke football movie that, despite their heroes throwing away a two-goal lead so dramatically, had the most perfect of endings. I'm not really sure I understand this game anymore.

*

After the match, I call for a friend – who doesn't particularly like football and was probably happily occupied with something far more enjoyable at the time – and drag him down to the local recreation ground with a football under my arm. Presumably, the reasoning behind this is to let off steam by kicking the last ounce of air out of the already misshapen ball, and of course, I'll need someone to go in goal. Though far from showing magnanimity in defeat, this seems like the most natural thing to do in the circumstances, but I'm about to learn another valuable lesson: when you're suffering the pain of defeat, the worst thing you can do is to go outside, especially with a football. As soon as we begin knocking the ball around, another boy our age walks over and joins in. He's grinning from ear to ear and, as if I couldn't have guessed the answer already, I ask him what team he supports.

"Arsenal," he replies.

I should probably ask him to go in goal at this point, thus turning the situation to my advantage by wiping the smile off his face with a few well-placed and thunderous volleys. That I don't do this may seem to indicate that, by nature, I am a good loser, but the truth is that my shyness wins the day and I end up between the goalposts as our guest does his best to re-enact the Alan Sunderland goal, my only consolation being that my friend couldn't cross a ball with his left foot if his life depended on it.

London SW6 — Saturday 15ᵗʰ September 1984

I'm feeling conspicuous already. I'm not sure that I have any business being here in the first place. It was with some hesitation that I'd agreed to come to London with my friends, Anthony and Steve, to see their beloved Chelsea play West Ham United, and now I'm standing behind a goal, surrounded by a few hundred complete strangers who all support a team that I've never really liked, waiting for the show to begin. This is the first time that I've been to a football ground. The closest I've been previously was to catch the briefest glimpse of Villa Park from a mini-bus while en-route to Snowdonia for a school trip. I've never had the opportunity to see a game; my Dad has never shown any interest in taking me and I've never asked to be taken. It's impossible not be aware of football hooliganism in the 1980s; these are the latter stages of the dark age of football violence and a football ground is far from being an ideal place for a father to take his son.

Football still only exists for me on television. Like TV presenters and cartoon characters, footballers inhabit a different world, and therefore, I still have no discernible proof that they actually exist. I know faces from watching *Match of the Day* and reading the sports pages, and I've had friends who've been to games and have told me how exciting it felt to be there, but I've never been particularly jealous and have had no more desire to see my footballing heroes in the flesh than I have in being in the same room as Han Solo nor any of my other childhood heroes. Somehow, that would ruin things; render them too *real*. Consequently, the fact that I've been asked along to see a game that doesn't involve Manchester United has probably swung it for me. Moreover, the trip involves going to London, a place that I already know to be real and exciting, so what is there to lose?

From the moment we make our way through the turnstiles, it's as if a switch has been flicked, pulling my senses into sharp focus. We are searched, which seems unnecessary, and Steve has his comb confiscated, which seems hilarious. Making our way down the steps of the concrete terrace, we can hear a chant of "*We love you Chelsea, we do*", and looking up, I can see that it's coming from a group of about 100 supporters, standing in the middle of the infamous area of covered terracing at one end of the ground known as "The Shed". Anthony motions for us to go and join the throng, which seems to me to be the one thing that we shouldn't be joining, but we do so anyway. As we take our place behind the goal, halfway up the terrace, I'm struck by both how vast the terrace is and how small the pitch seems. On television, a football pitch always looks enormous, especially at Wembley, but this one just doesn't seem big enough, and appears wider than it is long. Of course, this is simply a trick of perspective, but also has a lot to do with the pitch being so far away from the terrace. Stamford Bridge had once played host to both athletics events and greyhound racing, and the track around the pitch has remained in place ever since. The area between the goal and the Shed is so big that some people, presumably Club staff, have parked their cars there. In the future, when the track is eventually removed, it won't be the Shed itself that I miss, it will be the sight of the little pale blue disability car that is forever parked behind the goal, and that I see before me now.

This pitch-side car park forms a barrier that distances us from the football itself, so that the main sources of entertainment are the antics of those on the terracing around us. By the time the game kicks off, the crowd has swelled to fill the Shed, and although I'm interested in watching the game, the constant singing and banter is distracting. The lack of commentary is notable and takes a while to get used to, as does the lack of player close-ups. The first goal comes early on. Chelsea, attacking the goal that we are standing behind, are awarded a penalty in the 14th minute. Colin Lee takes it, the goalkeeper saves it, and then Lee scores from the rebound. Bedlam ensues as everyone around me goes berserk, and the crowd surges forward in a wave of collective delirium. Then, for some reason, the referee orders the penalty to be re-taken; Colin Lee takes it, the keeper saves it, Lee again dispatches the rebound, and again the crowd go bonkers. It's a bizarre introduction to the live game, almost as if I've been eased from my position of armchair supporter to paying punter by virtue of a helpful action replay to make me feel more at home. During the celebrations, I somehow manage to stay rooted to the spot and, as the only person not to celebrate the goal, I feel even more conspicuous. But gradually, as the singing is ramped up and the fans' exuberance is buoyed by their team's positive performance, I begin to enjoy the atmosphere, and the things that I once found intimidating now seem less so.

I still feel detached from the events around me, in spite of my closeness to them, almost as if I'm an unwitting extra in a potentially violent film. As I try to take it all in, the images are in slow motion one minute, twice the speed the next. The singing, the gesticulating, the latent aggression are so far removed from anything I've experienced before that I feel like a spectator on two fronts. I know, even as I stand here, that I can never be a part of it, but a part of me really wants to be. The songs are vicious but funny, but then again, some of the abuse is as unfathomable as it is unsavoury. The monkey noises made whenever West Ham's black winger, Bobby Barnes, has the ball seems particularly unpleasant. Thankfully, this level of moronic stupidity has no appeal whatsoever, but, to my impressionable teenage self, the camaraderie and the tribalism of it all definitely does.

Throughout the second half, there are sporadic bursts of fighting in various parts of the ground, the sight of which is met with a roar of encouragement from fans in other sections. I'm barely paying attention to events on the pitch at all now, but I do know that Chelsea are 3-0 up and looking more than comfortable. Then, towards the end of the game, there's a scuffle. The crowd in our section surge forward, and then to each side, before finally scattering in all directions. Not having any idea what's happening, I reach out and cling onto someone's jumper in a vain attempt to try and stay on my feet, and am swung around by the incumbent as he tries to break free. Although the fighting itself hasn't reached us yet, the infiltration of the Shed End by West Ham fans has caused a ripple of panic. Later, I am told by someone who'd been sat in the West Stand that, just before the end of the game, a small group of West Ham supporters behind him, some wearing suits, had calmly got up out of their seats and made their way toward the Shed, in an attempt to try to take the home end. One or two of those around us immediately ran toward the source of the trouble, but the majority have begun to jostle their way to the exit at the opposite end of the terrace. I've now become a part of the congealed mass of people trying to get to the exit, still not completely sure what's going on; I'm still moving, despite the fact that my feet are no longer touching the ground.

"Watch the barrier!" someone shouts, as my groin catches the top of a railing and is pressed against it by the force of the crowd behind me, and it takes all the powers of concentration and composure I can muster not to let out a high-pitched squeal as I ease myself free. By the time I'm outside the ground, I've long since lost sight of Steve and Anthony, but once I find them again, they are gibbering excitedly about what's just happened, and then saying that they've just seen someone sitting on the ground, nursing a stab wound.

As we make our way along Fulham Road towards the tube station, with the pungent combination of horse poo and fried onions filling our nostrils, we look up to see a crowd ahead, running in our direction. As those around us scatter, I realise that, momentarily, I'm alone again. Then I spot Anthony, sitting on the front wall of a house to my left, and I run over to join him. Steve is still missing and we're beginning to worry, until, amidst the chaos before us, we see a familiar figure emerge. Having only recently come out of plaster following a broken leg, running is still a problem for Steve, as is proved as he advances awkwardly toward us with a sort of Ministry of Silly Walks style straight-legged sprint. What should happen next is that we then hurdle the wall effortlessly, throwing in a forward roll or two, and land in the front garden of the house with both poise and grace, whereas what actually happens is that we just stumble down the front steps and land in a confused pile at the bottom. The plan is now to wait here until everything has quietened down a bit. We even ring on the front door bell in the hope that the nice residents will welcome us with open arms and give us shelter and a biscuit. There is no reply.

Dangerous Liaisons — 1986/87

As we take our places on the slope of concrete that stretches between the West Stand and the Shed End, I am feeling the first hint of nerves. They are nerves prompted partly by the possibility that fighting might break out around us at any moment, but more at the thought that I might be about to see my team lose. This is to be the first time that I've seen Manchester United play in the flesh, but as Brian Robson leads the United players out onto the pitch, I feel nothing. This isn't the same team that I grew to love in the mid-1970s. Greenhoff, Buchan and Pearson are long gone, and the way I see it, Duxbury, Blackmore and Whiteside aren't fit to lick the diminutive boots of Macari, Coppell and Hill. As a United player is sent sprawling in the Chelsea penalty area, and Peter Davenport dispatches the resultant spot kick, I say nothing, my only reaction being to pull my blue and white scarf tighter around my neck, partly in resistance to the inclement weather, but more in defiance of my former team. Nevin, Dixon, Durie and Pates are the new heroes. As the final whistle blows and we leave Stamford Bridge on this gloomy February afternoon in 1987, I feel happy that, with Mickey Hazard having secured a point, Chelsea, the team I now depend upon, haven't let me down.

*

I'm 17-years-old now. It's only eight years on from United's defeat to Arsenal at Wembley, but a lot has changed, not least my perception of Manchester United themselves. By leafing through my older brothers' football annuals from the late 60s and early 70s, I'd learned that they'd been a great side in the past, and that they'd been the first English club to lift the European Cup. But that was in 1968, a whole year before I was born. I read those books avidly, and with the same enthusiasm that I'd read books about dinosaurs a year or two earlier. Bobby Charlton and George Best were neatly filed next to Stegosaurus and Triceratops in my mind; awesome beasts that had once walked the earth but were now long since extinct. Bar one FA Cup, United had won nothing since '68 and, to most, they were underachievers. For me personally, they had only ever won that one trophy in 1977. The former glories had taken place in a Jurassic age long before I was born. Although I would still proudly point out to anyone remotely interested that the Club were originally called Newton Heath, I'd soon lost interest in the club's ancient past. As far as I was concerned, the Big Bang had occurred in 1974 and, on the eighth day, God created Steve Coppell. The team I'd fallen in love with were the team out there on the Wembley turf that sunny May day in '77, the plucky underdogs with the gung-ho style, the gang of Davids ready to slay the giant.

We'd met at a unique time, United and I. They were at a low ebb, a Second Division side for the only time in their post-war history, so in theory, a lot of teams were better than them. But they'd soon put the decline of the early 70s behind them and entered a new era of promise, with a squad of young starlets such as Coppell, McIlroy and Arthur Albiston pointing the way to the future. As the team grew in stature, it was increasingly apparent that they would rarely be seen as underdogs any longer. Whereas football had once revolved around the FA Cup Final for me – with that one match annually acting like the latest instalment of an exciting and colourful TV series – the older I became, the more interest I took in my team's welfare, and the more each and every game began to matter. They'd continued to compete at the top level, and had begun to challenge for the League title on a regular basis, whilst always just falling short, which became increasingly frustrating. The expectation that Manchester United, one of the biggest clubs in the world – if not the biggest – should be winning trophies on a regular basis was beginning to weigh heavily on my young shoulders.

Gradually, the players I'd developed a fondness for began to move on and were replaced by players with experience and big reputations, but although the Joe Jordans, Gordon McQueens and Brian Robsons of this world add a certain steel to a football team, as Macari, Pearson, McIlroy and the Greenhoff brothers left, so did some of the magic.

I'd soon learned that when your team lose, the derision meted out by school-friends increases in direct proportion to the size of the club, and there were none bigger than Manchester United. At such times, there will be nowhere to hide. When, in 1980, United lost 6-0 to Ipswich Town – despite Gary Bailey saving three penalties – it just so happened that the one and only 11-year-old Ipswich supporter in the whole of East Sussex was in my class.

And then, Brighton and Hove Albion materialised. Having risen rapidly through the divisions in the late 70s to find themselves in the First Division in 1979, it seemed that wherever I looked, friends, and even my own brother, began to defect from United, Liverpool or whoever they supported, in favour of Albion, their local team. People were dumping their former beaux just because another club were fluttering their eyelashes and whispering promises of a bright, more honest future. I thought this to be deeply immoral, but I could also see something honourable in their reasoning. Brighton still wasn't particularly close to us in Bexhill-on-Sea – being 30 miles away – but Albion were the only Football League club in the county, and were a hell of a lot closer than Manchester United. I began to question my own reasons for supporting United, and as such, I began to question my own sense of identity. It no longer felt as though owning the United Subbuteo team had been a good enough reason to have chosen them in the first place.

When United made it to the FA Cup Final in 1983 – their first since 1979 – there seemed an inevitably in the fact that it should be Brighton that they would face at Wembley. In what was thus far the most buttock-clenchingly, nerve-racking Final I had experienced, the Seagulls went ahead in the first half, and at that point, I was already contemplating taking a week off school. Although United regained their composure to take a 2-1 lead in the second period, I saw very little of their performance, having spent most of the game laying on my bed in the foetal position, with that being the safest and furthest point from the scene of the action, namely the television. Brighton eventually equalised and, but for a brave save at the feet of Gordon Smith by United keeper Gary Bailey, could have won it.

"*And Smith must score!*" radio commentator Peter Jones proclaimed.

He didn't – the neutrals were denied their storybook ending – and it was safe for me to go outside again.

*

The following Thursday evening, I sat and watched the replay in its entirety and felt proud that I'd managed to do so, although, admittedly, United being 3-0 up by half time – two goals from Brian Robson and one from Norman Whiteside – had made it a lot easier to endure. Arnold Muhren added a fourth from the penalty spot in the second half, and United had recorded one of the biggest scores in FA Cup Final history. This was far more than I could have hoped for, and as an unexpected consequence, I grew up a little that night and became a good winner.

The following day, I cycled to school with my friends as usual – one of whom was a nouveau Brightonian – and I hardly mentioned the game at all. The relief that I wouldn't have to put up with any mickey-taking was more important than the win itself. The ridicule that I'd imagined having to endure had been so horrendous that I took sympathy on Brighton supporters. A 4-0 win and the FA Cup were reward enough, and inwardly, I was embarrassed at the nature of the victory: this time, the plucky underdogs, the heroes of the people, had been royally duffed up, and I felt more than a little ashamed. I felt as though I'd become one of those snivelling, thin-lipped half-wits in *Grange Hill* who stood behind Gripper Stebson and giggled as he picked on another poor wretch and stole his dinner money.

But I knew that I couldn't give up on Manchester United. I'd already tried years earlier and failed. One Saturday in December 1977, despite United having lost 4-0 at home to Nottingham Forest that afternoon, I stayed up to watch the highlights on *Match of the Day*. Being allowed to stay up that late was a big deal for an eight-year-old so, not wanting to waste the opportunity, I duly sat and watched as my team were clinically deconstructed by Tony Woodcock, John Robertson et al., but, contrary to my wishes, the armchair failed to swallow me whole and spit me out into a twilight world where United were capable of turning a 4-0 humiliation into a win, or even a draw, in a game that had already been played.

On the following Monday, having jointly fielded the inevitable abuse from heartless classmates, a friend, and fellow United supporter, suddenly announced that he didn't support them anymore. He'd cracked under the pressure and announced, matter-of-factly, that he now supported Liverpool. I was aghast, and felt completely let down. I'd had no intention of turning my back on my team and switching allegiance in this way prior to his shocking announcement because I knew of the unwritten rule that made it clear that you could *never* change your football team. But I was so taken aback that anyone could do this, and so effortlessly, that I didn't quite know how to react. Shamefully, I took the "if you can't beat 'em join 'em" approach and announced that I didn't support United anymore either.

"I support Aston Villa now," I declared in a "so there" tone, and proceeded to etch ASTON VILLA in large block letters – in pencil, in case I changed my mind – into the back of my wooden ruler, and proudly flashed it around the classroom. (I'm not really sure why I'd chosen Aston Villa as an escape route, possibly because there was a character called Vila in one of my favourite TV programmes, *Blake's 7*.) Nobody seemed the least bit impressed at the behaviour of either of us and I was either ignored or met with well-earned derision for copping out like a wimp. At best, it was a cowardly reaction to a humbling defeat and basically amounted to the football supporters' equivalent of an ejector seat; you get taunted by your friends so you take the easy way out and support someone else. I knew it was wrong, and I felt ashamed.

*

I was only staying with Man United through a sense of duty. By 1983, I'd fallen out of love with them and I needed a way out. In this new age of uncertainty, I'd noticed that Oxford United had begun a Brighton-style rise of their own. Having been born in Oxford, this seemed a gift too good to refuse. Supporting your local team is one thing but supporting a team who represent the town of your birth seemed to make even more sense in terms of who you were as a person. My relationship with Oxford United was passionate and exciting for a short time, although we only met on the occasional Wednesday evening for highlights of their thrilling Milk Cup ties of 1983 and 1984 – which included a tie against Man United and two subsequent replays, with Oxford winning the second, 2-1. The fixture had presented me with a dilemma: I wanted both teams to win. Manchester United were still my team and everybody knew this, so, in the wake of Man United's defeat, any subsequent declaration that I was now an Oxford United fan would be met with contempt. In truth, Oxford's swashbuckling displays in the Cup runs reminded me of Manchester United's gutsy late 70's Cup performances, and inhabited a world where the underdog would either win the day gloriously, or fail with honours, heads held high. This was a world where the Royal Engineers could force a replay with the Zulu hordes at Rorke's Drift, against overwhelming odds, and Rocky Balboa could become the people's champion, even in defeat. Langan, Brock and Hebberd could ably fill the void left by Coppell, Macari and Greenhoff. But these meetings only ever really amounted to a holding of hands, a brief flirtation, and nothing more than that, and I returned to the United of Manchester each and every time, fully aware of my deceit and promising never to stray again.

Misfit

But all it took was that one trip to Stamford Bridge in September 1984.

There is an episode of the 1980's comedy series, *The Comic Strip Presents*, called *The Yob* – that parodies the famous science fiction film, *The Fly* – in which a pretentious and hyper-fashionable artist swaps personalities with a football hooligan as the result of a failed experiment. During the West Ham game, a similar metamorphosis had been triggered in me. In my case, the experiment was never likely to complete its cycle and succeed in turning me from a shy, middle class student into "the yob", but I began to make achingly pathetic attempts to look as though I belonged in the Shed End. Within months of that pivotal experience, I was borrowing my parents golf clothing, wearing bleached jeans and buying cheap gold belcher chains. Worse still, I was sporting a back perm, and though I felt sure it would help me to blend in, at best, it made me look like the gawky offspring of Paul Nicholas and Pat Sharp.

By '84, Manchester United had become a millstone around a neck that had long since seen the last of my grubby red, white and black scarf. It seemed to make perfect sense to add further confusion to the emotional turmoil of teenagehood by deciding to change my team. It was the ideal time to do so because, in the future, if word ever leaked out that I once supported United, I can put forward a convincing argument that I'd been a child and didn't know better. In fact, that's the truth: I was young and snotty-nosed and I really didn't know any better, but, amid the pubescent maelstrom, I'd had a change of heart.

I'd chosen to follow Chelsea on some subconscious level. As it had been with United 10 years before, the time was right for Chelsea and me to get together. I'd reached adolescence, and I was ready to move on. I'd enjoyed the experience at Stamford Bridge, however scared I'd been at times, and I liked the Chelsea team. John Neal had put together an exciting squad, who were promoted as Second Division champions in 1984, and combined experienced players like Mickey Thomas and Joey Jones with young stars in the making such as Kerry Dixon, David Speedie and, in particular, Pat Nevin, who with his skill, intelligence and discerning taste in music had quickly become my new footballing idol. The Club and I just seemed to click. There was no contact between myself and United, no explanatory letter, no awkward phone call; we'd simply grown apart and there was no real need for words.

Within 18 months, I was at Wembley Stadium for the first time, to see my new team beat Manchester City 5-4 in the final of the 1986 Full Members Cup. The brainchild of Chelsea's chairman, Ken Bates, and in its inaugural season, this new competition had been created with the view of compensating clubs from the top two divisions of the domestic league, following the tragic events at Heysel Stadium in May 1985 – in which 39 football fans lost their lives, prior to the European Cup Final between Liverpool and Juventus – and the subsequent ban on English teams competing in Europe.

Bizarrely, the competition wasn't open to the clubs who'd already qualified to play in Europe the previous season (they would instead play in a different tournament called the Super Cup) and only 21 clubs entered in total, and other than Chelsea, the only First Division clubs involved were Manchester City, Coventry City, Oxford United and West

Bromwich Albion. As such, the Full Members Cup was never taken seriously and could never be considered a bona fide major trophy, but I loved it. In the Final itself, Chelsea were 5-1 up at one stage, but three goals in the last five minutes made for a frantic and nail-biting finale, and as such, it was a shame that a game like that should occur in the final of such a third rate competition – it wasn't televised so nobody got to see it.

For Chelsea supporters, it was nerve-racking in the extreme, having been such a one-sided game for the most part. For it then to descend to such a level of panic had seemed unlikely. On a personal level, it seemed that the nightmare of 1979, and the "five-minute final", was happening all over again. I can only remember one goal of the five that Chelsea scored now – a long-range effort from Colin Lee – and that's largely due to the fact that I was once again spending as much time watching the crowd as the game itself. Although we were in a part of the ground designated to Chelsea supporters, minor scuffles were breaking out around us and a fellow Chelsea fan walked up to me and asked if he could take a pee next to my feet.

I said "No", which was apparently the wrong answer, so he lurched forward and took a swing at me, catching me on the cheek as I tried to duck for cover, at which point I realised for certain that I would never fully understand this world.

There was more trouble outside the stadium after the game, where the Chelsea Headhunters had supposedly joined forces with fans of other London clubs to teach the Manchester City supporters a lesson. Bottles were hurled, coach windows were smashed, and it seemed to take an age for ours to leave the ground. Had the gods of theatre been alert at this point, the chaos would have stopped suddenly and fans would have put away their fists and bottles in stunned silence as, at the end of Wembley Way, a group of 100 Manchester City fans stood in arrow formation and zombie make-up and, with a cry of "*Shamone*", advanced toward the coaches in perfectly choreographed unison, with dance their only weapon. But alas, that didn't happen and the fighting and glass smashing continued.

As much as I felt uncomfortable in these conditions, it still seemed glamorous to me in some strange way. I felt that just by being at the game and witnessing any form of crowd trouble, a little of the danger and aggression had rubbed off on me, and that this, along with a perm and a small collection of Lyle & Scott jumpers, would see me through life. Football hooliganism offered the tribalism that some people wanted in the 1980s, but I never got involved, and I can be thankful that, in my teenage years, the only damage it caused was to provide me with a repertoire of offensive songs, a low calorie cockney accent, and terrible dress sense.

That Sinking Feeling — 1987/88

"I'm afraid that Chelsea went out of the First Division with more credit and dignity than their fans. Players had no sooner left the pitch than the hoodlums attempted to take over. The invasion started from the Chelsea Shed End, but it was contained and turned back by a very calm response from the small body of policemen. But that precipitated the kind of thing we're seeing here... senseless, naked hatred that continues to stain English football." - Gerald Sinstadt - Stamford Bridge, 28th May 1988

As had been the case with United, Chelsea's history prior to 1984 was of little interest to me in the late 80s. If you haven't been around to witness a relegation or the winning of a trophy, you can't relate to it. Chelsea had last won a major trophy in 1971, when they beat Real Madrid to win the Cup Winners' Cup, and the previous year they'd won the FA Cup for the first time after a famous replay. Obviously, I'm pleased that England won the World Cup in 1966, but over the years, that success has only really served to make me more desperate to see them win it in my lifetime. Watching highlights of the '66 final, even in colour, is like watching footage from another world, one where footballers and civil servants look the same, and whose salaries probably aren't dissimilar either.

By 1986, two years into my life as a new-born Chelsea supporter, I was already tired of the same old clip of David

Webb barging home Chelsea's 1970 cup-winning goal. Although it had occured in my lifetime – just, 10 months into it to be precise – I felt no connection to it, and I was now eager to see them win a proper trophy under my stewardship. But Manchester United aren't in any mood to let it happen.

As Chelsea line up to face them in the fourth round of the FA Cup at Old Trafford on Saturday 30th January 1988, they are 13th in the First Division – having not won any of their previous 11 League matches. Meanwhile, United – under the guidance of Alex Ferguson, in his first full season as manager – are in third place and beginning to look like genuine title contenders.

The FA Cup has provided me with few happy memories in recent years. Chelsea haven't made it beyond the fourth round in either of our first three seasons together, and I haven't been able to watch a team of my own play in the final of the competition since 1983. By the time United met Everton at Wembley and lifted the Cup in May 1985, they had been out of my life for eight whole months. They have never lost to Chelsea in any major cup competition, and that trend looks sure to continue.

Whiteside has just been hacked down by Steve Clarke in the Chelsea box and Brian McClair is about to put the Reds one up from the penalty spot. But Roger Freestone saves it. Could it be? Will this be the year that my new team and I share our first proper success together?

No, it won't. Minutes later, Norman Whiteside heads United into the lead, and in the second half, his team continue to pile on the pressure and McClair adds a second. Chelsea go out of the Cup with a whimper, having been ruffed up by the big boys. Manchester United have upset me now and I no longer trust them. The fact that they miss out on the League championship to Liverpool is scant consolation.

*

Four months later, Chelsea were relegated to the Second Division. At the beginning of the 1986/87 season, a play-off system had been introduced for the first time, meaning that the club who finished third in the Second Division would no longer gain automatic promotion to the First. With the teams finishing in first and second place gaining automatic promotion, those finishing in third, fourth and fifth place were now given the opportunity to fight it out for the remaining spot. But the play-offs had to involve four teams, so it was decided that the team finishing in 18th place in Division One would also take part, so being faced with the possibility of four extra games with which to retain their place in the top-flight. When Chelsea beat Oxford United 2-1 on 31st October 1987, there was no reason to think that the Blues might go another six months without winning a game. By the time they beat Derby County on April 9th, they were involved in a relegation dogfight, despite being well clear of the bottom three – the traditional relegation places.

In the two-legged semi-final, Chelsea beat Blackburn Rovers convincingly, both home and away, 6-1 on aggregate, and were then faced with another two-legged tie against Middlesbrough, to try and stay in the First Division. Although they won 1-0 in the second leg at Stamford Bridge – thanks to a goal from Gordon Durie – having lost the first 2-0, it wasn't enough to save them. The squad of players that had looked so promising just two years earlier were relegated.

As the players left the pitch, Chelsea fans in the Shed End spilled onto it and ran to the opposite end of the ground to vent their anger at the Middlesbrough fans. The scenes made headline news, and images of supporters abusing police and throwing missiles at the away fans were relayed on television for the world to see. It was an ugly and embarrassing way to end Chelsea's stay in the top-flight.

*

I don't feel anger, only disappointment. As far as I am concerned, it's just one more change that I'll have to get used to. A month later, I finished my A-levels and just about managed to get the grades I needed to secure a place at Kingston Polytechnic, where I would be spending three years studying for a degree in estate management. It's a course that is intended to lead me to a career as a chartered surveyor; an option I've taken purely as the result of a computer-generated questionnaire aimed at finding my ideal job. Faced with the daunting prospect of moving away from home to embark on a vocation that I am yet to feel any enthusiasm for, I start to wonder whether I might have dismissed some of the questionnaire's other suggestions too hastily; maybe I should have opted to stay in Bexhill and work as a postal clerk instead. But, despite my nerves and reservations, I know I've got to try, and I don't want to let anyone down.

*

In September 1988, I leave home and move to Kingston-upon-Thames, to a life of lectures, shared accommodation, trips to the phone box, and a season, if not years, spent looking out for the Second Division scores on the Grandstand vidiprinter.

Part Two

Blue Is The Colour

Up For Grabs
— 1988/89

"Just a few seconds away now for Kenny Dalglish, unless Arsenal can launch something absolutely spectacular now in the few seconds that remain... And Arsenal come streaming forward now, in surely what will be their last attack." – Brian Moore, Anfield, May 26th, 1989

My love of Chelsea and my love for the game of football itself are two completely separate things. When I watch a Chelsea game on television, I'm not watching football, regardless how my team is playing. If they're playing in a fluid, entertaining manner and running rings around the opposition, it doesn't mean I'll enjoy the experience at all, it just makes it more bearable. The same can be said for any match that might have a bearing on Chelsea's fortunes. One might think that Liverpool versus Manchester United would be seen as a game to relish, but it isn't necessarily so. Depending on the implications for Chelsea, I will always take sides, one way or another, unless, of course, a draw is required. As such, I have never been as engrossed in a season as I am in this. Chelsea have spent the 1988/89 campaign in the Second Division and have taken it by storm, eventually winning it as champions with a record 99 points – 13 ahead of second-placed Manchester City, having scored a whopping 96 goals. In the process, they have lost only five times in the League. Not one top-flight game this season has had any effect on me, so in addition to my own team's success, the high drama that the race for the First Division Championship has offered has made this the most memorable of all seasons. I've watched *Match of the Day* each and every week, unconditionally, and read the sports pages frequently, and without wincing.

The climax to the season is so unimaginably dramatic that before long books will be written about it, and rightly so. The last goal of this most improbable, and tragic, of campaigns will forever give me goose bumps. As a result of the Hillsborough disaster on April 15th 1989 and the subsequent re-scheduling of fixtures, the two sides left with a chance of lifting the First Division Championship face each other in the final game of the season at Anfield on 26th May 1989. Arsenal need to beat Liverpool, away from home, by two clear goals to snatch the title on goal difference. With his team leading 1-0 – thanks to an Alan Smith header earlier in the second half – when Lee Dixon receives the ball deep in his own half, he knows that, with 90 minutes already up and the game in injury time, there is no option but to launch it forward, deep into the Liverpool half.

"*A good ball by Dixon finding Smith,*" Brian Moore declares.

Smith takes one touch, turns and flicks it on for Michael Thomas.

"*... for Thomas, charging through the midfield!*"

Thomas takes a touch, the ball hits a Liverpool defender, but falls neatly in his path, and he's through on goal.

"*It's up for grabs now!*"

He only has Bruce Grobbelaar to beat, but it's as if time is dwelling on the moment purely for dramatic effect. I'm on the edge of my seat, my Dad's on the edge of his. Come on... *come on...* and then it's there: Michael Thomas lifts the ball over Grobbelaar and the ball's in the back of the net. Arsenal are champions – in the last minute of the last game of the season. I'm out of my seat now. I never believed that it could happen like this. The League title is so often won with games to spare, and so often by Liverpool, that a result like this had never before seemed possible. It was like a Cup Final, and the underdogs won. I've rarely been happier for a team other than my own and I'm not alone in that: it's good to see someone else winning the title for a change. I go to the pub afterwards and I gladly allow myself to bestow congratulations upon Arsenal-supporting friends because I am genuinely pleased for them, and I want to share in their joy in some small way because I know that, barring a miracle of biblical proportions, there will never be an occasion when Chelsea might do the same.

Underground, Overground

I've been seeing someone else. I think that means I've been unfaithful already. I think so, but I'm not certain. It's complicated.

It started last season, 18th February 1989 to be precise. I had nothing to do on the day and thought maybe I'd go to see a game. It's FA Cup fifth round day so, having already been booted out by Barnsley in the third, Chelsea aren't playing, but I'd noticed that Wimbledon, the Cup holders, were to entertain Grimsby Town. Wimbledon is only down the road from where I'm living, which helped persuade one of my housemates to come along too. It soon became clear that this was to be a football experience quite like no other.

Not having been to the ground before, we parked in Wimbledon town centre, obviously assuming that Wimbledon was the size of a Sussex hamlet. Having been surprised not to see any supporters making their way to the ground, we wandered aimlessly through unfamiliar streets for a while, before asking a couple of amused pedestrians for directions and eventually making our way along the endless thoroughfare they call Haydons Road. After a few hundred yards, a car passed us and, from the open windows, we could make out what appeared to be the heads of some large, man-sized fish that were cheering loudly whilst the driver pumped the horn. Further on another car passed us, again with the cheering fish, and then another. As we finally approached the ground, we saw more fish, dozens and dozens of them, this time on foot as well as in cars. Once deprived of their vehicles, it was clear to see that they were the soon-to-be notorious inflatable haddock, proudly sported by the Grimsby fans as mascots in honour of their town's proud fishing heritage. Inside the ground, the away supporters' terrace was teeming with haddock. I'd yet to see anything quite so strange at a football match. Away from the pitch, there didn't appear to be a hint of trouble anywhere – just schools of bouncing fish.

The ground itself was tiny. Having only been to Stamford Bridge and Wembley previously it was natural for me to think that at all football grounds there should be a yawning chasm between the pitch and the terraces, but at Plough Lane you could pat a player on the back of the head as he took a throw-in, should you feel the need to do so.

In 1989, Wimbledon had been in the top division for three years, were more than holding their own, and had quickly become a thorn in the side of the bigger clubs. They had a reputation for an uncomplicated style of play, generally involving what's known as "route one" football, which, put simply, involved hoofing the ball forward from the back for one of the imposing centre forwards to chase and bully his way onto. They were universally criticised for this, but it had proved effective, as their League position testified. So they might not have played the most attractive football but there were plenty of reasons for me to like them. For one thing, their nickname was The Wombles, after those furry, eco-friendly creatures from the TV series who made their home on Wimbledon Common, and who released a few singles and albums in the mid-1970s that led to them becoming my first favourite band. There was also a cartoonish quality about the club, helped by the team having acquired the nickname, "The Crazy Gang", as a result of their madcap off-field antics. Yet, at the time, I liked them purely because, in the previous season's FA Cup Final, they'd beaten Liverpool; a team who had dominated the domestic game in the 1980s. I always like an underdog, and Wimbledon were the most ferocious of them all.

But on this day, it was Grimsby Town – then of Division Four – who were underdogs and, spurred on by the haddock, it was they who took the lead. Gradually, however, Wimbledon overpowered their opponents to win 3-1, with a direct and entertaining style of football that was exemplified by a move that concluded with a superb diving header from Terry Phelan, a left back.

It helped that a few goals were scored and that an upset had been on the cards for a short time, but everything about the game seemed to epitomise what, as an entertainment, the game of football should represent. I had no preconception that it's right and proper for supporters to be within hair-ruffling distance of the pitch, but following that game, it just seemed obvious. There was a lack of animosity between fans, the haddock won the day on the terraces, and it was clear that surrealism and football were made for each other. But the mere fact that a First Division side, containing household names such as Dennis Wise, John Fashanu and Vinnie Jones, who were playing week-in, week-out in such a small and unfussy ground, seemed to me the oddest thing of all. Enthralled and seduced by the convenience of it all, I attended more games over the course of the year. Plough Lane was easy to get to once you knew how, and for £6, you could see the country's best teams in just a short bus ride away, all of which helped persuade others to go with me.

During this time, I saw Dennis Wise pull on an invisibility cloak to cheekily head the ball out of Bruce Grobbelaar's hands to score against Liverpool, cheered on a handful of Sheffield Wednesday fans as they performed a conga across a deserted away fan's terrace, and stared into the abyss whilst looking Vinnie Jones in the eye as he drew on an imaginary post-goal cigarette. I even managed to chalk up my second TV appearance as Wimbledon scored their fourth goal of the day against Newcastle as I, wearing a naff cream jacket and fully aware of the position of the TV gantry, was to be seen grinning inanely at the camera and punching the air unconvincingly, whilst my friends did the decent thing and applauded the goal, ignoring the spotlight (my TV debut, an equally brief and innocuous appearance in the crowd at a primary school maypole-dancing exhibition aired on *Play School*, had been far more impressive as an exercise in studied disinterest). In addition to all these attractions, with the average crowd being so small in comparison to other clubs in the top division, it was easy to spot the characters, my favourite being a vocal man in his 60s who would shout "confusion and nuisance" in the general direction of the pitch for no apparent reason, following this up with other more pedestrian, but less wholesome statements. When asked by the stewards to keep the noise down and cut out the swearing, he would proceed to shout "Oh come along chaps, jolly well try harder".

My trips to Plough Lane were purely about being entertained. I enjoyed the Don's "Looney Tunes" style and loved the way that it would befuddle the big teams. But I felt guilty about going too. I recalled the derision I'd suffered at the hands of school friends, following my briefest of dalliances with Aston Villa in 1977, and wondered whether I was doing the same thing again. And I recalled another of football's unwritten rules; the one that states that you can't support more than one team. Chelsea were my team and there was no reason why I would want to abandon them. Watching another team had begun to feel sordid. So I stopped going, and now they're out of my system. Or so I think. Years from now, Wimbledon FC will have left Plough Lane to play at Selhurst Park as part of a controversial ground-sharing deal with Crystal Palace, made necessary, it will be claimed, as a result of the Taylor Report – a report published in 1990 that contained the findings of Lord Taylor of Gosforth's enquiry into the causes of the Hillsborough Stadium disaster on 15th April 1989, which had claimed the lives of 96 Liverpool supporters. The report recommended that all fans attending football matches should have a seat, so as to avoid a repeat of the horrific events that occurred that day, and that all stadia should therefore become all-seaters. It was a recommendation that The Football League subsequently made compulsory for all of its clubs, and the Wimbledon board considered that any redevelopment of Plough Lane to meet the new requirements would be uneconomical. Eventually, there will be a vast and generically modern development of flats standing on the site, and whenever I drive past, I will hear a voice from beyond the walls whisper "confusion and nuisance".

Wise and Lows — 1990/91

The Blues have now been back in the top division for two seasons. 1990/91 began with the stellar pre-season signings of Andy Townsend and Dennis Wise – the latter a purchase that I was especially pleased about and helped me get over the disappointment of England's heartbreaking penalty shoot-out defeat in the semi-final of the World Cup in the summer. I had long admired Wise. Watching him in his Wimbledon days at Plough Lane was like watching a schoolboy who'd won a competition in *Shoot* magazine to find the country's cheekiest and most gifted young footballer, with the top prize being a run out for a First Division side. In the previous decade or so, the biggest signing Chelsea had made, in terms of the player's experience and stature in the game, was that of Graham Roberts in 1988. But, for all his experience, he was still a player approaching the end of an already successful career. Dennis Wise, however, was still only 24 when he signed from Wimbledon for £1.6 million in July 1990, and I was hopeful that his transfer to Chelsea, and the level of ambition that it represented, might signal a new dawn.

Despite the arrival of Townsend and Wise, Chelsea still aren't seen as serious challengers, and as a result, their matches are rarely televised. But this, their first, momentous TV appearance of the season, has given me the perfect excuse to take an extended break from an assignment I'm due to hand in tomorrow. As I settle down to see Chelsea take on Manchester United at Old Trafford on Sunday November

25th 1990 – two weeks after I've witnessed a disappointing 1-1 home draw with Norwich City, and one week after a 2-1 defeat at Wimbledon – I'm expecting them to lose. In contrast to Chelsea, United are riding high in the League at this point of the season, but, despite my pessimism, I'm in the middle of a miserable final year at Kingston Polytechnic – made more difficult by a lack of focus and commitment to my studies during the first two years of a course that I am still unsure about – and I watch purely in the hope that something might happen to cheer me up.

When Gary Pallister slices the ball into his own net to put Chelsea ahead after just 15 minutes, although I am suitably cheered, I still feel certain that we'll lose. But when Andy Townsend carves open the United defence to put them two up just minutes later, in contrast to Townsend's joyless but determined post-goal facial expression, I begin to dream of the impossible – a draw at Old Trafford – but just a couple of minutes later, a United corner causes confusion in the Chelsea penalty area and Danny Wallace pounces to head his side back into the game. When, in the second half, Wallace hits a cross beyond Chelsea keeper, Dave Beasant, and Mark Hughes heads the equaliser, it seems obvious that United will now go on to win at a canter. But they don't, and instead, Chelsea manage to get a winner.

Wise scores from the penalty spot and the Blues have scored a famous victory, famous perhaps not in the history of the sport as a whole, but to me, it represents a welcome flash of light amid the academic fog and autumnal gloom. It also appears that the post-match euphoria instils in me a previously untapped enthusiasm for property law or residual valuations, or whatever subject I should've been giving my undivided attention to, as I proceed to breeze through the assignment as if I'm writing a letter to Santa Claus.

*

Although my brother, Ian, has supported Chelsea most of his life, we had never been to a match together, so we decided to put that right on Saturday 12th January 1991 by visiting Stamford Bridge to see Chelsea entertain local rivals, Queens Park Rangers. Having splashed out £15 each for tickets in the upper tier of the East Stand – which, on my meagre student income, meant foregoing fast food for the next week – we watched with relish as Gordon Durie scored both goals in a 2-0 victory, although I couldn't help feeling a little sorry for the Rangers players, clad as they were in shirts, shorts and socks of the most violent shade of orange.

It was good that we'd made the effort to go to The Bridge together at last. Within a few months, Ian moved to France to live and work. He'd always been a dependable ally, ready to hear of my regular Chelsea-themed frustrations and anxieties whenever needed because he felt the same way. He'd left the family home and moved to London in 1974 when he was 18-years-old and I was only five, so I'd never really been as close to him as I was to my other brother, Andrew. However, Ian lived only a few miles from Kingston, in Weybridge, and as a result, we'd got to know each other better in the last few years. Although he's not exactly moving to the other side of the world, I'll miss him, not just as a brother, but also as a football confidant.

*

It's the evening of Monday 6th May 1991, and I'm standing on the famous North Bank as all around me are united in celebration, with Arsenal having just clinched the League title for the second time in three years before they've even kicked a ball. Liverpool had played Nottingham Forest beforehand, and I'd watched the game in The Plimsoll Arms with my old friend, Ashley, a lifelong Arsenal fan, to see the Merseysiders lose 2-1 to hand the First Division Championship to Arsenal. As we wait for the teams to take to the field, I am struck firstly by the compact, old school magnificence of Highbury Stadium, but secondly, by just how relatively calm those around us seem. Obviously, fans are jubilant, but the celebrations are conducted with the controlled nonchalance of those who know what it's like to win a title; a feeling that is capped, literally, by the sight of Lee Dixon ambling onto the Highbury turf for the warm–up, wearing a yellow hat. No doubt winning the League with two games to spare is fantastic, but it clearly doesn't warrant the same wild, untapped celebrations that a first title win in 18 years, won in the final seconds of the final game of the season, will encourage – as had been the case two years previously. I try to imagine the euphoria that would ensue on the terraces at Stamford Bridge had Chelsea won the League tonight, and I just can't. It's just too big a stretch of the imagination to envisage such a thing ever happening. I love the atmosphere and I am happy for Arsenal, but my congratulations are tinged with envy for their achievement, and I promise myself that, should the unimaginable one day happen, and Chelsea win the title, I will run naked through the streets of South London, whatever the weather.

Arsenal's opponents tonight are Manchester United, my original fondness for whom, after just seven years, now feels as though it belonged to another life. When reflecting upon this former life, I'd realised that it hadn't been the club that I'd fallen for as a boy, but the team of the mid-to-late 1970s itself. As Coppell, Macari, Buchan and the Greenhoffs began to leave, so did my interest in the club. With Chelsea, things had been different. I'd loved the team that I'd first seen in September 1984, and that had competed so well for the following two seasons, but although I'd been sad to see those players leave, especially Pat Nevin, I'd still cared about their replacements. In May 1990, Manchester United had drained all the romance out of the FA Cup by first equalising in extra-time in the final, so denying Crystal Palace their first major trophy, and then beating them 1-0 in the replay, so becoming spoilsports of the highest order. They've lost to Chelsea twice this season – 3-2 on both occasions – and that's softened my attitude toward them slightly; we are no longer friends, but they are yet to hurt me enough to be enemies. Four days after the home defeat to the Blues in November, United played Arsenal in a League Cup tie at Highbury and walloped them 6-2. A month earlier, the two teams had met at Old Trafford and a 21-man brawl ensued, as a result of which, Man United were deducted one point and Arsenal two, making their title-winning triumph all the more impressive. As a result, there is now a bitter rivalry between these two clubs, but, had I still been a United fan, I would never have forgiven Arsenal for the way they'd toyed with United during the '79 Cup Final, a game that had left me heartbroken. I should at least want them to beat the Gunners just for old times' sake, particularly as Arsenal now have nothing to play for, but in the event, thanks to an Alan Smith hat-trick, Arsenal win 3-1, and I think it's fitting that the new champions should continue their night of celebration in such a way. It's probable that United's performance had been hampered by thoughts of their impending European Cup Winners' Cup Final appearance against Barcelona a week later; a game that, as England's representatives, I want them to win without question, and I'm happy when they do so.

Groundhog Day — 1992/93

In my time as a Chelsea supporter, a pattern has emerged. Each season typically starts with the disappointing news that the Club have sold a couple of players who you really liked, and may include at least one promising young player who was making an impression in the first team, but then they make a couple of interesting signings that you hope might help compensate for this. There is then an indifferent start to the season with a couple of uninspiring draws, an encouraging win, and an alarming defeat. As the season unfolds, the team's League form will continue to frustrate, with a lower mid-table finish looking inevitable. They will beat a couple of the top teams – Manchester United, Tottenham Hotspur or Liverpool – but will have depressing defeats at home to teams who are struggling. As early in the season as October, all thoughts of perhaps finishing in the top four or five in the League are extinguished, and instead, hopes of an appearance in the final of either the League Cup or FA Cup are all that's left. But before Christmas is upon us, they are out of the League Cup, having suffered the embarrassment of being knocked out by a team from a lower division – Scunthorpe United, Reading or Scarborough, for example. Then all that's left is the FA Cup, and having been given a decent draw in the third round, hopes are high that perhaps this could be the year that, finally, talk of the Club's last major domestic cup triumph in 1970 will end. Then a lower division team like Oxford United or Luton Town will knock them out before the competition has begun in earnest, and so begins a string of meaningless League games that Chelsea make hard work of, as if to give the fans a relegation dogfight to think about, just to keep them interested.

Last season – 1991/92 – proved no exception to this. During pre-season, they'd made some impressive signings in Paul Elliott, Tom Boyd, Clive Allen and Tony Cascarino, and a more surprising one in Vinnie Jones. They had also, sadly but predictably, sold two of their star players – Gordon Durie left for Tottenham and Tony Dorigo signed for Leeds United. In the League, they were typically inconsistent and began the campaign with disappointing draws at home to Wimbledon and Notts County, and a 3-0 defeat at Oldham, but over the course of the season, they managed to beat Liverpool at Anfield and Tottenham, home and away, but otherwise struggled and eventually finished 14th. The team were knocked out of the League Cup at the first time of asking by Tranmere Rovers. Unusually, they did have an impressive run in the FA Cup, before being knocked out in the quarter-final by another Second Division team, Sunderland.

Having scraped a second-class honours degree in estate management, I'd left Kingston in the summer of 1991 and moved back in with my parents in Bexhill. Returning home had helped me to emerge from a state of total post-adolescent confusion as a person who, though still generally confused about adulthood and what it expected of me, was far more relaxed now in the company of family and familiarity. 1992 was a wonderful year in many ways. My girlfriend, and soon to be fiancée, Vanessa, and I had got together in February, and I had a job working in an off-licence, where my old school friends – Ashley, the Arsenal supporter, and Steve, my Chelsea cohort – also worked, and I loved it.

The majority of the year felt like one long summer holiday, and if I could have found a way to have stayed there for the next 40 years, playing storeroom football, swapping Euro '92 stickers with the younger customers, "product testing" cigarettes and bar snacks, and chatting to the cast of colourful characters that regularly shopped there, I would have done so. But I knew all along that it couldn't last and that I was really just delaying adulthood. By the end of '92, I had swapped my carefree lifestyle for a more responsible one that involved Vanessa and I sharing a flat in Bexhill and a full-time job working for the civil service in Hastings in order to pay both the rent and a car loan. My extended childhood was over.

What hadn't changed was my dependency on football. If anything, the fact that I was no longer studying for impending exams had given me more time to think, so I had even more time to listen to radio coverage of matches and football chat shows, and to read the sports pages in the newspapers. I was reliant on Chelsea's fortunes more than ever, but after the FA Cup defeat at Sunderland, I just couldn't see their luck changing.

*

This season, however, I have a feeling that things might be different. After a couple of heartening victories over Newcastle United and Everton, they've made it to the quarter-final of the League Cup and I'm now thinking that 1993 could be Chelsea's year. They're to play Crystal Palace, a team who are struggling in the newly-formed Premier League at present, and I'm hopeful that we can beat them and get to the semi. It's a miserable January day but I've already decided that I'm going to the game, and my Dad has agreed to come with me.

Dad had enjoyed a long and successful career as a mechanical engineer but had also spent many years as an amateur footballer, and had played to a good standard. Eventually, in his mid-30s, his playing career was curtailed by a combination of sore knees and a love of golf, but his love of football hadn't diminished. Although he hasn't been to a football match for over 20 years (his non-attendance having had much to do with the reputation of supporters), he still watches televised games whenever possible, and, with restless frustration and enthusiasm, in his mind, he will kick every ball whilst doing so, particularly when watching England.

My Dad's fondness for the game is clearly something that I've inherited, but his relationship with the sport is different to that of my own. For one thing, his lack of a clear allegiance to any one side other than the national team seems thoroughly alien. Indeed, he can no more fathom my continuing loyalty to one club any more than I can understand the regular re-branding of his favourite team, most usually Tottenham Hotspur or West Ham, depending on who is playing the more attractive football at the time. My constant reference to Chelsea in the first-person plural – "we" – in particular causes him much amusement. And so it is that we pack our similarities and differences into the car and make the long journey up the A22 to Selhurst Park on this wet and dreary Wednesday night; me with my first-person plural tucked loosely into my pocket and Dad holding his neutrality close to his chest.

I should've known how the game would pan out even before we set off. Having taken a shower at my parents' house prior to leaving, I'd slipped on an errant bathmat and, in a frantic attempt to steady myself – my legs lost in a Road Runner blur – I'd grabbed at the shower curtain, an action that the curtain rail put up very little resistance to and came away from the wall, bringing at least one cracked tile with it. Owning up to this wanton act of destruction immediately seemed only fair, but added a tension to the evening that was hardly called for.

Being a London derby, and a quarter-final, the game is all-ticket, and by the time we arrive at Selhurst Park, they've sold out, leaving us to pay a tout an inflated price of £45 for two tickets. The conditions are atrocious and we're told that the game was only given the all-clear half an hour before kick-off. As we reach the top of the steps that lead from the Glaziers lounge to the stands, and the pitch reveals itself before us in all its floodlit and rain-soaked Technicolor glory, the look on my Dad's face is one of pure childlike wonder. He'd never taken me to a game when I was younger, but in that instant, I feel as though I am the parent witnessing the awe that he might have seen in me years earlier, and that memory will come to be one of my fondest.

We take to our seats just as the game kicks off. As the rain continues to lash down and the pitch fails to deal with it, the surface water threatens to turn the game from the free-flowing, technically proficient spectacle that both teams have undoubtedly rehearsed, into a comical combination of pinball and water polo. As players splash haplessly, the ball skims across puddles, and passes fail to reach their intended destinations, the men in blue aren't able to cope. In the fourth minute, a ball is hoofed into the Chelsea half, but there's no danger because Frank Sinclair will deal with it, no problem. He passes it back to Kevin Hitchcock, the Blues' keeper, the way that he always would, the way he was taught to as a youth player, but this time the ball doesn't do what he expects it to, what any of us expect it to, and it gets stuck in the mud on the edge of the penalty area. The only person to have expected the ball to act in this way is Chris Coleman of

Palace, and he slides five yards on his backside and knocks it through Hitchcock's legs.

But the comedy isn't over, and the ball teases the 28,000 present by stopping just short of the goal line, waiting for a couple of seconds, and then spinning over. It's the worst possible start for Chelsea. It's already clear that there is only ever going to be one winner, and it won't be the game of football itself, nor its mutant hybrid. Then Chelsea pull a goal back, by virtue of a tremendous strike from Andy Townsend, who belts the ball with such purpose, as if to punish it for its high jinks earlier in the game, and sends it skimming past Nigel Martin. I'm out of my seat and punching the air, and then I remember that my Dad's sitting right next to me, and manage to stifle a celebratory swear word just in the nick of time. But 17-year-old rookie striker, George Ndah, then puts Palace 2-1 up before half-time. As the second half progresses, it's becoming clear that Chelsea's ability to cope with both the conditions and Palace's youthful endeavour will not improve. Nineteen-year-old Grant Watts then adds a third for the home side, and I spend the rest of the game just trying to stay dry. The final whistle blows and, with the team having been knocked out of the FA Cup by First Division Middlesbrough four days earlier, the 3-1 defeat spells the end of Chelsea's hopes of a trophy for another season and, as we drive home through torrential rain, I am consumed by thoughts that I will probably never get to experience Chelsea winning a major trophy in my lifetime.

Tumbleweed — 1993/94

There has never been, and may never be, a better opportunity than this. Chelsea are 90 minutes away from a place in the 1994 FA Cup Final. Their opponents are Luton Town, of what is now called Division One, but, following the formation of the Premier League in 1992, is actually the second tier of top-flight football. Of the four semi-finalists, Luton Town are the only team who aren't playing in the top division. And the game is being played at Wembley.

Three months ago, following a 0-0 draw in the third round at home to Barnet of Division Two, and with Chelsea in the thick of a battle against relegation, this all seemed highly unlikely, but now I'm sitting in a pub, watching my team playing in an FA Cup semi-final. I'm not confident, of course: Town have already knocked out West Ham and high-flying Newcastle United, so another so-called giant-killing is far from inconceivable. Also, to add some romance to the fixture, Kerry Dixon – a Chelsea legend, and one of my favourite players from the 1980's team – is now playing for Luton. Now this, combined with the fact that there is no such thing as a foregone conclusion when you follow Chelsea, makes me even more nervous. Players always come back to haunt their former teams. "*BLUES KO'D BY KILLER KERRY*" is the only headline I can foresee in tomorrow's papers: plucky Luton continue their glorious run in this year's competition by making it to the final. In the event, however, I needn't have worried, as Gavin Peacock scores one in each half in what turns out to be a relatively comfortable 2-0 win.

*

With thoughts of yesterday's triumph temporarily cast aside, I'm now watching the second semi-final, hoping and praying that Oldham Athletic, at present an established Premier League side but who are facing relegation, will overcome Manchester United, who are, at this point, well on their way to winning a second consecutive Premier League title, and who I do not want Chelsea to have to face in the final. Anything's possible, obviously, but they are so dominant in the English game right now that I can't realistically foresee anything other than a United win. But 90 minutes are almost up and it's still 0-0: a little piece of magic or a mistake by either team at any point now could prove decisive. I still know that United are more likely to produce the magic and Oldham the mistake, so I'm still resigned to the inevitable victory for the Reds, but time is slipping away. Then, in the second period of extra-time, I notice Andy Ritchie on the touchline, getting ready to come on for Oldham. Ritchie was a young striker at United in the late 1970s and I was a fan, thinking him to be something of a potential super-sub and lucky charm in the way that David Fairclough was for Liverpool at that time. Perhaps he might fulfil that potential for me at last. As he's still getting ready to make his entrance, Oldham have a corner. As the ball is whipped in, Peter Schmeichel races off his line to gather it safely, but he does nothing of the sort. He makes a complete hash of it, spilling the ball at the feet of Neil Pointon, who swivels, shoots, and scores! I'm out of the chair, arms aloft and staring out of the window, presumably in search of someone to whom I can proclaim my newfound love for Neil Pointon. Ritchie has worked his magic without even taking the field.

Oldham only have 10 minutes to hold out. United look shell-shocked, as their dream of winning the League and Cup double for the first time in their history slips from view. There's only one minute to go now and we've reached that point in a game where, to tease the crowd and delay the final whistle, time appears to slow to a tenth of its normal speed. I am standing up in restless anticipation, screaming at the TV screen for the Oldham players to hoof the ball out of play to waste more time. There's a United throw. It's their last chance. All the Oldham players are behind the ball. It breaks for Lee Sharpe midway in the Oldham half, with every player lining up as if it's a United free kick. Sharpe knocks it forward, it's headed away. A United player heads it back to the edge of the penalty area. It's hooked on. It falls to Mark Hughes, and, with the rest of the Universe on hold, he volleys it goalwards. It hits the back of the net. The game ends. Oldham's chance of glory has gone.

Three days later, United win the replay, 4-1.

*

I am sitting in a worn but comfortable armchair in the middle of a vast and barren Dali-esque landscape, containing nothing but a television screen (that's big enough to take notice of but small enough to ignore, as necessary), a small selection of refreshments, and only a sparse scattering of tumbleweed for company. The physical science of this place has also determined that a portal to another dimension is handily placed next to the chair in case of the need to escape to somewhere even more isolated.

At the end of the 1994 FA Cup Final, that is a scenario that I will crave with some desperation.

*

I wake on the morning of 14th May 1994 in a state of some excitement. It's a sunny day. I pop down town in the morning to buy the commemorative Cup Final magazine. I have my lucky Chelsea shirt on – the one from the 1990/91 season with the red trim on the collar – and I've never felt more at one with the world. At last, after a gap of 11 years, I am watching a team I support, playing in an FA Cup Final. It's enough that Chelsea have reached the Final and I genuinely don't mind that they will probably lose. In the event, this game more than any other will come to prove that there are many shades of defeat. It isn't just that they lose the game 4-0; it is the horrific way it has all unfolded. They're giving a good account of themselves against the newly crowned Premier League champions in the first half, and are unlucky not be 1-0 up at the break after Gavin Peacock almost chips Peter Schmeichel for the third time this season, only to see the ball hit the crossbar and bounce away to safety. It is the ease with which the team's performance has created such a false sense of security that makes the second half so agonising. At least they'll only lose by the odd goal now, I think to myself at half-time, and better still, they might just nick it.

I will never again afford myself such confidence. To say that the sky has caved in around the team might sound a bit dramatic, but in a metaphorical sense, it really has, as one goal follows another and then another in the space of what feels like just a couple of minutes. Some friends are watching the game with me, one of whom is a United fan, and with every goal scored, he is out of his seat in celebration and flashing taunts in my direction. The goals are so frequent that he hardly has time to sit back down. I can't understand why I might have entertained the notion that watching any game, let alone a Cup Final, in the company of an opposing supporter might be a good idea. From this day on, I will do my best to ensure that if I can't be alone when watching Chelsea, then only fellow Chelsea supporters or sympathetic neutrals may be present.

*

The irony inherent in Chelsea having to play Manchester United in the Final hasn't been lost on me. That the team I'd supported through most of my school years now stood in the way of the team I'd chosen to spend my adult life with – and ready to shatter the dream that I might finally get to see them win something – was too obvious an outcome not to happen. It is one of those occurrences that I could quite easily take to mean something profound, although, for Manchester United, the best team in the country, to make it to the Final is hardly a surprise. But for the game to finish in a 4-0 defeat for my team, the same score by which United had beaten Brighton in our last final together 11 years earlier, adds excessive weight to the irony. It's as if karma has dealt me such a cruel and personal blow, purely in order to teach me a lesson, even though I'd been on my best behaviour following United's win in '83 and had hardly gloated at all.

*

The defeat, and the manner in which it occurred, hurt badly, and yet I still feel proud to be a Chelsea supporter and am robust enough to not fear the inevitable fallout at work as

I make the long, lonely walk to my desk this morning. I'm still working for the civil service in Hastings and my desk is at the far end of a long open plan office, which seems even longer and more open in the current circumstances. I naturally assume that there will be sniggering and finger-pointing as I make this endless walk of the damned, but I will not rise to it: I will hold my head up high and take it all on a chin left fully exposed. A friend from work had called round to our house yesterday – the day after the game – proudly wearing his Man United shirt (that grim green and yellow vertical-halved away shirt with the lace-up neck from the early 1990s that was supposed to be a reproduction of the original Newton Heath strip from a century before, but looks more like a giant boiled sweet). I didn't acknowledge this blatant act of provocation, however, and although at first he was disappointed to see that I didn't seem too bothered by it all, he at least had the good grace to concede that the score line didn't reflect the game as a whole, and that Chelsea were a little unlucky: United didn't really deserve to win by four and, but for the timing of the first goal – a blatant penalty, converted by Eric Cantona – and the highly dubious award of a second penalty soon afterwards – Cantona again with a goal that broke the Chelsea players' spirit completely – it might have been different. But right now, at work, I'm surprised to find that I don't receive much stick at all. The walk that I dreaded is just as it would be on any other Monday. There are two other Chelsea supporters on my floor and they help to absorb the blast, and although there is the odd visit from a smirking United supporter during the day, those who understand football and actually watched the match seem mildly embarrassed at the nature of the victory and, thankfully, keep their gloating in check.

This experience of a post FA Cup defeat workplace reaction is a far cry from the mauling I would have experienced had I still been at school. Had my school years extended into my mid-20s, there is little doubt that I would've considered feigning illness by adopting a pathetic, gravelly voice – somewhere between Orville, the ventriloquist's duck, and Linda Blair in *The Exorcist* – in order to convince my Mum that I'm in no fit state to go anywhere, and instead spend a day at home watching *Picture Box* and *The Flumps*. That I was expecting to be ridiculed but haven't been proves that, firstly, fewer people than I think are that bothered about the result or football itself, but also that children become adults; the savage childhood barrackings eventually give way to the comparatively mild-mannered banter of adulthood. But past experiences still prompt temporary agoraphobia following any defeat. To my mind, all those people out there, they are all children, and they are all waiting in their masses, like hordes of the undead, baying for my humiliation.

The Butterfly Effect — 1994 to 1996

The 1994 World Cup has everything. Except England, which to me means everything. Of course, it's disappointing that they failed to qualify, particularly given their impressive display in 1990, but such is the infrequency of international fixtures that, as a nation, we have had a long seven months during which to digest the misery of England's failure before the start of the tournament itself on June 17th 1994. In the beer-stained, tear-drenched aftermath of the shoot-out defeat in 1990, as we sat in a pub in Bexhill, myself and a few friends had made a pact – Blood Brothers style (but without the blood) – that in four years' time we would fly out to the USA to follow our gallant heroes go one step further and lift the famous golden trophy. Not only did England's failure save me a fortune – or rather spared me the guilt I might have felt for having backed out of the deal – but it has me excited about football again, the way that I had been about the World Cup in 1978; the last time England had failed to qualify. I read World Cup magazines cover to cover, diligently filling out wall charts, admiring talented footballers from far-off lands, and all with the relaxed disposition of one who doesn't have to worry about England's next game, because there won't be one. Teams like Romania, Colombia, Nigeria, Bulgaria and Sweden seem colourful and exciting, particularly in the US sunshine, the intensity of which just emphasises how different it all is to our own domestic league.

When the tournament is over, I am amazed to see some of the stars I have so admired turning up in Merseyside, Yorkshire and North London. Daniel Amokachi has signed for Everton, Dan Petrescu for Sheffield Wednesday, and greedy Tottenham Hotspur, despite starting the new season with a 12-point deduction, having been penalised for financial irregularities, have managed to lure Petrescu's fellow Romanians, Gheorghe Popescu and Ilie Dumitrescu, to White Hart Lane, as well as Germany's star striker, Jurgen Klinsmann. Suddenly, the Premier League seems, if still not quite exotic, at least more interesting by way of its doors having been flung open to usher in such notable international players. Their welcome appearances brighten up *Match of the Day* and extend the kaleidoscopic festival that was the World Cup into the domestic footballing calendar. Chelsea's defeat at Wembley the previous May belongs to another era now and, with the Blues also playing in European competition, my footballing world has gone widescreen. The game is changing and will never be the same again.

More stars make their way to Premier League sides the following season, including twice former World Player of the Year, Ruud Gullit, who, incredibly, signs for Chelsea. It follows that one man does not make a team, and yet Gullit's signing already feels bigger than the acquisition of just one player. Mark Hughes, Terry Phelan and Dan Petrescu then follow him to Stamford Bridge, and for Chelsea to sign three of my favourite players seems eerie; almost as though the club has read my mind to seek inspiration as to who to sign next.

*

Having had Sky TV recently installed, for the first time, I am able to watch Chelsea games live on a comparatively regular basis in my own home, which has proved both a blessing and a curse. Over the years, I've become used to performing a bizarre ritual that involves having the game showing on one television, and another, in a different part of the house, switched to a channel that is broadcasting a programme as innocuous and far removed from sport as is possible. I will then sit down in a semi-relaxed position, although probably with arms folded in the early stages of anxiety or annoyance, and watch the build-up to the game. As it kicks off, I will begin a slow slide toward the edge of the seat that will end in me standing up, the timing of which will depend on how early in the game Chelsea's opponents threaten to score. Inevitably, within minutes of kick-off, I will be making my way hurriedly to the security TV, desperately trying to immerse myself in whatever documentary or chat show is on at the time. Unable to concentrate, I will then revert to the game, turn the volume down to a level that is barely audible until such time as there is a key change in the commentary that indicates that a goal has been scored, and I then go and make a cup of tea. I will only allow myself alcohol at the final whistle, and then only if Chelsea have won the game or earned a creditable draw against a decent team. This mad and un-merry dance will last the full 90 minutes, plus stoppage time, and I will only watch the half-time analysis if Chelsea aren't losing.

Right now, whilst watching Chelsea entertain Middlesbrough on a Sunday afternoon in February 1996, I'm getting ready to abandon ship and head for the security TV. But I might not need to just yet. Chelsea came under some pressure early on so I spent a minute or two standing up in readiness, and yet the Blues have just gone 1-0 up through

Gavin Peacock and things are looking good. They're on the attack again, it's opening up. Dan Petrescu picks out John Spencer unmarked in the Middlesbrough box, and he scores: 2-0 up already. Gullit breaks clear, squares it for Peacock, who only has to tap it goalwards. 3-0; it's not even half-time and I'm rubbing my eyes in wonder. I'm still grinning as the half-time pundits wax lyrical about the quality of Chelsea's football – or at least that's what I hear – and I ignore suggestions that Gullit may have been in an offside position for Chelsea's first.

In the second half, Chelsea are in such complete control that I don't want to leave the chair for fear of my movements triggering a 'Boro comeback. Then Paul Furlong adds a fourth, and before long, Peacock completes his hat-trick to make it five. It's unfortunate that the game has to end, but when it does, I'm already comparing what I've just seen to the fluid, intricate and incisive "Total Football" style of the great Dutch teams of the 1970s; in Ruud Gullit, they do have their own Dutch maestro after all. This is every fan's dream: a team featuring a blend of home-grown players and seasoned internationals turning on the style to completely embarrass the opposition, and it should be added that Middlesbrough are no slouches themselves.

*

"And so it came to pass... the Almighty Hod maketh a side in his own image."
> – Brian Woolnough, 6th February 1996.

So reads the headline to Woolnough's report on Chelsea's stunning victory yesterday. I've already photocopied the piece and will keep it always, preserving it for posterity as a reminder of a period when, under the guidance of Glenn Hoddle, Chelsea became capable of some sublime and clinical football, and this one game has crystallised their evolution to that level, from previously being a team who were as capable of being hammered as they were of scraping a victory.

Last month, I went to Loftus Road with Steve and QPR Chris to see Chelsea take on local rivals, Queens Park Rangers. It was the first time I'd had a chance to see first-hand evidence of the revolution that was occurring at Chelsea. The football they played that night seemed staggering at times. There was a composure about the way they passed the ball and retained possession that just hadn't seemed possible before Hoddle had arrived at the start of the 1993/94 season. It was clear that he had transformed the young David Lee from a rough diamond into a player of genuine quality and panache, who could orchestrate play from his role as sweeper, in the style of Hoddle himself. It would be interesting to know how the stats read for that game, but all I do know is that Chelsea were in such control of it that, even when QPR took the lead in the 70th minute, I wasn't too worried. As it turned out, Chelsea eventually had to rely on an own goal and the relief of a 90th minute winner, so it was clear that, no matter how good their football, some things would never change. I will forever recall that performance in gushing terms, so much so that to me it really was just like watching Brazil. The only blot on the memory is that this is 1996, so the players were forced to wear that shocking orange and grey away strip.

And yet none of this would have happened if it hadn't been for the result of the Blues' fourth round FA Cup replay at Sheffield Wednesday on Wednesday 9th February 1994. Chelsea won the game 3-1 after extra-time, and it was a match in which everything seemed to click into gear for the team. Hoddle's midfield diamond formation

– comprising Eddie Newton in the defensive role, Gavin Peacock in front with Craig Burley, and Dennis Wise either side – had born fruit at last, and continued to do so for the remainder of the season. If they hadn't won the game, they would have faced a battle against relegation and, with nothing else to play for and morale low, they might well have gone down, and Hoddle might well have lost his job: there would have been no FA Cup Final appearance, no European Cup Winners' Cup adventure the following season, and no foreign superstars.

I admire Hoddle in his time at Chelsea. He experienced a religious epiphany during his playing career and had become a born again Christian, and this resonated with me because I'd wrestled with similar theological issues myself in recent years. I'd been to Sunday school as a child so I believed in God, but only in the sense that I didn't know there was an option not to. Once the usual teenage pre-occupations had kicked in, atheism had become a far more attractive concept. But during my final two years at Kingston, a few good friends of mine had become Christians, which had led to my thinking a lot about Christianity, and religion in general, and after much deliberation, questioning and discussion, I'd come to embrace it in my own private way. As such, Hoddle's appointment felt as though it had a personal significance, and, at the time, there might even have been the odd moment when I thought it might be an indication that the club and myself were somehow spiritually in tune.

I took my girlfriend, and future wife, Vanessa, to Stamford Bridge in August 1993 to see them entertain Blackburn Rovers, in what was Hoddle's first game for the Club. This was to prove her one and only visit. Her subsequent non-attendance had much to do with finding no entertainment value in watching grown men kicking the modern equivalent of a pigs' bladder around a park, but had she watched more of the game and less of the antics of the Rovers supporters, I'd like to think that she would have found a lot to admire in Hoddle's performance. He had poise, finesse, vision and, it seemed, the ability to think four times quicker than anyone else on the pitch. It was, as somebody else at the game pointed out, like watching a PE teacher strolling around with all the time in the world, while the rest of the players harried like lunatics.

I hadn't played football much in my youth, other than jumpers-for-goalposts kick-arounds in the park, but once in my 20s, I began to play regularly. As soon as I'd seen Glenn Hoddle play for Chelsea, I'd taken it upon myself to try and emulate his performances on a Saturday or a Sunday. It was on these occasions that his talent became most apparent. I'd quickly discovered that, rather than buying me time to think and to slow the game down as Hoddle did, trying to play at a fraction of the speed of the other players around me would nearly always result in my losing the ball and, when playing as a sweeper, giving a goal away. But Hoddle managed to do it successfully and without fail, and not just against pot-bellied amateurs, who at best could claim that they once had a trial with Eastbourne United under-14s, but against talented and well-paid professionals. I have been known to argue unswervingly that Hoddle is one of the greatest managers of all time – most notably in a pub in the West End of London when two bemused Norwegians were unwittingly dragged into the debate – and very few people will agree with me at such times, and, to be fair, most of the time, I wouldn't either. But the reality is that, despite all the reservations people may have about his methods and beliefs, he moulded a ramshackle Chelsea side into a stylish team and took them into Europe for the first time in 22 years, and gave me the belief that something special was about to happen.

Cash and Kids
— 1996

In 1991, Jack Walker, a multi-millionaire who made his fortune in the steel industry, took control of Blackburn Rovers, then of the Second Division. Born and bred in Blackburn, and a life-long Rovers supporter, Walker was the country's first footballing superfan; a man with the will and financial means to back the club he supported and to help bring them the level of success that he, and every other Rovers fan, aspired to. His entrance into the public consciousness, and the consequent emergence of Blackburn Rovers as a major footballing force, bore a simmering envy as well as a grudging admiration in fans of other clubs. On the one hand, it hardly seemed fair that a club who had little or no hope of achieving success at the top level of the game should suddenly acquire the financial muscle to outbid Manchester United, Liverpool and every other club who'd spent years in the top flight for all the top players. On the other, who wouldn't wish for a similarly wealthy benefactor to appear in a puff of smoke to help out their club and make their dreams a reality? Envy was further tempered in most supporters' minds because Walker was a true fan of the club he'd bought.

For a Chelsea fan, in a glass half-empty, half-full predicament, Rovers' newfound wealth could either represent one more big scalp to claim, or a further diminishing of any chance of ever winning a trophy. For myself, the glass was as good as dry. There was just no way that Chelsea could compete without a serious injection of cash, and the occasional mugging of a top five club wasn't enough anymore. The club's appearance in the '94 Cup Final had raised expectations to such heights that a shadow was cast over the willingness to accept anything less than silverware itself. But, as luck would have it, Chelsea were soon to unearth a sugar daddy of their very own. Matthew Harding, a lifelong Chelsea fan, and now a successful businessman, had stepped in to answer Ken Bates' call for financial investment in the club in 1994. In the short time that he served on the board, both as director and then as Bates' vice-chairman, he committed millions to Chelsea. Though not sufficient to challenge the financial clout of Blackburn Rovers perhaps, his money not only contributed to the purchase of several high profile players, but also helped finance the construction of the new North Stand and the acquisition of the freehold of Stamford Bridge, so securing the club's immediate future.

*

1995/96 will turn out to be the only full season in which the "Four Hs" of Harding, Hoddle, Hughes and Gullit are in co-operation at the club, which is currently in rude health, and the future looks bright. Brighter still today because Chelsea are about to play in another FA Cup semi-final.

It's Sunday 31st March 1996, and I am on the verge of seeing my team progress to another Final, or at least would be if it wasn't for the fact that their opponents today are Manchester United. There are certain patterns that become apparent in football, perhaps the most obvious being that old saying, "what comes around goes around": if one day you get walloped, you will soon get your own back. Thanks to the '94 Cup Final spanking, one small portion of my mind is clinging to the hope that this might be the day that the saying will prove its worth. However, if anything, United are even stronger now. They still have midfield hard-man Roy Keane, the outstanding Peter Schmiechel in goal, and the ever-inspirational Eric Cantona playing wherever he chooses, but now they also have prolific striker, Andy Cole, along with a host of young stars in their squad, including Ryan Giggs, David Beckham, Paul Scholes, Nicky Butt, and the Neville brothers, Gary and Phil. But the real inspiration behind their success this season appears to be *Match of the Day* pundit and former Liverpool player, Alan Hansen. More specifically, his comment that "You can't win anything with kids", following United's 3-1 defeat at Aston Villa on the opening day of the season, seems to have inspired the team to achieve great things, so, effectively, he has created a monster.

Before winning a replay at St James' Park, Chelsea had almost been knocked out of this year's competition as early as the third round. Leading Newcastle United 1-0 at Stamford Bridge and heading for the fourth round draw, Dmitri Kharine had a goal kick for the Blues in the third minute of injury time. He only had to hoof it into the Newcastle half, or even into the stands, and the final whistle would have blown. Instead, he scuffed it straight to Phillipe Albert, who nodded it forward to Les Ferdinand and, whilst frozen in terror, I watched as the Newcastle striker side-footed it through the Chelsea keeper's legs and into the net. I turned the TV off and stood in silence in the kitchen, feeling more alone in the world than I had felt since I swapped my whole collection of Topps football cards for one Lou Macari when I was eight-years-old. I can't concentrate on anything in the few days before a cup game. I have now reached a stage where I don't just want the FA Cup, I *need* it.

I'm watching most of the first half from various locations, both seated and standing, with United having already hit the post and Giggs having had two point-blank efforts saved by Kharine's replacement, Kevin Hitchcock. It's not looking good. Then, in the 35th minute, Mark Hughes wins the ball and muscles his way into the United area, crosses beyond two defenders, and Gullit rises gracefully to head Chelsea into the lead, leaving Peter Schmeichel performing a flailing star jump as he watches the ball fly past him. I'm still on my feet and my arms are raised. I daren't say anything out loud, partly because I'm alone, but perhaps what's already gone around is about to come around after all. If that is to be the case, and Chelsea are to knock United out of a major cup competition for the first time ever, then they need to score another couple of goals soon, otherwise I'll be out of here. I barely watch the second half at all, unable to overcome the tension, and only occasionally switch the TV back on to check the score. The game turns in United's favour the moment Terry Phelan appears to pull a hamstring when chasing a through ball from John Spencer in the second half.

Minutes later, Andy Cole prods home the equaliser at the far post after Phil Neville's cross is headed back across goal by Cantona. Just four minutes after that, Chelsea self-destruct when an inexplicable back-pass from Craig Burley falls to David Beckham and he slides it past Hitchcock. Chelsea try to push for an equaliser, but it's not to be. No doubt it's been an entertaining game for some, but what was the point in United winning? They'll go on to win the Premier League, they've appeared in the last two Cup Finals, and do they really need to become the first side ever to win the League and Cup double twice? After 1994, I've had a major grudge with United, but now they've hurt me once too often. From this day on, we are mortal enemies.

*

I start to wonder whether I need some sort of lucky charm. Perhaps it would help spur my team on a bit, give them that edge they need to go one step further and actually win something. The "lucky" shirt was consigned to the loft soon after the Cup Final in 1994, having proved that it was nothing of the sort. Glenn Hoddle has himself proved lucky at Chelsea, but his work at the club hasn't gone unnoticed by the FA, who lured him away this summer to become the new England boss. As unfortunate as this is for Chelsea fans, as one legend leaves, another takes his place. Ruud Gullit has no managerial experience, but his is an exciting appointment nonetheless. Aside from his immense success on the field, he has always won things with teams who wear white socks, as he himself has pointed out.

Not long into the 1996/97 season, I am given a Ruud Gullit Corinthian figure – one of those two-inch tall figurines with the disproportionately large heads – and it immediately takes pride of place on my desk at work, forming a sparse but respectful altar to the new manager, and to hopes of a glorious future for Chelsea. Known simply as Little Ruud, the figurine has already proved lucky. By November 1996, it had managed to spirit Gianluca Vialli, Roberto Di Matteo, Frank Leboeuf and Gianfranco Zola to the club, so lending a glittering international sheen to the Chelsea squad that was hitherto unthinkable. In years past, the signing of just one of those players would've been enough to set pulses racing and conjure thoughts that this, yes, this *at last* would be the year when the doors to the trophy cabinet could be opened once again. With all four players arriving in the same season, surely everything is now in place to guarantee success:

financial backing, white socks, and a team that can compete with the best. On 2nd November 1996 they beat Manchester United 2-1 at Old Trafford, and it is now that anything seems possible.

Other than the fact that a win at Old Trafford isn't in itself a great rarity, the only flaw in this spontaneous eruption of optimism and its attendant plan for national domination is the fact that other teams are making some stellar purchases of their own. Middlesbrough, not famed for its glamour, does now however boast a football club with lofty ambitions. In 1995, having just been promoted, they'd signed the Brazilian starlet, Juninho. By the time they kicked off against Liverpool in the first game of the 1996/97 season, they could also name Juninho's fellow Brazilian, Emerson, and Italian international striker, Fabrizio Ravanelli, in their squad.

Newcastle United, with the flamboyant Frenchman, David Ginola, and the artful Colombian, Faustino Asprilla, already at the club, had bucked the international trend and splashed out a massive £15 million on England's own Alan Shearer. Aside from the North Eastern threats, Manchester United are now beginning to look invincible. The mark of a truly great side is one that can not only win the major trophies, but also continue to do so consistently, and with the achievement of their second League and Cup double in three seasons still a recent memory, United don't appear to be in any mood to relinquish either honour; the Premier League title in particular. Despite suffering what, for United, represents a major blip in the autumn, with a run of three successive defeats that began with a 5-0 humbling at Newcastle, followed by an infamous 6-3 defeat at Southampton – in which the team were forced to change their kit at half-time from a grey strip, that apparently rendered the players invisible, to a more obvious blue one – and ending with the defeat at home to Chelsea, like a wounded animal, they've come back with a vengeance. They don't lose another game until March, by which time they're top of the League and on course to win it once again. Having seemingly kick-started United's charge to the title with the 2-1 win at Old Trafford, any fanciful hope Chelsea have of competing for the League has gone before the year is out. Which, once again, leaves just the FA Cup.

Blue Day
— 1996/97

As I am driving past the post office in Cambridge Road, Hastings, during my lunch break on 22nd October 1996, it is announced on the radio that Matthew Harding has been killed in a helicopter crash whilst travelling home from Chelsea's 2-1 defeat at Bolton. It would be conceit to suggest that I'm devastated – I'd never met the man after all – but all Chelsea fans feel a very real and personal sense of loss upon hearing that news, I'm sure. He was a true supporter, dedicated and passionate, rarely missing a game, and had the courage to help the club he loved try to achieve the success we all wanted for them. My memory of his passing will be crystallised as a four-way split-screen image with, clockwise from top left: a typical image of Matthew Harding wearing a Chelsea shirt and his trademark cheeky grin, Scott Minto scoring Chelsea's only goal of the game against Bolton, a street view of Hastings General Post Office and, finally, the scene outside Stamford Bridge in the following days, with the poignant image of Terry Phelan laying flowers amid the thousands of wreaths, shirts and scarves already laid in tribute. At such times, any thoughts of self-pity following a Chelsea defeat become trivial, and all thoughts of my visit to the Bridge three days ago to bear witness to Wimbledon's 4-2 dismantling of my team evaporated in an instant. Within two months, I am to receive news that, on a personal level, is so distressing that it will prove to have the opposite effect.

*

Harding's death has cast a huge cloud over Chelsea's season, and yet in the following weeks, the club appeared to galvanise in the most positive way. A team who had been under-performing thus far have now wiped the slate clean and, starting with an emotional home victory against Tottenham four days after the accident, their League form has improved enough to raise anticipation for a decent cup run. Side-stepping the potential banana skin that a home tie in the third round against West Bromwich Albion might normally have represented, with a 3-0 victory, further increases optimism. But then comes the draw for the fourth round; on 26th January, Chelsea will have to entertain Liverpool. Although the Blues beat them 1-0 at the beginning of the month, they also lost 5-1 at Anfield earlier in the 1996/97 season, and Liverpool have proved harder to beat than Manchester United in recent years. The Merseysiders also have a point to prove in this season's competition, having lost out to United in the Final last year. I am certain we'll lose, and, to make matters worse, the game is televised, meaning that I have an obligation to sit and watch it for as long as physically possible.

Before 10 minutes are up, I am too, as Robbie Fowler prompts my exit with a simple tap-in. By the time I can look again, Stan Collymore has made it 2-0, and by the interval, it could've been more. Within 45 minutes, a season that had begun in August with a flurry of illustrious signings and a bucketful of hope has already ended, in embarrassment, and the start of the next sits on a horizon that's barely visible. What I haven't bargained for is the possibility that, unlike myself, Chelsea haven't given up hope of turning the game around.

At half-time, Ruud Gullit faces his biggest test yet as a manager in trying to lift the players after such a turbulent first period. Whatever it is that he has said or done during the interval, the only conclusion I can draw is that, thinking outside the box, and with a stroke of managerial genius, he has adopted the guise of the shopkeeper in the 1970's cartoon series *Mr Benn*, so as to usher the players onto the pitch, not via the usual doorway, but through a new and magical one.

The pitch they step onto for the second half is different somehow, and alive with glorious possibilities. Last to take to the field is substitute Mark Hughes, cast in the role of Mr Benn himself, and tasked with the job of restoring the equilibrium. Hughes' impact is immediate. Within five minutes of the re-start, a long ball is played into the Liverpool box, he takes it on his chest, swivels and fires it beyond David James. Eight minutes later, he tees-up Gianfranco Zola, who equalises with a belter from 20 yards. In the 63rd minute, as Gianluca Vialli toe-pokes the ball past James, the comeback is complete, and then confirmed in the 76th when Vialli scores again. I've never known a game quite like it. It just seems unfeasible that Chelsea could overturn a 2-0 deficit, let alone against a team of Liverpool's stature.

So buoyant am I in the immediate aftermath of the match that I do something that I will soon feel thoroughly ashamed of. My first thought is to expunge myself of all those years of grief suffered at the hands of Liverpool, whilst a supporter of both Chelsea and United, by phoning an old school-friend, who to me represents Liverpool Football Club more than anyone else I know, and who'd been a chief antagonist in my school years. In the event, when he comes to the phone, I can't quite bring myself to indulge in full-on gloating by adopting the parlance of a 12-year-old and saying that Liverpool are rubbish and Chelsea are magic, and instead choose to offer my thinly-masked condolences, whilst he proceeds to berate Ruud Gullit, whose face has just appeared on screen.

*

Toward the end of 1996, Dad begins to feel unwell. A few days before Christmas, it is confirmed that he is suffering from stomach cancer, from which there will be no hope of a recovery. The news comes as a complete shock to us all, and this is the first time that I've felt the closeness and stability of our family unit to be threatened in any way. Being the youngest by several years has always seemed to infer a lesser responsibility upon me, and this has never been more apparent than now.

I feel a numbness in the following months and, although I do go home regularly and can see for my myself just how quickly he is deteriorating, I feel a detachment from the situation, as if in some way it just can't be real. As a parting gift to the family, Dad wanted for us all to have a holiday in Florida, himself included, despite his physical fragility. So in February, we spend two weeks together, visiting Disney World, Universal Studios, MGM, SeaWorld and Epcot. It is a wonderful trip in so many ways, but against such a desperate backdrop, it further adds to the incongruence of the whole situation.

*

A million miles away, in another concurrent reality, Chelsea are progressing well in the FA Cup and have overcome Leicester City and Portsmouth to set up a semi-final showdown with Wimbledon. Emerging as the surprise package of the season, Wimbledon have reached the semi-finals of both domestic cup competitions and are competing well in the League, prompting talk of the Dons achieving a possible trophy treble. As outlandish as that may seem, they are an imposing and fiercely competitive side in 1997. They knocked Manchester United out of the FA Cup in February and are the one team that I had hoped Chelsea could avoid in the latter stages. The other possible semi-final opponents had been Chesterfield, of Division One, and Middlesbrough, who had begun to struggle in the wake of their recent League Cup Final defeat to Leicester City, and a three-point deduction handed out for failing to field a team for a League fixture against Blackburn Rovers, due to having had a squad depleted by illness and injury on the day of the game.

I hear a news story in the days leading up to the semi-finals that a celebrity, I don't recall who, possibly Mystic Meg, had dreamt that a team with the letters CFC on their shirts would lift the FA Cup in May. This gives me a welcome crumb of hope initially, until I realise that CFC also stands for Chesterfield Football Club.

On 13th April, Chelsea, in yellow, line up against Wimbledon, in red, at Highbury, and I'm watching the game with friends at a pub after playing a Sunday League match. In such surroundings, there is nowhere to hide, but if the might of Ekoku, Jones and Gayle torment Chelsea the way that I expect them to, I will still make my excuses and take my leave early in the game. But once Mark Hughes scores to put Chelsea one up, the game becomes easier to bear, even more so in the second half, once Zola skilfully wrong-foots Dean Blackwell to make it two. Hughes then adds a second late on to make the final score 3-0, and Chelsea are one step closer to glory.

Chesterfield play Middlesbrough later that afternoon, and are magnificent. They're 2-1 up and 20 minutes from victory against a team reduced to 10 men, and I begin to think that perhaps the celebrity dreamer has been correct, and that I will now have to suffer the ignominy of my team losing in the Final to a team from Division One. They're eventually beaten in a replay after the game finishes 3-3, and I can now look forward to the Final, safe in the knowledge that Chelsea are the only CFC to which the dream could have referred.

*

The following day, my father died. Given the pain that he'd been suffering in the final weeks, and the strain that Mum had been under, initially, it was something of a relief when it happened. Seeing the bed now empty and the family in relatively good spirits made the events of the preceding four months seem implausible. I'd had some nice things happen to me during his illness – such as becoming a godparent for the first time, and winning a Cup Final with one of the football teams I played for, after many years of trying – and I'd love to have shared those experiences with him, but the stark contrast between our family's situation and my personal life away from it made it all seem less and less real. I've spent much of the period in a state of denial, which is to continue for some time, and football is once again providing a major distraction.

*

Thoughts of the impending Cup Final, to be played on 17th May, are now promoted to a more prominent central role. With the squad they have, and the way they've been playing under Gullit, there is every chance that Chelsea can win. Unlike three years previously, when Chelsea had been obvious underdogs against United, it's recognised that this represents their best ever chance of the Blues laying to rest the ghosts of 1970. At work, Little Ruud serves as a constant reminder, as if I really need it, of Chelsea's date with destiny. He remains unmoved for the next five weeks, as if disturbing a two-inch representation of a footballer would somehow distract the real Ruud from the job at hand, namely coaching his team to glory.

In the run-up to the Final, everything seems to be going smoothly. There are no injuries to key players, Chelsea have been playing well – winning three of their last four games of the season and drawing the other – and confidence is high, which worries me greatly. Five weeks isn't a long time in the universal scheme of things, but it feels like five months when your team is due to play in an FA Cup Final, and allows the mind far too much space in which to run riot. Of the host of possibilities entertained, the most likely seems to be that, given the famed romance of the Cup and the part that fate will undoubtedly play, Middlesbrough, having already been beaten in the League Cup Final, and having suffered the pain of relegation on the last day of the Premier League season, are destined to end the campaign on a high by beating Chelsea to lift the FA Cup in an inevitable third-time-lucky plotline. Once born, this possibility has quickly become a probability, and I then spend the week leading up to the game, hoping for news from the Middlesbrough camp of training ground bust-ups or freak injuries to key players; obviously not serious injuries, but perhaps just bruising to a toe, caused by a fumbled bottle of ketchup in the canteen that, though seemingly innocuous, causes enough discomfort to render the supremely gifted Juninho, for example, temporarily immobile. There is to be no such news from Middlesbrough, but, thankfully, not from Chelsea either. There is another possibility that would fit with the romantic nature of the competition perfectly, and that has occurred to me, but that pessimism and caution will not permit me to dwell upon: the late Matthew Harding, who would have loved to see the Blues lift the Cup more than anyone, would tragically be denied the chance of doing so, just months after his life had been taken, but what more fitting tribute could there be than for his heroes – whom he had helped to assemble – to go and win the famous trophy in his honour?

It's the night before the game and we are at a friend's wedding party. Although I should be doing nothing but projecting glad tidings toward the happy couple, all I can bring myself to do is talk about my concerns for Chelsea tomorrow. It's all I can think about. Towards the end of the evening I stand at the bar with a couple of long-suffering friends and proceed to deliver what feels like a speech of Shakespearian magnitude and that deserves a far larger audience, in a bid to explain the importance of tomorrow's Final. In reality, it's just a minutes worth of slurred words, arranged in something resembling sentences, that can be paraphrased simply by saying that, should Chelsea win, I would be able see out my days in perfect contentment, having lived a life fulfilled.

*

It's May 17th, 1997. The big day has arrived, at last. Ashley, the Arsenal-supporting friend who introduced me to the delights of Highbury in 1991, has invited Steve and I around to watch the Final, and now I'm sitting in his front room, waiting for the horror to unfold. So all-consuming is my concern that I will soon be feeling as bad as I had at the end of the Cup Final of '94, I would promise vast sums to anyone who can offer me a way to take a peek an hour or two into the future, just to see what the result will be, and enable me to either stay and enjoy the game, or leave quietly. I don't think I'll be able to cope if Chelsea lose again. To exacerbate my fears of defeat, our Sunday League team's end of season awards night, which I am helping to organise so have to attend, is being held tonight, and a Chelsea loss will not be ignored. Watching the build-up on TV – in which several references to Matthew Harding are made – helps calm my nerves slightly, as does the relaxed demeanour of Steve, who always has a far more realistic and mature attitude in the wake of a Chelsea defeat than I do. But nothing relieves tension quite like a goal in the first minute of a Cup Final.

When Dennis Wise wins the ball and feeds it to Roberto Di Matteo, still in the Chelsea half of the pitch, there is no cause for excitement. But then, Roberto keeps running, and the 'Boro players keep letting him. And then he stutters, pulls back his boot and, still unchallenged, prepares to shoot. Expecting the ball to sail high over the goal only heightens my surprise as it brushes the underside of the bar and hits the back of the net.

"Oh what about this?! What about this? It's possibly the quickest ever goal in a Wembley Cup Final! It's Roberto Di Matteo inside 45 seconds," John Motson cries.

But I barely hear him. My reaction to the goal is curious; I leap from my seat, run out of the room unchallenged, and keep running until I reach a wall in the hallway, which I high-five. From this day on, and for many years afterwards, I will repeat this celebration unconsciously following the most important goals, only failing to complete the ritual if I am denied a clear run at a wall. The last opportunity I'd had to celebrate my team scoring a goal in an FA Cup Final had been in 1983. But that was Manchester United, and they were expected to win trophies. This was Chelsea; the team that I'd started to think might always be the bridesmaids at a miserable and badly-organised wedding. So I can forgive my own bizarre post-goal antics on this occasion, because this could be the moment that I have been waiting for.

But, once the euphoria has lapsed and the game has re-started, it dawns on me that scoring a goal after 43 seconds, the fastest in Wembley Cup Final history, might not be such a good thing. It could have an adverse effect. Middlesbrough are likely to wake up now, take advantage of the Chelsea players' physical exertions during their goal celebrations, and win the game. But the Middlesbrough players look shell-shocked following the goal, and they remain so for much of the first-half. Their star striker, Fabrizio Ravanelli, wasn't fully fit prior to kick-off and, during a rare sprint toward the Chelsea goal, he injures himself further and is substituted after just 24 minutes. Middlesbrough are then forced to make another change just six minutes later as Robbie Mustoe is also replaced. It's been a terrible start for the team in red, and, therefore, the perfect start for me.

But then the team in red equalise.

"The linesman on the far side is flagging. Brian Robson's team have not equalised."

Yes! Thank you John Motson!

Middlesbrough defender, Gianluca Festa, was in an offside position as he headed the ball beyond Chelsea's keeper, Frode Grodås. Or was he? It looks marginal, but who cares? It doesn't count, and I love both John Motson, for announcing the news, and the linesman, for raising his flag. And then, the half-time whistle blows. With the exception of the disallowed goal, Middlesbrough have rarely threatened Chelsea. I'm feeling calm, but in the back of my mind I know that there is still a catastrophe waiting to happen.

Middlesbrough may have lost two important players early in the game, but they still have Juninho. As the second-half progresses, the little Brazilian is looking as though he will be the instigator of my imagined catastrophe as, time and again, he attempts to take Chelsea on single-handedly, and looks increasingly likely to do so. I'm not sure I can take much more of this. On the whole, Chelsea are controlling the game, but they're not controlling Juninho. Di Matteo is booked for bringing him down on the edge of the penalty area, and I'm relieved to see that the referee only shows him a yellow card, as is Di Matteo. Thankfully, the resultant free kick comes to nothing.

We're into the last 10 minutes of the game and I'm considering my options. I could walk out now, which would look cowardly. I could hold a cushion in front of my face, which, again, would look less than dignified. Or I could stay perched on the edge of my seat, hoping that Chelsea might grab a second goal, and in so doing, force Juninho to finally give up hope.

"*And Chelsea come forward again with Newton. Petrescu is to the right. So is Hughes. This is Petrescu; he's gone for the far corner, and Zola came in. And it's there! It's Eddie Newton!*"

It's the 83rd minute. Surely that's it now. There is no repeat of the high-fiving celebration from myself following that goal, nor, 10 minutes later, at the final whistle; just a feeling of elation – which I vocalise by shouting an expletive – tempered by overwhelming relief. The camera pans to Ruud Gullit, and to Ken Bates, and to Ruth Harding, Matthew's widow.

"*And it's a moment for Chelsea to cherish. Their first major trophy for 26 years.*"

Motson's right. I've seen my team win a trophy, better still the FA Cup, and it feels so much better than '77. This time,

I've put the work in, done the time – not as much as other Chelsea fans by any means, but anyone who sat through the horror of '94 deserves this moment.

*

When I'd arrived home after the game, I'd remembered with some disappointment that, for reasons of superstition, I hadn't recorded any of it. Later, when Vanessa and I get home from the club awards night, I hasten to the video recorder to watch the *Match of the Day* highlights. I'm not sure how I expected it to feel. I'm still happy, obviously, deliriously so. But amid the delirium and the alcoholic haze, I am also aware that something is missing. Perhaps I'm already concerned that there's nothing to worry about anymore: Chelsea have won a major trophy at last – something that I've wanted for 13 years – and I feel pride, pleasure and relief, but I'm not sure what comes next. I know that the ecstasy of that one moment when the final whistle blew can't last forever. I watch the highlights, and then I watch Dennis Wise lift the FA Cup. Then I hit rewind and watch him lift it again, and again, and again. As I do so, for the first time in my adult life, football makes me cry, although, after such an emotionally-bewildering five months, I'm certain the tears are shed for my Dad as much as for the boys in blue.

New Europeans
— 1997/98

I want more. Traditionally, the final has always been the last game of the domestic season, and for a football fan, that is what makes winning the FA Cup unique. Given that a team is only as good as their last result, it means that your team are officially very good for three whole months. As I recalled from United's win in 1977, the effect this has is for summers to flash past in a glorious blur, leaving you wishing that all future football could be banned to prolong the victory. But in August 1997, the prospect of a new season was exciting and I couldn't wait for it to get underway. Chelsea had a manager who was now not only experienced, but successful. He had signed some new players – including the returning Graeme Le Saux – and despite their penalty shoot-out defeat to Manchester United in the Charity Shield, there seemed every reason to be optimistic for the coming campaign. As it progressed, the assumption I'd previously made, that once I'd seen them win a major trophy, I would be quite content to put up with a lifetime of trophy-free mediocrity, seemed increasingly preposterous. Success is addictive, and when experienced once, it has to be experienced again.

The FA Cup as a competition begins when the Premier League has barely kicked off, with six qualifying rounds to be played before top-flight teams enter the fray for the third round proper in January. When the draw for the third round is made, clubs from the non-League and lower divisions will be praying for a draw against a big club, and in particular,

Manchester United, the biggest of them all. I'll be praying for the exact opposite, as I was when the draw was made for the 1997/98 competition. Please let Chelsea be drawn against Hereford United or Emley, home or away, I don't mind which. In fact, anyone would be okay, but not Manchester United. Oh, it's Manchester United. Great. At Stamford Bridge? As if it matters.

I watch only bits of the first half – mainly the bad bits. I see David Beckham score a tap-in following all sorts of defensive confusion. I cringe as Ed de Goey tips Beckham's free kick into the net to make it 2-0 to United. I miss Cole's breakaway goal just before half-time, and Chelsea are 3-0 down already. It's a living nightmare. If we'd drawn Emley instead of this lot, at least we might still be in with a fighting chance.

I hardly watch the second half at all, only returning to the TV to see that Teddy Sheringham has just scored from a corner to make it 5-0 with quarter of an hour left to play, having missed Cole's fourth for United 10 minutes earlier. Graeme Le Saux then chips the ball over Peter Schmeichel from 20 yards, but it's no consolation and I'm left wondering whether there's any way to exchange that goal for Peacock hitting the bar at Wembley in '94 just to see what might have happened.

Three minutes later, Gianluca Vialli grabs a second for Chelsea, but again, too little too late. But hang on, when Gary Pallister makes a mess of a back pass with two minutes of normal time remaining, parts of my life flash before my eyes: Pallister's sliced own goal against Chelsea in 1990, the 4-2 Cup win over Liverpool last year and, better than that, Chelsea's comeback against Sheffield Wednesday at Hillsborough in the League Cup in 1985, when having been 3-0 down at half-time, they came back to draw 4-4 and take the tie to a replay. Pallister hits it straight to Vialli, who plays a one-two with Dan Petrescu and knocks it into an empty net. 5-3. Game on. This could be the greatest comeback of all time. As it turns out though, United were just toying with us, and now I dislike them even more.

*

With retaining the FA Cup now an impossibility, greed demands a trophy. Any trophy will do, but the Premier League is a dream too far. At the beginning of the season, it seemed that only Manchester United and Chelsea's own inconsistency could prevent the Blues from adding the League title to the previous season's Cup Final success. But then Arsenal began to rise from the shadows, under the guidance of Arsene Wenger, who'd been in the job for barely a year. Chelsea were still hanging in there until February and were still in with a shot, until, on 11th February, disaster struck; for a joke, two of my work colleagues stole Little Ruud.

Chelsea sacked Ruud Gullit the very next day and Little Ruud's kidnapping sprung to mind immediately upon hearing the news. The two events seemed both coincidental yet uncanny. Little Ruud had hardly moved for 18 months, in which time Chelsea had won their first major silverware in 26 years. Whilst at work the following day, I jokingly voiced my displeasure to the kidnappers, who had already admitted their guilt and returned Little Ruud without the need for a ransom, and I blamed them for big Ruud's sacking. I thought that I'd done this with my tongue held firmly in my cheek, but when one of the protagonists later had a quiet word with me to express her disbelief that I could seriously believe that their prank and Gullit's dismissal could really be connected, it was clear that I'd actually sounded serious in my accusation, and it occurred to me that perhaps a part of me really did.

It was immediately announced that Gullit was to be replaced by Gianluca Vialli, another current squad player now promoted to player-manager, but this wasn't the cause for concern that it might have been a few years previously. The club had proved that the appointment of player-managers could work, and with wonderful consequences. With Gullit having already retired as a player the previous season, the playing staff were still intact, so an already impressive squad was still more than capable of picking up at least one of the two trophies that they still had a realistic chance of winning. In a daunting baptism of fire, Vialli's first game in charge was to be against Arsenal, in the second leg of the League Cup semi-final at Stamford Bridge. With the Gunners leading 2-1 from the first leg, and having also beaten the Blues 2-0 in a League encounter at Highbury 10 days earlier, there is a daunting challenge ahead for Vialli and his men.

I settled down to watch the game, fully expecting to be turning the TV over within minutes, with Arsenal having stretched the aggregate score beyond the reach of my team. But Mark Hughes put the Blues ahead in the 10th minute, and within an hour, they are 3-0 up on the night – Di Matteo and Petrescu – and Arsenal are down to 10 men. The game ends 3-1, Chelsea have won 4-3 on aggregate, and they are through to another Final.

With all hopes of a title challenge now gone for sure, Vialli's next big test is to guide his team past Spain's Real Betis in the quarter-final of the UEFA Cup Winners' Cup. This he manages comfortably as Chelsea win 2-1 away, and they then seal their place in the semi-final with a 3-1 victory in the home leg. Ten days later and they are once again playing Middlesbrough in a Final at Wembley, this time in the League Cup. On this occasion, I wasn't thinking about the game at all – I was at a family memorial service in honour of my father – but yet again, they win 2-0 and Di Matteo scores, although on this occasion, extra-time is needed for the Blues to lift the Cup. Whereas most managers will spend years trying to win a trophy, Gianluca Vialli has won one within his first two months in charge. What's more, he has an opportunity to win another as he prepares his Chelsea team to face Vicenza in the Cup Winners' Cup semi-final.

The first leg is played in Italy on 2nd April, only days after the Wembley Final. Perhaps unsurprisingly, the Italians win 1-0; a far from unassailable lead with the home leg still to come. I am hopeful more than optimistic as the game kicks off, knowing that Italian sides are famously hard to beat. Vicenza score in the 32nd minute and the goal comes as the result of some comically naïve defending. I immediately turn the television over to watch a documentary about pigeons. My brother remonstrates with me and can't understand why I should've given up on my team so soon. I admire this attitude but when my team concede a goal, the only eventuality I can consider is that the opposition will score the next goal as well. However, Andrew seems intent on watching the match rather than an informative program about the breeding habits of one of Britain's most common birds, and insists that I turn back. Reluctantly, I comply, but only because it is his house and, therefore, his television.

I've barely taken my finger off the channel selector when Zola fires in a shot from outside the penalty area, which the Vicenza keeper parries only for Gus Poyet to let loose an acrobatic volley and put Chelsea back into contention. I will thank my brother for days afterwards because, as a result of his insistence, I am to witness one of Chelsea's great comebacks, and two superb goals. Surprisingly, given the international look of Chelsea's team, both goals are typically English. The first is a thumping header by Zola from a powerful and rangy cross on the run by Vialli. The second is classic route one – a huge punt up the field from Blues keeper, Ed de Goey, then Hughes nods the ball upward, spins and fires it into the far corner. 3-2 Chelsea on aggregate, and they're in another Cup Final. An exhilarating performance of this fashion is something I've rarely seen from my team, and the Manchester United nightmare of three months earlier has been wiped from the memory, temporarily at least.

The final is to be played in Stockholm. Ian, my eldest brother and fellow Chelsea supporter, is living in Sweden now, and he and a friend have bought tickets for the Final. I haven't once considered it an option to fly out to see the game myself, which surprises the friends I speak to the week before the game. I point out that there is simply no way that I could afford to go, to which one points out that I should just stick it all on my credit card and worry about it later. This would seem like an obvious thing to do, and I do feel a little ashamed that my dedication to my team won't extend to entering a period of short-term debt, but my relationship with Chelsea isn't like that. They don't need me there; they'll be fine. The ticket allocation will all sell out and the support in Stockholm will be tremendous. Instead, I go to Mum's house and watch the match with Steve and Ashley. Andrew joins us, along with a lucky mascot in the form of my nephew, Ben – aged three-and-a-half – resplendent in full Chelsea kit. The final itself is tense and unenjoyable until the 70th minute. Zola has been on the pitch for less than a minute when Dennis Wise chips the ball forward. Zola collects, and he's one on one, in almost exactly the position that Michael Thomas was in 1989. He catches it perfectly on the half volley and the ball's still rising as it hits the roof of the net, and I am off, arms outstretched, running out of the lounge, through the dining room and into the kitchen, the wall of which I high-five. Gianfranco has won us the game.

Two trophies in one season. For a short time, the club are actually the holders of three, as it is still two weeks before they are to relinquish the FA Cup to Arsenal. The Gunners also go on to win the League title, and so win the double for the second time in their history. I look over in their direction briefly and envy their achievement. We've won two trophies, but then so have they, and arguably theirs are more significant.

But then I snap out of it and, figuratively speaking, remember exactly where I am. Five years ago, I was at a wet and windy Selhurst Park, watching the Cup dream die once more, feeling despondent, but Chelsea have now not only repeated their success of the early 1970s by winning the FA Cup one season and the Cup Winners' Cup the next, but have surpassed it by winning the League Cup as well. Three months later, on 28th August, the Blues beat Champions League winners Real Madrid 1-0 to lift the UEFA Super Cup. I don't believe that it can ever get any better than this.

But still I want more.

Part Three

Where The Grass Is Greener

Wombling Free
— 1998/99

I've done it again, I know. This time it was worse though. This time I made no attempt to hide it. But I really don't think that I'm the one to blame...

*

For a young football supporter, the perfect scenario would be this: you're born somewhere that has a little-known football club. When you're old enough to make choices of your own, you choose to support that football club. You then watch them rise from respected non-League stalwarts to top-flight mainstays in a matter of nine years, and finally, you see them lift the FA Cup two years later (having beaten a team who some of your friends support and who just happen to be the current League champions). It sounds implausible, but that is exactly the experience that my friend, Skip, had enjoyed.

Born in 1970, at a time when Wimbledon were a successful team in what was then called the Southern League – one division below full League status – he would've been just about old enough to be aware of their legendary FA Cup run in 1974/75, as they beat First Division Burnley away from home, and then held the First Division champions Leeds United to a 0-0 draw, also away from home.

In 1977, when Skip was just seven-years-old, Wimbledon were elected to join the Football League, so beginning a meteoric rise through the divisions that ended with them winning promotion to the First Division in 1986. When they beat the mighty Liverpool at Wembley to win the FA Cup in 1988, Skip was still a teenager. The club's achievements in such a short space of time were impressive enough, but, although it is statistically probable that he wasn't the only person to be born in Wimbledon in the early 1970s, and who spent their formative years in Sussex, to me, it still represents an extraordinary and enviable synchronicity, and one that might never be repeated.

*

Five minutes ago, I was a neutral. I was enjoying the fact that I was feeling neither nerves nor anxiety. I'd been looking forward to watching the game, and all subsequent games this season, through the eyes of a purist: it won't be the result that matters, just the quality of the football. But it wasn't to last. Something changed the moment Efan Ekoku headed Wimbledon's second goal, at which point I leapt from my seat, becoming airborne for a second or two, and cried "Yes!"

I've remained impartial for much of the game, and though I've never been particularly fond of Tottenham Hotspur, I'd been enjoying watching Spurs stars such as Anderton and Ferdinand without experiencing that familiar leaden-stomached feeling every time they had the ball, and I have nodded approvingly whenever David Ginola has turned on the style. Even when Robbie Earle put Wimbledon ahead in the second half, I merely clapped politely.

But now, as Wimbledon are put under increasing pressure, I begin to chew my nails nervously, or grip my seat until my knuckles turn white, and then raise both hands to my head in horror as Ginola or Fox threaten the Dons' goal. I cheer every Wimbledon tackle and Tottenham fumble, and clap vociferously when Ginola is booked for diving: where once I'd admired, now I scorn. Obviously it's entirely normal to form an allegiance in whatever sport you might be watching – be it choosing the horse with the funniest name, or the team that haven't won a game for six months – yet, until this match, I had genuinely thought that remaining indifferent for the whole season, let alone for just one game, would be easy. But what worries me more is the detachment I feel as I sit through the highlights of Chelsea's defeat at Coventry on *Match of the Day* later in the evening, which I do purely in order to watch 30 seconds of action from the Wimbledon-Spurs match right at the end of the programme.

*

In 1998, Vanessa and I left Hastings and moved to the London Borough of Sutton, temporarily staying with my brother, Andrew, and his family whilst we looked for a permanent home. I'd decided to finally try and make use of my estate management degree by gaining the requisite work experience to become a chartered surveyor, whilst working as a self-employed surveyor and draughtsman, and Andrew, a structural engineer, had kindly offered to put some work my way whilst I did so. I'd been struggling with what I assumed had been stress for a while at the end of '97 and, having seen a doctor, assuming that he'd sign me off work for a few days, he instead prescribed a six-month course of Prozac and advised me to go back to work because it would be good for my self-esteem. It was obvious that my father's passing had affected me more than I'd realised. Football, and more specifically Chelsea's march to FA Cup glory, had given me a welcome escape from the stark reality of Dad's illness, but had really only delayed the inevitable. As my mind cleared,

Vanessa and I began to discuss our future and decided that we needed to make a change. We made the move mainly to be closer to the city for work opportunities, but for a long while, we'd both had a secret yearning to live near the capital on a permanent basis, and we'd finally got around to telling each other after five years together, and thought it best to do something about it before we reached 30.

Since leaving Kingston in 1991, I'd managed to uphold a pledge to get to a Chelsea game at least once a season, but now that we were living just a few miles away from Stamford Bridge, I was looking forward to going more regularly. Ideally, I wanted a season ticket, as I viewed this as a necessary step to take in order to become a true supporter; to celebrate Chelsea's increasingly frequent victories with a greater sense of having earned the right to do so, and to take my loyalty to another level by paying for the privilege. But Chelsea raised their season ticket prices by almost 50 per cent for the 1998/99 season, and that seemed like a high price for loyalty (and it was money that I didn't have because at the time I was earning very little). Then, when phoning the Club to ask for a reserve team fixture list, I'm told that I can only have one if I send them a stamped addressed envelope first, and my annoyance at this far outweighs the price of a couple of second-class stamps. Petty perhaps, but in the meantime, having bemoaned the Club's stellar pricing to anyone who would listen, I learned that you could get a season ticket to see Wimbledon FC for a mere £180. This represents incredible value for money and means that I can see all 20 Premier League teams in a season for the price of five or six trips to the Bridge. Wimbledon, by now, are playing at Selhurst Park, the home of Crystal Palace, and to be within easy reach of a Football League club, let alone one who are playing in the Premier League, is a great novelty.

I quickly got in touch with Skip to see whether he'd be interested in making the long trip from East Sussex every couple of weeks to see his team, and he was. So that was that; we bought tickets for the Players' Lounge – deciding that we would splash out the extra £60 for a tad more luxury than the Holmesdale Road end could offer; namely a bar and the opportunity to see some of the players having a drink after the game.

When I mention it to my brother, Ian, he says he thinks it strange that I've bought a season ticket at a club other than Chelsea. I can't disagree with him because I'm not really comfortable with it either. Once again, the memory of my Aston Villa moment of shame in 1977, coupled with that of my visits to see Wimbledon between 1989 and 1990, have made me feel as though I'm betraying Chelsea in some way. I'd already flirted with the Dons before and I thought I'd got them out of my system. There had been no love letters to dispose of, or photographs of the two of us to tear in half, and I'd been left with just a scarf that I'd since given away, but whereas our previous relationship had only amounted to the occasional rendezvous behind the bike sheds, this seems more serious. It involves commitment.

Obviously the honourable thing would be to go to see Chelsea when I can afford to, or to not watch live football at all, but instead, I've convinced myself that by overcharging their supporters, my Club are the ones who have betrayed me, and I've run straight into the arms of another. I explain to my brother, and others, that going to see Wimbledon is purely about watching and enjoying football, and nothing to do with allegiance, which satisfies them, but I'm not sure that it really convinces me. There had come a point in 1992 when, with Dave Beasant and Dennis Wise already at the club and Vinnie Jones having just been signed, it seemed as though

Wimbledon were attempting a takeover at Chelsea, with Beasant the Trojan Horse, and it made you wonder exactly when Alan Cork, John Fashanu and Carlton Fairweather might pitch up too. Perhaps I should have wanted that, because it would make my current concerns a complete non-issue.

In some ways, I feel as though, being relative newcomers to League football, Wimbledon need protecting, and I feel protective towards them. In that sense, our relationship is more paternal than romantic: we spend a day out together every other weekend, sometimes midweek, for a treat, I give them money and, in return, they either irritate me, make me laugh, or give me reason to feel proud. I don't like them being criticised. From the moment they were promoted to the top division in the mid-1980s, the Club had been regularly criticised for the style of football they played. They've now been playing in the top-flight for 12 years, so the critics would have us believe that, throughout that time, the club have only managed to retain their lofty League status via a combination of overt physicality and route one football. Obviously, the Wimbledon of the mid-to-late 80s were a physical side who knew how to wind up the opposition – players like Jones and Wise could hardly be described as shrinking violets after all – and they deserved their reputation to a degree, yet it seemed to me to be based primarily upon the playing reputation of Vinnie Jones himself – and, in particular, one famous photograph of him grabbing Paul Gascoigne's privates – and their performance in the FA Cup Final in 1988. Jones should've been booked within the opening minutes of that game for what can at best be described as a late challenge on Steve McMahon, and that set the tone for the rest of the match as the Dons chased shadows, nicked a goal from a free kick, defended as if their lives depended on it, and clung on to win the game. It didn't matter that they rode their luck and had to rely on their goalkeeper saving a penalty, because I got the story I wanted as a supremely talented, all-conquering Liverpool team were beaten by the no-hopers. There were plenty of neutrals and fans of the beautiful game who I'm sure were outraged at the manner of Wimbledon's victory, whereas, at the final whistle, I applauded and could only dream of a day when Chelsea might be outplayed in a major Cup Final, score a timely but unlikely goal, have their goalkeeper save a penalty, and, against all the odds, go on to lift the trophy.

*

This is a test. I know that. It's a cold December evening in 1998 and Robbie Earle has just scored for Wimbledon to put them 1-0 up at Selhurst Park against Chelsea. I don't celebrate the goal but I'm not disappointed either. This conflict of interest is easy to manage. Chelsea are having a great season in 1998/99, putting in a genuine and very realistic challenge for the League title, whilst Wimbledon, though firmly in the top half of the table, are focusing on the cups and qualification for Europe, and are taking points off Chelsea's rivals in the process. Also, this is the quarter-final of the Worthington Cup, which Chelsea won last year, so I'm not quite as hungry to see them win it this time around. This unique set of circumstances may never repeat itself. I try to explain to a Chelsea supporting friend who's at the game with us that it's actually a good thing if the Blues are knocked out of the competition if it somehow contributes to the club winning the League at the end of the season, but he doesn't understand my reasoning. Michael Hughes makes it 2-0 from the penalty spot in the 75th minute and it looks certain that

Wimbledon are in the semi-final. Then Vialli scores to make it 2-1 five minutes from time, and now I'm confused. Would it be good for Chelsea to win the League Cup again this year? It might actually, but then it'd be good to see the Dons get to a final too. Help me referee. Do something. He blows the whistle. Chelsea are out, and Wimbledon march on.

✶

Darren Huckerby is walking towards me, holding a celebratory finger in the air. He's actually walking toward the Coventry fans in the away enclosure at Stamford Bridge, but I'm right in the middle of them, and it's as if he's singled me out for a personal goading. It's 16th January 1999, and Huckerby has just put his team 1-0 up early in the first half against a lacklustre Chelsea side, who seemed to have put their recent good form behind them the moment I walked through the turnstile. He is making it clear to me that it won't be the last time that he scores today, or at least I think he is. I'm sitting here because my friend, Chris, a Coventry fan, bought the tickets, and so I now have to endure the wild celebrations as Huckerby continues to coolly stroll past us. To add to this, another friend, Mike, a Manchester United fan, is standing next to me and is obviously struggling to disguise his delight that Chelsea are about to blow their title chances. This is only the ninth minute, and I then have to suffer another 35 minutes of excitable banter, and although I've always quite liked a Midlands accent, it soon begins to grate. Watching a game as a neutral is easy: you can appreciate the football being played, devoid of all frustration and stress, and your own neutrality is emphasised and heightened by the frustration and enthusiasm of those around you. Sitting with away fans, watching their team playing yours, on the other hand, can be agonising in the extreme; like having an itch that you can't scratch.

Following what seems like an eternal period of huffing and puffing from Chelsea, which includes Gianluca Vialli violently miskicking in front of goal and cork-screwing himself into the turf, Frank Leboeuf finally equalises with a stunning strike on the stroke of half-time. It's not easy hiding your emotions in these situations, but it's a sacrifice that is not only necessary when you're surrounded by a few hundred disgruntled Midlanders, but also well worth the effort. Despite increased pressure from Chelsea in the second half, they aren't getting the breaks. We're in stoppage time. We need a win to stay top of the League, and Aston Villa and Manchester United are waiting for us to slip up. A draw is no good at all.

But wait; the ball is laid off on the edge of the Coventry penalty area and there is Roberto Di Matteo, just back from injury, waiting to do what he does best. He strikes it beautifully, and Magnus Hedman is beaten, and so are Coventry City. Although I am denied the explosion of joy that such moments demand, it isn't a problem. As the game ends and we leave our seats to a soundtrack of anti-Chelsea vitriol, I know that, despite having experienced severe emotional anxiety for most of it, the result has ensured that I won't enjoy another game more for the rest of the season.

The moment I'd entered the ground, I'd felt at home, despite the fact that I knew only two other people in the whole stadium and spent the afternoon in the most hostile part of it. My experience of Wimbledon and Chelsea is very different. Whereas I like to see Wimbledon win, if they play well but lose, I might still be happy. Watching Chelsea, however, is like watching a best friend or a member of your family placed in a position of mortal danger whilst being unable to help them in any way, and most of the time, I can't handle it.

*

As the season progressed, and with Chelsea's challenge for the Premier League title looking increasingly realistic, my regular trips to Selhurst Park were a godsend. Although they ultimately failed in their title bid, the stress that the Blues' good form had put me under would've been unbearable if it hadn't been for the distraction that Wimbledon provided. For the Dons and I, life had rarely been dull. There were the backs-to-the-wall victories over Liverpool and League champions, Arsenal; Schmeichel's cock-up in the first few minutes that gifted Jason Euell the opening goal against Manchester United; the bugle call for every corner kick for the home team; the game against Coventry City in which both sets of players seemed to have spoons strapped to their boots; and my lucky escape from injury as our adopted hero, Carl Leaburn, swept into the car park before a match.

And then there was our pre-match ritual. This involved a series of daft superstitions that we had developed during the course of the season and would begin with us meeting at Carshalton Beeches station, where we would scan the platform in the hope of catching sight of a character that we'd affectionately named Mister Wimbledon. We first spotted him early on in the season and made a link between having seen him before games a couple of times and the fact that Wimbledon had gone on to win those games. He was a mysterious character; always alone, which wasn't strange in itself, but such was our experience of him, that I'm not sure we ever saw him move – he just seemed to pop up on railway platforms or in seats at the stadium. He was physically unassuming, slim and of average height, with thinning hair and the sort of face that is difficult to age, and below this ageless face sat a proud and tightly-wound Wimbledon scarf. To add to his enigma, he had also begun to randomly appear to me, ghost-like, in the run-up to games, sometimes a few days before in a shop or a post office queue, or sometimes on the morning of a game itself, all of which I would take as a sign that Wimbledon were subsequently sure to play well. So he became our very own lucky black cat. Though we would've loved to seek him out, the sightings could never be predicted and, short of trying to find out where he lived, we preferred to believe that the search for the real Mister Wimbledon would be futile and that he only really existed when he needed to.

Whether or not we had caught sight of our mysterious friend, our ritual would continue on to "Prediction Bridge"; a bridge over a junction just before Selhurst Station at which the train always stopped, and at which we would both take turns to predict the score that afternoon or evening. Then, having made our way to the ground, we would ensure that we entered the stadium via the one turnstile that always seemed to get stuck and clip us on the back of the ankle as we pushed our way through. Once inside the ground, I had to drink Murphy's whether I wanted it or not, and we had to stand at the bar, regardless of whether there were seats available. Amongst the motley collection of behaviours that we had accumulated between August 1998 and May 1999, one or more had proved surprisingly ineffective. More specifically, whichever had made its way into the mix at the end of January or beginning of February had proved costly, as between their FA Cup fourth round replay at Tottenham on 23rd January and the last game of the season, away to Liverpool on 16th May, Wimbledon managed just one win and three draws.

At the end of January, the Club had been seventh in the Premier League and, competing for a place in Europe, were still in the FA Cup, and a major Cup Final beckoned as they were well-placed to win their forthcoming Worthington Cup semi-final second leg at home to Spurs. I can only assume that we should actually have sat down in the bar whenever a seat became available, or that I should have drank anything *but* Murphy's, as an excellent season fizzled to an anti-climax as the Dons finished just two places above relegation.

The Chelsea-Coventry match at the Bridge in January was instrumental in my decision not to renew my season ticket at Wimbledon for 1999/2000. Wimbledon have done nothing wrong – on the contrary – it's just that my attachment to another is too strong for me not to forgive them for perceived misdemeanours, namely overcharging their supporters. This is a different age for football as a commodity and I, and many fans, have come to accept that the days when you can get into a game without a pre-booked ticket and for less than £20 are long gone. I will retain my membership and continue to go to see the Dons, but now my time is to be balanced between the two. Wimbledon will always be a social event, whereas, if I go to Chelsea, I'll go alone. It's better that way.

The Promised Land — May 1999

"Robert Wurtz looks at his watch... and his whistle signals that the European Cup has come back to Britain, and has gone to Liverpool." – Barry Davies, Stadio Olympico, Rome, 25th May 1977.

This is a very strange feeling. I've spent the last few days worrying about Manchester United. That's not unusual in itself by any means; I worry about them every time they're about to play Chelsea, but that's different. Tonight, I'm worried that they might not win. In less than two hours' time this date, the 26th May 1999, could either be etched forever on the minds of Manchester United fans the world over, or it'll be quickly forgotten. I don't like Manchester United anymore; that much is clear. They knocked Chelsea out of the FA Cup again this year – 2-0 in a quarter-final replay at Stamford Bridge – going on to win the Cup last Saturday, having already won the League the week before – pipping Chelsea by four points – meaning that they've now won the Double a record three times. They're so good these days that when playing in a domestic competition, they will always be the pantomime villain. But, for some reason, I still think of them differently when playing in Europe. They represent England now, and they're about to play Bayern Munich, who represent Germany. For a football fan, it's a no-brainer. The two sides have already played each other in the group stage of this season's competition, with both games ending in a draw. I'm worried because they're missing two of their most influential players. Having both been booked in the semi-final second leg at Juventus, Paul Scholes and the captain, Roy Keane, are both suspended and will miss the game.

United kick off, Giggs is on the right and Blomqvist on the left. Within a couple of minutes, former Reds' manager, Ron Atkinson, tonight's co-commentator, is stressing the importance of their wide men pinning back the Bayern full-backs, and as he says this, I'm growing more concerned than ever. The Germans always look so imposing. And now, Carsten Jancker's through. Ronny Johnsen collides with him on the edge of the United box and the referee's given a free kick. Stefan Effenberg, as imposing as any, steps forward to take it. No, hang on, it's Mario Basler who'll take it... and he's scored. What a soft goal; Schmeichel just stood there as Basler passed it into the net. 1-0 Bayern. Only six minutes gone, but I can't see United getting back into this. There's the occasional flurry of activity around the Bayern box, but it comes to nothing. These are Germans after all; they know how to control games. It could be the last game Lothar Matthäus ever plays, and what a fitting end to such an illustrious career. Even more reason why Bayern won't slip up now.

The game's starting to drag. They've run out of ideas. Cole and Yorke, one of the most effective striking partnerships in the world this season, are either having a bad night or they're being expertly contained by the Bayern defence. Ferguson's bringing Sheringham on with just over 20 minutes left. Basler's away, he cuts inside, leaves it for Scholl, he chips it... over Schmiechel... off the post... and back into the keeper's arms. Commentator, Clive Tyldesley, seems to think that this might represent some kind of turning point for United. I can't see it myself. I've never seen a European Cup final killed off as early as this. It was all over in the sixth minute. But wait; Butt's running for the touchline, inside the box, knocks it across – it only needs a touch but there's no one there. Solskjær with a header! Saved. He's only just come on. Scholl! Close. End to end stuff now. It's still too late for United though. Jancker – off the bar! Bayern have to add a second goal at this rate. Solskjær back-heels to Sheringham! Saved by Oliver Kahn. Yorke! He's mishit it. It really hasn't been his night. Basler's off and acknowledges the Munich fans on his way to the bench, as if to cue the celebrations.

Ninety minutes are up. The fourth official indicates three minutes of injury time to be played. United have to throw it all at Bayern now. Beckham does well, lays it off to Neville who gets a cross in, put behind by Effenberg for a corner. This is what you might call the "Last Chance Saloon", and Schmeichel knows it. He's running up for the corner.

"Can Manchester United score? They always score," declares Tyldesley.

No chance. Beckham takes it, to the far post, Yorke gets there. It's cleared, but only as far as Ryan Giggs on the edge of the penalty area. He hooks it towards the goal. Sheringham's in the way, and he turns; it's in! They've taken it to extra-time!

But hang on a minute: I've seen this one before. This is the one where Sammy McIlroy equalises at the end of the game after his team have been outplayed for most of it, and the United fans go crackers, thinking it'll be extra-time and the other team go and score right at the death. Bayern will get a winner now. On the bench, Lothar Matthäus looks dejected, but he needn't worry. Solskjær doesn't seem to have given up yet though. He wins another corner. There can't be any time left.

"Is this their moment?" the commentator asks.

Beckham with the corner, Sheringham flicks it to the far post – SOLSKJÆR! It's in the roof of the net. What?? I'm on the floor, staring at the carpet and shouting something. Whatever just happened has done something to my brain. I can't get any part of my head around it. I phone Andrew, I know he's seen it. Perhaps he knows. My sister-in-law, Lisa, answers. She supports Manchester United and what follows is a series of high-pitched noises that generally indicate that neither of us can quite believe what we've just seen, but that we're both quite pleased about it.

"*United have reached the Promised Land.*"

After an ending to the match that was as thrilling as Arsenal's win at Liverpool 10 years before, as I watch Alex Ferguson and Peter Schmiechel lift that gargantuan trophy, inwardly, I applaud their success. They're the first team ever to win the Treble: FA Cup, Premier League and Champions League – a feat that they themselves had prevented Liverpool from achieving in 1977. I'm envious of course, but I have no thoughts about what might have been for me. If I'd sat and thought about it, I would have worked out that, had I not switched teams in adolescence, and had instead stuck with United through the Atkinson years and beyond, by now, I would have celebrated winning the FA Cup seven times, the Premier League five times, the League Cup once, and now the Champions League; the ultimate prize. When they won the FA Cup in 1985, I was happy for them for old time's sake. Tonight, I'm happy for them purely because they're an English club. Although we've fallen out in a big way in recent years – with my distaste for the Reds having grown in direct proportion to the frequency with which they've beaten Chelsea when it's really mattered – Chelsea never played in the European Cup, as it was previously known, and have never come close to qualifying for the Champions League. Therefore, in this competition, we have never been rivals.

Video Nasties and Lucky Rooms — 1999/2000

By finishing third in the Premier League in 1998/99, Chelsea have qualified to play in the Champions League for the 1999/2000 season. This has occurred as a result of UEFA awarding the English FA an extra place for their clubs, but the Blues aren't granted direct qualification to the group stages, so instead, need to play in a qualifying round, against a team from another European League, in a fixture to be held over two legs. Wanting to be there for the club's historic first European Cup tie at Stamford Bridge, I bought a ticket. Without meaning any disrespect to their opponents, Chelsea are lucky to have avoided drawing any of the big name teams – the likes of PSV Eindhoven, Rangers, Spartak Moscow and Parma – and are instead drawn to play the Latvian champions, Skonto Riga. Despite a tight 0-0 draw in Latvia, and a frustrating 80 minutes at the Bridge, Chelsea eventually win through, having scored three times in the last 10 minutes, in a game that is so dull for long periods that I am reduced to entertaining myself by conducting a head count of the intrepid Riga fans in a near empty away enclosure. There are 17.

*

Anticipation was then mounting as to whom Chelsea would be drawn to face in the first group stage of the competition. By the time it had transpired that they were to entertain AC

Milan in the very first fixture, I'd already made my mind up that I wanted to attend all three home games. Naïvely, I'd assumed that I'd be able to just pitch up at the ground and buy a ticket without queuing, as I had done for the Riga game. How wrong I was. Having stood in a queue that snaked around two floors of the Shed End, I finally acquired my tickets for all three games three-and-a-half hours later, and I was then charged £10 for four hours' worth of parking in the stadium car park. But I was happy and, unlike other people in the queue, I hadn't complained about the clubs' stinginess at not wanting to pay for more cashiers to handle the obvious clamour for tickets once. Nope, not me.

Chelsea went on to exceed all expectations in the Champions League. They not only won their group in the first group stage – which included the most entertaining 0-0 draw I have ever seen, at home to Milan – but they also finished second in the next group stage, so qualifying for the quarter-finals. In 2000, the novelty of playing a club of Barcelona's stature in a European Cup quarter-final was almost beyond comprehension. I'm sure there weren't too many Chelsea fans who, despite the team's previous performances, genuinely felt that there was much hope that Chelsea might actually win the tie and book a place in the semi-final, particularly as the second leg is to be played in Barcelona.

Yet optimism makes a rude and unexpected appearance in the first half at Stamford Bridge on 5th April as, following a blistering eight-minute spell, during which Chelsea scored three times – through Zola and Flo, twice – suddenly, the impossible dream seems anything but. The Champions League, that big and beautiful trophy, currently in Manchester United's possession; could it happen? This is when football is at its cruellest, when euphoria overcomes reason, raising expectations to such levels that you release your grip on reality, forgetting all previous calamities and the fact that there are at least 142 minutes of football still to be played. I am amazed to find myself still sat in front of the TV in the 63rd minute with the dream still alive. Figo scores in the 64th and I leave the room, knowing that Chelsea now have no hope of reaching the semi-final.

The excitement of the Champions League run has left everyone wanting more. The atmosphere at Stamford Bridge for the European games has been incredible, and playing on the biggest stage has proved addictive, but the Club's League form seems to have suffered as a result of their exploits in other competitions. With Chelsea too far off third place in the League to qualify automatically, the only way to ensure more great European nights the following season is to win the Champions League this time around.

On April 18th, Chelsea are in Barcelona, hoping to cling onto their 3-1 advantage in the second leg. They're under pressure early on, with the home team knowing that if they win 2-0, they're through. By half-time, Rivaldo and Figo have each scored and Barcelona have the score line they need. It's just past the hour mark and home keeper, Ruud Hesp, comes under pressure from Gianfranco Zola and, in an attempt to clear the ball, hits it straight to Tor André Flo, who slides it into a gaping net. Get in! Half an hour away from a place in the semi-final! Barcelona now need a goal just to level the aggregate scores. Chelsea just have to prevent them getting through, which they manage, until the 83rd minute, when Dani heads his side back into the game. Two minutes later, Frank Leboeuf concedes a penalty, which, if Rivaldo converts, will send Barcelona to the semis. He puts it wide.

Extra-time, and Chelsea are under intense pressure, even more so as Babayaro himself concedes a penalty and is sent off in the process. Score this and the home side have surely won it. This time, Rivaldo makes no mistake. 4-1 on the night, but if Chelsea score once more, they'll be through on away goals. Won't they? It's confusing now. And then, it's irrelevant. Dani crosses for Kluivert and it's an easy header. Barcelona 5; Chelsea 1. Game over. 6-4 on aggregate. A brave attempt, but the Blues have just fallen short. To be within seven minutes of reaching the semi-final was agonising. Defeat has ended the possibility of more Champions League football for at least another season, but the possibility that the club might have to wait a lot longer is all too real. Manchester United and Arsenal are dominating the Premier League, Liverpool are still strong, and Leeds United seemed to have acquired a limitless transfer kitty, meaning that the magical third League position could prove elusive for some years to come.

I blame myself for the defeat in Barcelona. I forget exactly when the superstition first saw light, but at some point, I'd recorded a televised Chelsea game on video, and they hadn't won. I think it may have been the Sunderland FA Cup quarter-final in 1992, but either way, it had been a game that I'd been unusually confident of them winning. As a consequence, I vowed never to record another, so depriving myself of the opportunity of repeatedly watching any number of great performances in the intervening years.

However, in October 1999, when Chelsea had travelled to Istanbul to play Galatasaray in a Champions League group match, I'd taken the reckless decision to record the game, and Chelsea won 5-0. I can understand why I had chosen to do so no more than I can understand how the Blues had managed to win so convincingly at a ground in which it was notoriously difficult to get a result. Whatever the reason, one thing was certain; the superstition was dead and I was now free to record games at will. The next game I chose to record was the away leg in Barcelona, and the superstition was reborn. The only plausible explanation for this blip in the natural order is that a Galatasaray fan, having the same superstition as I, but with a stronger bond with supernatural causality, also chose to record the Chelsea-Galatasary game, and his breaking of the taboo had trumped mine in spectacular fashion.

*

Following their impressive performance in 1998/99, Chelsea's League form in '99/2000 hasn't met with the expectations of neither fans nor, more noticeably, the media. Throughout the course of the season, there are constant mentions by pundits and reporters of, firstly, Chelsea going one better and winning the League this time and then, when results suggest that they've blown their chance of doing so by the turn of the year, that they need to qualify for the Champions League at the very least. In six short years, Chelsea have evolved from a club playing in a venue more suited to greyhound racing, and whose realistic goals would be retaining top League status and a decent Cup run, to a team who are expected to be competing on equal terms with Manchester United and Arsenal, and who are considered to be one team who could break that increasingly formidable duopoly.

The reality, however, is that whilst Chelsea have now rediscovered the glitz and swagger of the early 70s period (after which some fans still hanker) – and have even surpassed the success of that era – Arsenal and United have already moved up a gear. The former have acquired a level of stability and professionalism under the guidance of Arsene Wenger – who has still barely been at the Club for three seasons – that has seen them become, to my mind, the best and most complete team in the country, which I find irritating and often leads to a heated retort whenever anyone lavishes praise upon Arsenal and speaks of how well they are playing, how attractive their football is, and then remarks "And aren't they nice to watch?" And yet, spurred on by the new threat from the Gunners, Alex Ferguson and United have upped their game and won everything. The Reds of Manchester have become an increasing annoyance to me since the Great Wembley Tragedy of '94. In three of the five subsequent seasons, they've knocked the Blues out of the FA Cup, and have lost only once against them in all competitions. United are the ultimate spoilsports; it's official now. So, on Sunday 3rd October 1999, when the international superstars of Chelsea lined up to face the immovable Red Machine in a Premier League fixture at Stamford Bridge, I held little hope of a happy ending.

Of all the supposed mythical, utopian lands, you can keep your Shangri-La's and Atlantis's; the one I covet the most is the Lucky Room: a place in which you can relax and watch a game, secure in the knowledge that it holds a power within it to ensure that you will always leave with a gladdened heart and a happy tale to tell. On the day of the game, we had been visiting our parents in Bexhill for the weekend, and were at my Mum's, getting ready to travel back home, as the game kicked off. Had I taken time to consider the historical facts, it would have occurred to me that, to date, I hadn't seen Chelsea lose whilst watching a game in the living room of my family home. In fact, it might also have become unnervingly apparent that I had never seen any team of mine beaten in that room, certainly not in a game of any great significance. In my youth, my parents had been in the habit of moving the one television set they owned from the large lounge, which held one extensive radiator that stretched for the entire length of one wall, to the much smaller study every autumn, in order to save on heating bills during the winter months. It was common for them to forget about moving the TV back to the lounge in the spring, sometimes leaving it until as late as June or July. That is how I came to witness Man United's defeats in the Cup Finals of 1976 and 1979 in the study, whereas the lounge had bought me success in both 1977 and 1983. As it was, I was oblivious to such truths, as if superstition would really have provided any comfort in the circumstances, and so I settled down to watch the match with the usual sense of trepidation.

I needn't have worried. After only 27 seconds of the game had passed, I was on a victory sprint and headed for the kitchen, having just seen Gus Poyet head Chelsea into the lead. Naturally, I was certain that this would only serve to sting the United beast into action, but by the time Jody Morris made it 5-0 toward the end of the game, we were gliding up the A23 and I was luxuriating in the words of the commentator as he declared that, for Chelsea, this was payback time. I'm not sure that's true though: it's not a Cup Final, and ultimately, it won't stop United winning the Premier League, but it's a start.

The victory, coupled with their fine displays in the Champions League, further prompted pundits to claim that Chelsea could achieve great things this season. Similarly, whereas a win against United, let alone one so convincing, might once have proved satisfying enough, over the course of the season, the fans probably expected more.

*

By March, the European exploits had taken their toll, and Chelsea were adrift in the League, but the FA Cup was still a possibility. Manchester United had caused much controversy by opting not to enter the competition for the 1999/2000 season, upon the FA's request, due to their participation in the World Club Championship in Brazil. To many, this was considered hugely disrespectful to the history of the great competition, depriving the smaller clubs of a chance to pit their wits against the champions and earn some much-needed revenue in the process. But from my perspective, their non-involvement was a gift from above. With Arsenal having been knocked out by Leicester City in January, and Liverpool having succumbed to Blackburn Rovers in the same month, the path was clearer than ever before.

In early April, Chelsea beat Newcastle in the semi to reach the FA Cup Final; the last to be played at Wembley Stadium before it is to be demolished and rebuilt. At around that time, during a post-match interview, Dennis Wise was asked how it feels for the team to have had such a disappointing season, to which he sarcastically replied, "What, fifth in the League and in the FA Cup Final? Yeah, what a terrible season," which neatly summed up just how unrealistic the expectations for the Club have become.

*

Aston Villa will undoubtedly prove tough opposition in the Final – arguably with their best squad for at least a decade – and have finished just one place below the Blues in the Premier League, in sixth. It's bizarre, therefore, to think that I have never felt more relaxed about a big game involving Chelsea. It's Saturday 20th May, 2000, and I'm watching the final in the front room of my great friend and neighbour, Mel. I'd met Mel when we moved into the flat above hers in Wallington in April 1999. In our first conversation, football had been mentioned, and she had admitted to being an

Arsenal fan. It turned out that it had all been the fault of Charlie George. As the Arsenal striker lay on his back on the sun-baked Wembley turf with his arms above his head in celebration, having just scored the glorious extra-time goal that would see Arsenal beat Liverpool 2-1 to win the 1971 FA Cup Final, something had clicked in Mel's mind. She was already fascinated by the game enough to watch it whenever possible, but had yet to pick a team to call her own, and Charlie sealed the deal. She would support the Cup winners; a team who had already won the First Division Championship that season, so becoming only the second club to win the Double in the 20th century.

But little was she to know that she wouldn't get to experience that same sense of euphoria every year, or even every two or three years. The next time she'd get to see an Arsenal player lift a trophy would be after Alan Sunderland had picked Manchester United's pockets at Wembley in 1979, by which time she'd suffered a lifetime's worth of frustration and disappointment.

The chaos and calamity of the last five minutes of the '79 final had turned to ecstasy for Mel and Arsenal, whereas I had been left feeling utterly deflated. But we had both been permanently scarred by the experience. Mel could barely watch Arsenal anymore, in fear that something that horrific might happen again, and that the next time it wouldn't end as happily. She'd go to see games occasionally, but she would go more through a sense of duty, in fear that she might have her licence to support them revoked if she didn't make at least one appearance at the Club every couple of years.

Living so close to a fan of an opposing club isn't the ideal ingredient for a cordial neighbourly relationship, but Mel has always been so magnanimous in the wake of an Arsenal victory over Chelsea, which are frequent, that it has never really been a problem.

Despite her passion for Arsenal, as we're watching the game, she seems more nervous than I, so much so that I end up watching much of the game alone (although it might just be disinterest on her part because, as far as Cup Finals go, this is hardly what you might call a classic). On the other hand, I am able to watch the game calmly and without hiding in the bathroom or changing channels once. It remains goalless for 72 minutes, which makes my sanguine state of mind even more surprising. Then Chelsea have a corner; the Villa defence panic; David James spills the ball; and Roberto Di Matteo pounces to lash home his third consecutive goal in a domestic Cup Final. I celebrate as one who knew it was about to happen. Whatever magic has descended upon me to give me such confidence and foresight will desert me as soon as I leave here. As Dennis Wise is presented with the trophy – the Cup in one hand and his infant son in the other – it occurs to me that I have never seen Chelsea lose in the room in which I am sat, and Mel's lounge is now that most hallowed of all things; the Lucky Room. It's an assumption that will one day prove to be categorically and catastrophically false.

Travellers

This isn't what it looks like. It's a different world, so think of it like a holiday. We've known each other a long time; we meet up and have a laugh now and again. Honestly, it's nothing more than that...

Through the medium of television, I have probably been to a couple of hundred football grounds across the world. Purely in physical terms, I have visited the grounds of 16 current football League clubs. According to the laws of The Traveller, I have been to none.

*

Looking around me, I'm hoping that, come the end of the game, I'm the only one here who'll be left smiling. I'm sat in the home end at Ashton Gate, surrounded by Bristol City fans, and I'm hoping that their team will lose to Kingstonian, who are, at present, my non-League team of choice. It's January 2001 and this is the fourth round of the FA Cup, and the competition needs an upset. Kingstonian have become something of a force at non-League level, having performed well in the GM Vauxhall Conference for two seasons, and winning the FA Trophy in both 1999 and 2000. In January, the Ks knocked Southend United out of the FA Cup at the third round stage to set up this opportunity to make history. If they win this afternoon, they will become only the sixth club from non-League football to reach the fifth round of the FA Cup, and none have ever made it beyond that round to the quarter-final. As my friends and fellow former students from my Kingston days, Katharine and Eric, live in Bristol, I'd managed to persuade Eric that we should go to the game for old time's sake to support what was once our local team. We could only get tickets for the home end though, hence I am keeping quiet, despite the fact that Kingstonian are looking as though they might be the team making all the headlines tomorrow morning.

*

I was aware that a whole different footballing universe existed beyond the confines of the football League from a young age, but only because, at the end of each season, there would be a brief mention as to whether or not a club from the non-League had been elected to the Fourth Division. This unknown territory seemed distant, mysterious and impenetrable, but also insignificant enough for me to give it no further thought until I moved to Kingston-upon-Thames. I'd seen snatches of County League games in my youth, but a quick glance over at a Little Common Albion match, whilst having a kick-around at the local rec, doesn't really count. In any case, it seemed a world away from the brightly lit version of football on TV.

During my second year at Kingston Polytechnic, I'd noticed a football ground hiding behind a row of shops and houses that I passed whenever I went to lectures. Its presence would have gone completely unnoticed were it not for the floodlights poking above the rooftops, and that invited passers-by to take a look down the small side road called Jack Goodchild Way, the end of which revealed a patch of green grass belonging to Kingstonian Football Club. With our curiosity peaked, my housemate, Rich, and I decided to investigate further by going to see a midweek game there. On the night we chose to go, Kingstonian were hosting Farnborough Town at Kingsmeadow Stadium, and other than the fact that Town won (3-1 I think), my only memories of the game are of a tricky little Farnborough forward called Roddy Braithwaite, and the fact that Mickey Droy was sent off for Kingstonian. Not only was a former Chelsea player now seeing out his playing days in a pokey little non-League ground, but the ground was, in itself, far from being pokey. Aside from the aforementioned floodlights, there were turnstiles, a coffee bar that also sold food – both cold *and* hot – and a stand that not only had a roof, but also row upon row of seats; their fixed nature signifying that they wouldn't be hastily removed after the final whistle in order to accommodate a keep-fit class. This was a proper stadium, more modern and luxurious than Wimbledon's Plough Lane, and yet it belonged to a club that plied its trade in something called the Isthmian League Premier Division. A whole new world was revealing itself to me, beckoning me to learn more and, better still, hardly anyone seemed to know of its existence. There were so few people in attendance that we could've chosen to sit virtually anywhere in the stand or, such was the emptiness of the rest of the ground, we could have taken a picnic in, along with a couple of sun-loungers, picked a nice spot pitch-side, and treated it like a county cricket match, and I'm sure nobody would have objected too strongly.

Subsequently, it transpired that there was something called a League Pyramid that exists in England, which is basically a hierarchy of football Leagues, both professional, of which there are four, and amateur, through which clubs could be promoted and relegated. In 1989, the peak of the Pyramid was the First Division (and is now the Premier League), and at the foot of the structure sat the teams that spent their Saturdays playing in the local parks and recreation grounds, who had to change in their cars, would wash their own kit, and were only one step beyond using jumpers for goal posts. The system whereby a team from the uppermost amateur division, the Football Conference, would have to seek election to the Fourth Division, the lowest professional League, had ended in 1986, thus ensuring that movement between the leagues from top to bottom was now more fluid. Prior to this, from the perspective of amateur clubs, the top four divisions were uncharted cosmic territory, the exploration of which could only be made possible by acceptance from the necessary authorities. From 1986 onwards, however, a system of straightforward promotion and relegation was introduced, meaning that any club with pockets deep enough to ensure that its ground met the required standards and that its team were good enough could send its boys skyward, simply by winning the Conference.

All that mattered to me was that there was a part of the footballing cosmos beyond that which I knew, that remained undiscovered, and that yielded former Chelsea players, seats, burgers, was within walking distance, and all at a student-friendly price of a few pounds. Occasionally, small hordes of football fans would descend upon the Town from exotic and far-off places such as Cheltenham or Barrow for Cup ties at Kingsmeadow and, at these times more than any, non-League football seemed to offer a truly viable alternative to the professional game.

But as it turned out, the Farnborough game was to be both the first and the last Kingstonian game I would attend in the 1989/90 season, instead opting to invest my emotional energies in Chelsea's glorious charge to Wembley, and the Zenith Data Systems Cup (formerly the Full Members Cup), but my interest was such that I now had another team's results to look out for. I genuinely cared about their progress, not as much as that of Chelsea by any means, but enough that, rather than throwing the local paper straight in the bin, I would now head straight to the back pages to check for the K's results and news of upcoming fixtures first – and then throw it in the bin.

Once I'd returned to the South Coast, I re-engaged with the non-League universe. Hastings Town had a decent side in the early 1990s and, for the 1992/93 season, had secured promotion to the Southern League Premier Division; one league below the Football Conference. Their ground, The Pilot Field, was vast in comparison to Kingsmeadow, the area between the pitch and the terraces being almost as expansive as that of Stamford Bridge. I'd occasionally get to see Town play, particularly when they played pre-season friendlies against the top clubs such as Arsenal and Nottingham Forest, but with that pocket of East Sussex being something of a footballing void – given its lack of professional clubs – even Hastings Town seemed like giants of the game. I took an interest in the whole non-professional spectrum, avidly leafing through copies of *Team Talk* magazine, not only to see who was progressing well in the Ryman (née Isthmian) or Southern Leagues, but the Sussex County and Hellenic Leagues too. Having played for local teams during this time, I'd also acquired the habit of stopping off at a local petrol station on the way into work every Monday morning just so that I could buy a copy of *The Argus* to check results from that weekend's fixtures in the East Sussex or Hastings Sunday Leagues, and to see how the competition had fared in matches between teams who could only dream of being watched by the fabled One Man and His Dog. So, when we moved to South London in '98 and I was introduced to the concept of The Traveller, I had some empathy.

As well as going to see Wimbledon, I'd also started to go to local non-League and reserve team games with a friend and colleague, Barry. I enjoyed going to games and watching teams I felt no affection for, no matter who was playing – even badly-organised kick-arounds in a public park can be fun to watch; observing grown men sporting replica Arsenal or Brazil shirts and pretending to be Denis Bergkamp or Romario always has tremendous entertainment potential. Reserve games were often played on weekday afternoons, which required me to take full advantage of my new self-employed status and the flexibility it gave me. Whilst attending these matches, some faces in the stands grew increasingly familiar. There would be men, usually over the age of 60, sometimes on their own, but often in small clusters, at every game, whether it was at The New Den to see Millwall reserves, Motspur Park for Fulham, Kingsmeadow for Chelsea, Bromley Town, Croydon Athletic; it didn't matter, they would be there. It was then that Barry explained that these entities were known as Travellers, a community not reviled like their namesakes, but then few knew of their existence. Initially, this fascinated me and I would watch as they furiously scribbled notes on their programmes – usually just a photocopied sheet of A5 paper – whenever a goal was scored or a corner was won. When I asked why they might be doing this, I was told that Travellers like to keep a record of any significant event in the game, no doubt to be filed away in one of many neatly-kept storage boxes when they got home. It then became clear as to why, before one particular game, I'd seen a disgruntled man remonstrating with a club official about why it was that there were no programmes left, meaning that he was left without one, having not been one of the lucky and organised few who had arrived at the game a full hour before kick off in order to secure one of the 20 or so that had been printed.

Though I could never quite see myself becoming a fully paid-up member of the Travelling fraternity, at least until retirement, I recognised that the level of obsession required wasn't beyond me. For the time being, I was satisfied with simply enjoying the pleasures to be had from reserve team and non-League football, of which there were many. I'd learned early on, at a Wimbledon reserve game played at Sutton United, that a quick flash of a season ticket would result in my being waved through the turnstiles with a smile and an approving nod, and led me to walk tall as I picked out one of the few hundred empty seats to call my own. A quick scan of any programme-come-team-sheet would reveal some high calibre players, who would either be out of favour with the first team manager, or returning from injury. But there were usually more famous names off the pitch than on it, as managers and staff from other clubs were sent to scout for talent or assess the competition, meaning that you could rub shoulders with the stars, or at least stand in a tea queue with Peter Beardsley. The sparsity of the crowd would lay bare the eccentricities of the most hardened supporters, as exemplified by one poor Fulham fan whose constant frustration at the efforts of Steve McAnespie would result in his screaming "MCANESPIE!" in a soprano so ear-poppingly shrill that all around him, including Sam Allardyce on one occasion, would quake at the sound. Players had such wonderful names and much entertainment was to be found in picking out the best, leading to an ultimate "best names" 11 that included Byron Bubb, Barrington Belgrave, Nayron Nosworthy, and the less alliterative but no less splendid, Lemano Trésor LuaLua and Toby Oshitola. Yes, this was a world both simple and pure, light years away from that of first team professional football, and I enjoyed it hugely. Travelling is football's equivalent of trainspotting, and whole weekends are organised on an annual basis purely for Travellers, allowing them to spend three whole days visiting one non-League ground after another in the North East of England, for example, for games that had been scheduled for their benefit. And yet it was clear that, even if I'd wanted to, I would never be accepted into the Travelling fold, and this saddened me. You see, once I had learned that one cannot claim to have been to a football ground until one has actually walked at least once around the pitch, I knew that I would never have the courage required.

*

Little Kingstonian are playing like champions. An upset could be on the cards here. The Bristol City fans are looking nervous. As Phil Wingfield scores in the 57th minute to put Kingstonian 1-0 up right in front of us, I can't say a thing, but for the following 36 minutes, I become as tense as I have ever been at a football match. Every Kingstonian tackle and clearance is met with an internalised yelp and I am becoming increasingly convinced that we are about to see non-League Kingstonian reach the fifth round of the FA Cup for the first time – and I am witnessing history being made first hand. The referee has got to blow the whistle for full-time now, surely. But he doesn't, and as City equalise in the fourth minute of injury time with what literally proves to be the last kick of the game, I am oblivious to the raucous celebrations that have undoubtedly ensued around us, and I feel dejection for the poor Kingstonian players, most of whom lay slumped on the Ashton Gate pitch, trying to come to terms with just how close they've been to making history. As the gloom lifts later in the evening, I can reflect that it's been an enjoyable day, despite its end, and at least I've been to a ground that I'd never been to before. But then it occurs to me that, in effect, having not taken the trouble to risk arrest by circumventing the pitch, I haven't been there at all.

The Wonderless Years — 2000 to 2002

A sunny day. Wembley Stadium. Chelsea versus Manchester United. A trophy awaits the winners. This is the moment I've been waiting for: six years have passed and I need wait no longer. It starts well enough, Gianfranco Zola torments the United back four. He chips one over for Stanić! Surely! He's headed it wide. The 22nd minute; Leboeuf knocks it forward, Poyet wins it well in the air and Hasselbaink is through – Jimmy Floyd Hasselbaink has scored on his debut for Chelsea. That'll repay a bit of his £15 million transfer fee. It's all looking good.

It's just passed the hour mark and it's looking even better: Roy Keane is off – given a red card for a challenge on Gus Poyet. United are down to 10 and it must be plain sailing now. Twenty minutes left. Come on... Melchiot is going all the way... *and it's there!* 2-0 Chelsea. That'll do, thank you very much. Full-time, and the Charity Shield, and revenge, is ours. Except that it isn't. The Charity Shield doesn't mean anything. It's a nice occasion, and it's nice to win something, but does this make up for 1994? Hardly.

I don't realise it yet, but victory in the Charity Shield on 13th August 2000 spells the end of the golden era. Gianluca Vialli is sacked in September, after only five League games have been played, and Claudio Ranieri is appointed as his replacement. It's probably a measure of the club's recent success and the resulting growth in expectations that the most successful manager in Chelsea's history should be dispensed with so early in the season after what was perceived to be a bad start – they have lost only once in the league, albeit to Bradford City. The arrival of Ranieri, an established and experienced non-playing manager, marks the end of a trend of appointing established stars as player-managers, and seems to signal the beginnings of a more pragmatic, less glamorous approach by the Club.

For those missing the frustration and inconsistency of yesteryear, and who have been left dazed and confused by success, the 2000/2001 season marks a welcome return to form. Although they beat Liverpool and Tottenham (twice), and are unbeaten against Manchester United and Arsenal, as well as the defeat to Bradford City, Chelsea also lose to Sunderland, Leicester City and Charlton Athletic, home and away. But rather than being a comforting return to more innocent times, this return to haplessness is just upsetting. They are also knocked out of the UEFA Cup, European football's secondary competition, in the first round, by Swiss side, St Gallen, nearly a year to the day since the Blues had beaten Galatasaray in the Champions League. It's also a night that ultimately signals the end of Roberto Di Matteo's playing career, after he suffered a broken leg during the game. Thanks to recent successes, Chelsea are considered a big club now and are easy targets for the so-called smaller clubs, and their inconsistency made them a laughing stock in the process. The poor form in the UEFA Cup continues for another two seasons, and following another first round defeat in 2002 – this time at the hands of Norwegian part-timers, Viking FK – I am awoken the next morning by an excerpt of the match commentary, describing Eric Nevland's winning goal for the Norwegians, followed by the voice of Danny Baker, declaring that Chelsea are "the exploding cigar of the Premiership". From now on, I will become more accustomed than ever to avoiding all forms of media the day after a Chelsea defeat. They, and I, are on a downer; paying the price for the glory years.

*

In 2002, Chelsea once again have a good run in the FA Cup and, by beating Fulham in the semi, are set to play Arsenal in the final at the Millennium Stadium, Cardiff on May 4th. I'm at my brother's house, staring at his new and gargantuan television, waiting for the suffering to begin. Only Manchester United and Arsenal have managed to beat Chelsea in the competition since 1995, so it follows that as long as we avoid those two sides, we will surely win the Cup. Therefore, unlike the finals of 1997 and 2000, this time, I am certain we are going to lose. On top of that, our top scorer this season, Jimmy-Floyd Hasselbaink, isn't match-fit and, even more worryingly, John Terry, who despite being only 21 has already proved to be an invaluable member of the first team, won't be playing, having been struck down by a mystery virus. But my concern is not so much for my own welfare as for that of my nephew, Ben. He is seven-years-old now and has been a Chelsea supporter since the age of six months, a choice that it's just possible he had little to do with, and in which I played a part, having once presented him with a bright yellow Babygro, emblazoned with the words "Chelsea's Next One Million Pound Striker". Today, memories of the harrowing finals of 1976 and 1979 are foremost in my mind, and I know that there's a chance that if Chelsea don't win, Ben might quickly reconsider his position as a lifelong Chelsea fan. Knowing, as I do, that Chelsea will lose, I'm just hoping for some sort of damage limitation in the form of a good performance and a respectable score line.

When I arrived, it was revealed that Ben had shown concerns that Arsenal might be too good for Chelsea, and that to allay his fears, Andrew has promised him that Chelsea would win. This doesn't help at all. Not being a father myself, I can imagine that the easy way out when a child seems scared or fearful is to reassure them by telling them something wholly unrealistic. But this isn't like the Tooth Fairy or Father Christmas: Arsenal are very real – the equivalent of the bogeyman under the bed – and Ben has been left cruelly exposed.

Chelsea are actually playing well and don't seem to be under anywhere near as much pressure as I'd expected, all of which raises the suspicion that my brother has made a *Rosemary's Baby*-style bargain with some local occultists. The sight of former player, Roberto Di Matteo, leading the Chelsea players onto the pitch has also given me a sense of hope. He's been a talisman for Chelsea in the past, and perhaps he will be now. Ben seems to be enjoying the game and is clearly taking his father at his word; but then disaster strikes, in the form of Ray Parlour. When he receives the ball 35 yards from goal, he runs with it, but there seems to be little danger – as Tim Lovejoy alludes to during his soon-to-be infamous Sky Sports commentary: *"It's alright, it's only Ray Parlour"*. Ray Parlour finds the top corner from 25 yards. Poor Ben is distraught, and when Freddie Ljungberg curls in Arsenal's second 10 minutes later, he goes to pieces. Empty cries of "There's still time for Chelsea to score twice," fall on two sets of deaf ears. There are still 10 minutes left, but there's no way back now, and I don't think Ben fully understands this. As the final whistle blows, he runs out of the room crying and, although I feel I might want to do the same, I know that time is short. If I don't act quickly, young Ben might do something stupid, like tear his Chelsea shirt to shreds or deface his Club calendar. I make my way downstairs and find him sobbing in the kitchen.

"You told me they'd win," he blubs, but rather than point out that it was actually his dad who had misled him, I just try to console him as best I can. At once, I realise how difficult these situations must be for Andrew and several million fathers around the world. Recalling my own previous FA Cup experiences, and Bobby Stokes in particular, I try to assure the poor, broken lad that Chelsea will win it the next time – itself a rash, unfounded claim – at which point he abruptly shrugs me away and wails, "I don't care! I support Arsenal now!"

I would love to say that what happens next is that I deal with this shocking declaration with dignity and restraint, gently placing a reassuring hand on his shoulder and telling him that he'll feel differently in the morning and that losing can only make us stronger somehow. What I actually say, in a fit of disgust, is, "If you support Arsenal then I won't be your uncle anymore." Not the most mature response perhaps, and it could quite easily have backfired had Ben then called my bluff by saying he was quite happy for me to absolve myself of all my responsibilities as an uncle and skipped away singing, "There's only one Ray Parlour". But thankfully he doesn't, and he's still a Chelsea fan. And perhaps Chelsea really will win the Cup the next time.

*

In the summer, when our friends, Mel and Dave, return from a holiday in Benidorm, they present me with an unofficial bottle of Chelsea Football Club wine. It has the Chelsea crest and CFC painted proudly on its label, and will come to be known simply as The Bottle. It would appear that The

Bottle contains red wine, but there is no further clue as to its vintage, alcoholic percentage or anything, which further adds to the magical aura that it will come to adopt. Little Ruud went missing a couple of years ago, and I need another lucky charm. As they hand it to me, I am genuinely touched, and vow that I will open it and share it with them upon a suitable occasion, preferably the next time Chelsea win a trophy, and even more preferably, when they win the League; a suggestion at which I am the first to laugh.

Womble Dawn
— 2002

Alright, alright, I know. But it's different this time. Things have changed. What's that? I'm weak? Maybe, but I can't ignore them now.

*

As I watch a newly-re-formed Siouxsie and the Banshees performing at the Shepherd's Bush Empire on Wednesday 10th July 2002, 12 miles to the south, a crowd of 4,500 have gathered to watch AFC Wimbledon playing their first ever match, at Sutton United. That's a staggering number of people. I've been to games at Selhurst Park with lower attendances.

Wimbledon's decline since 1999 had been drastic. Since the double blow of a League Cup semi-final defeat to Spurs and Joe Kinnear suffering a heart attack in the spring of '99, the team had been relegated to the First Division in 2000, and narrowly missed out on a play-off place the following year. By 2001, rumours of relocation to another part of the country, or even a different country altogether, had already been hanging over the club for a few years. There had been rumours that both Hull and Basingstoke were among the preferred destinations, but the one option that endured above all others was a move to Dublin. How the idea of yanking a club out of South London, where they'd been for over 100 years, and displacing them to Ireland's capital, whilst still allowing them to play in the English Premier League, could be given any credence is hard to understand. It reached the stage where the concept had been taken seriously by the Football Association of Ireland and a new name had been chosen: The Dublin Dons. A move of this scale had no historical precedent in this country. The highest profile relocation of a football club to date had been Arsenal's move from Woolwich, South London, to Highbury, North London, in 1913. This had also occurred as the result of a takeover by a businessman who felt that low attendances warranted such a measure, but whereas existing supporters still continued to travel from Woolwich to see their team play at the club's new home (and apparently there is a lineage of fans who still do so), at least it was within the same city. It was impossible to imagine that supporters of Wimbledon, or of any club, would be willing to make the trek from London to Dublin on a regular basis, and why should they? It felt like the Club was dying and, even as I went to games at Selhurst between 1998 and 2001, it was always in the back of my mind that the Wimbledon move would definitely happen one day; the plan was skulking in the players' tunnel like a cowardly Grim Reaper.

The Dublin plan did itself die a death eventually, but a move to the Emerald Isle was soon replaced by talk of a move to the concrete utopia of Milton Keynes. On 2nd August 2001, all Club members and season ticket holders received a letter from the Club, confirming that the potential relocation to Milton Keynes, previously thought to have been just another daft notion, was actually going ahead. The way that the Club's supporters reacted to this devastating news should serve as an inspiration to all. Protests were held, including an eight-mile march from Plough Lane to Selhurst Park prior to one match, and fans of other clubs joined in solidarity against a move that symbolised not just a slap in the face for one club, but for the game as a whole: if it could happen to one football club then a dangerous precedent might be set. Even after the Club's announcement, the FA had unanimously voted against the move to Milton Keynes, but the Board were determined to make it happen and the Club's chairman, Charles Koppel, then lodged an appeal against the decision. From the outside looking in, all the evidence seemed to point to the move being blocked. Nevertheless, on 28th May 2002, the verdict was announced; Koppel had won the appeal and the fans had lost the battle. Wimbledon would be moving to Milton Keynes.

I hadn't renewed my membership at Wimbledon in 2001/02 so I didn't receive the letter from the Club. Any details of Wimbledon's plight I had gleaned from the media or heard from others. I didn't go to see them play at all that season because, as far as I was concerned, the Club didn't exist anymore. Whilst the true supporters fought for their club, I, a mere admirer, dismissed Wimbledon more out of disappointment than protest. To my mind, there was already a hole where the Club used to be. At the time, I had little or no idea as to just how proactive the fans had been since August 2001, until I heard that they'd formed a new club. Although it'd been buried amidst news of the impending World Cup, I heard about the formation of AFC Wimbledon sometime in June, and I was delighted. Here we go, a team I can get behind this season who'll help take my mind off Chelsea's on-and off-field decline. They had no players as yet, but the new club had wasted no time in securing a place in the Combined Counties League and arranging a series of pre-season friendlies. The first of these was at Sutton United. It was the perfect choice for such a historic game; the fixture having a history dating back decades to a time when both clubs competed at non-League level. I desperately wanted to go, if only to show my appreciation of the new Wimbledon and what they represented the only way I could, and obviously to associate myself with this bit of history too – to say "I was there". But I'm not there. I'm in Shepherd's Bush with my friend Tim, watching Siouxsie and the Banshees at what's turned out to be a memorable concert, and for all the right reasons. I'd already bought the tickets and, although I wanted to be in both places at once, despite all the technological advancement mankind has made, I couldn't find a way to make it happen.

With that opportunity missed, I vowed not to miss the first competitive home game. The Club had managed to secure a deal to ground-share with Kingstonian Football Club and so would be playing their home games at Kingsmeadow Stadium; the same cosy and well-appointed ground that I had grown fond of over the years. It's Wednesday 21st August, and The Dons are playing host to Chipstead FC for their first home League fixture. Skip, Barry and I decided to get here early in case there were queues outside, and it was lucky we did. The official attendance figure tonight will reach 4,142. There would be more, but the ground reached full capacity long before kick-off, so some poor souls are left outside and unable to get in. The atmosphere is one of celebration; tonight is the culmination of a lot of hard work by a lot of dedicated people. This is a new dawn in the history of, not a new club, but a club re-born. It's a new Wimbledon in the sense that it is now a club owned and controlled by the fans, and as such, it really feels as though we are standing in the only place in the world this evening where any significant history is being made. People are singing, laughing, some looking a little bemused, but everyone is happy, and it's infectious. This is the answer. I can come and watch Wimbledon on a Saturday and then watch *Match of the Day* in a mature and rational way, even if Chelsea have lost.

The convenience offered by Wimbledon and non-League football joining hands in this way – these two worlds that I'd become so fond of over the past few years – seems surreal, but then this is Wimbledon. The club may have changed in so many ways, but it's clear that the world of Wimbledon is still a weird and wonderful one. There has always been a quirkiness about them, from the days when they played at Plough Lane, when the likes of Liverpool and Manchester United would turn up to play a top-flight fixture at a rickety old ground a fraction the size of their own iconic stadia, to more recent times when they shared a stadium and the fans would constantly be outnumbered by those of their opponents. But Chipstead can't have been fully prepared for what awaited them tonight.

Chipstead is a small village in the Surrey commuter belt with a population of less than 7,000 people, very few of whom turned up at Kingsmeadow. A friend of mine, Jon, lives in Chipstead, and had been to see them play for the first time early this season, when there had been a crowd, or should that be a clump, of just 18 people. Other than himself, the remaining 17 were all friends and family of the players. This is to be the future for The Dons; when once they had been the minnows, they will now be giants. But clearly the atmosphere is too joyous to prove intimidating, and far from choking at the occasion, the Chipstead players have risen to it and win the game 2-1. To lose is disappointing, but at the same time, tonight wasn't really about that. Had they won the game, it would've been too perfect somehow, and defeat served as a reminder that AFC couldn't expect to rise through the divisions with ease; there would be a lot more hard work to come. This is just the beginning of a story; there'll be plenty more opportunities for happy endings. The club is now barely two months old after all, and in comparison, Chipstead are seasoned campaigners.

In another quirk, Kevin Cooper scores The Don's only goal of the game. Not the Kevin Cooper who won the fans' award for Player of the Season the previous year – whilst the club was still in its Selhurst Park guise and playing in Division One – but a different Kevin Cooper who had already ensured himself legendary status by scoring AFC's first competitive goal the previous week in an away game against Sandhurst Town. To add to his legend, he had also scored the first ever goal *against* AFC Wimbledon whilst still playing for Sutton United six weeks earlier. Of a more personal resonance to me is the presence of Joe Sheerin, the new Dons' captain, who has until recently been playing for Chelsea reserves at this very same stadium. To have a player of his experience turning out for them is a clear statement of the club's intent as well an indication of their potential. The fans have already made up a new song for him too, to the tune of *Volare* – *"Joe Sheerin whoa-oh, Joe Sheerin whoa-oh-oh-oh, he used to play for scum, and now he's Wimble-dun"*. Although nice for Joe, it proves that The Dons supporters' attitude toward Chelsea hasn't thawed, much as I'd hoped that their ire might now be turned towards either Chipstead, Walton Casuals or Chessington & Hook United instead.

The rest of the season proves enthralling as The Dons fight hard to win promotion. Ultimately, they just miss out, eventually finishing third behind AFC Wallingford and the champions – the slickly named Withdean 2000 – but it's been an amazing experience for the Club and the fans. The Combined Counties League is the ninth tier of the Football League Pyramid, five tiers below full League status. We go to the final game of the season, a 5-1 home victory against

Raynes Park Vale, and the crowd totals over 4,500; even larger than that against Chipstead nine months previously. They regularly attract over 1,000 fans at away games, against teams who are used to playing to crowds of less than 50. When AFC meet Chipstead in the return fixture in December, Chipstead opt to play the game at the ground of Whyteleafe FC, feeling that it would be safer. A crowd of 1,777 – myself and Chipstead Jon included – turned up to see The Dons overturn a 2-0 deficit to win 3-2. But spare a thought for the now legendary tea ladies of Merstham, who, expecting 1,500 away supporters to descend upon them the following day, got up in the early hours to begin the production of cheese rolls, enough for one per punter. To the ladies' disappointment, the 1,500 fans who duly arrived clearly weren't hungry that day and they sold only a fraction, leaving them with blisters on their fingers and a cheese roll mountain.

Meanwhile, up the road in SW6, Chelsea have a mountain of their own to climb.

Jesper, and Marcel, and Nicolas — 2002/03

"They know what they have to do, and the atmosphere's at fever pitch. Big names for the big game. And it's not just about finance – these players want the competitive element of competing with Europe's finest next season."
– Rob Hawthorne, Stamford Bridge, 11th May 2003

*

The English FA had been awarded a fourth qualifying spot for its clubs in 2001, meaning that for the 2001/02 season, the teams who finished in the top four places in the Premier League would qualify to play in the Champions League the following season. This opened up the possibility of qualification for a number of clubs who would previously have had little or no hope of doing so, and who would've spent the second half of the season either attempting to finish high enough to qualify for the UEFA Cup, or just keeping out of trouble. Chelsea was just such a club, and finished sixth in the League in 2002, having never realistically looked likely to threaten the top four. They did in fact qualify for the UEFA Cup on two counts – through both their League position and also as runners up in the FA Cup, with the winners Arsenal having already won the League – but for some reason, they weren't allowed to trade those places in return for a more lucrative Champions League birth in a unique two-for-one swap deal.

In 2002/03 however, despite having bought no new first team players, the Blues started brightly and have been competing at the top of the League for much of the season. Leeds United, until recently such a potent force in the Premier League (having spent huge amounts on transfer fees and players' wages), are by now paying the price for their profligacy and, having sold many of their key players, are struggling to avoid relegation.

Chelsea have accrued huge debts themselves and, in order to avoid falling into the same trap as that of Leeds, success is crucial, and success means securing the financial rewards of Champions League qualification. Their unexpectedly good form has meant that I've once again begun avoiding highlights of defeats and the more infuriating draws, Every game counts now. If they don't qualify for the big one this year then who knows what might happen? It's becoming obvious that Gianfranco Zola will be leaving at the end of the season, and without him, we won't be as good. I might as well open The Bottle now; they'll never again be in a position to win the League. As the season nears its end, the race for fourth place has been reduced to a straight battle between Chelsea and Liverpool. As I drive home on Saturday 26th April, I listen to the radio for news of Chelsea's game with Fulham, and I hear the heart-stopping announcement that "*There's been a goal at Stamford Bridge!*" Who for? Get on with it! It's then reported that Luis Boa Morte has just scored an equaliser for Fulham. I'm so certain that Chelsea have blown their chances that I pull over and stop the car. Even though I feel like getting out and smacking the bonnet repeatedly with the nearest inanimate object, like Basil Fawlty but with less comedic grace, instead I just sit and stare at the windscreen. It's all downhill from here.

*

A week later, they lose at West Ham and their chance has gone for sure. At the same time, Liverpool are beating Manchester City with just minutes to go, so it's game over. But it isn't over at all. Thanks to two fist-pumpingly late goals from Nicolas Anelka, City win 2-1, and it is all to be decided in the final game.

And so it's come to pass that when Chelsea meet Liverpool at Stamford Bridge on the final day of the season, it is dubbed "The £20 million match" and is imbued with the drama and expectation once reserved only for Cup Finals. With both teams locked on 64 points, history will have a tendency to recall that only a win would ensure either of claiming that hallowed fourth place. In reality, Liverpool need a win but Chelsea only require a draw. Either way, Chelsea's chief executive has apparently made it clear to the players that, should they lose, the Club would be forced to make drastic cuts and so face a stark future. My memory will eventually rearrange the details of the game such that I recall it like any football film or *Roy of the Rovers* story you could care to mention. Yes, there is an unlikely hero – in this case, Jesper Gronkjaer – but no, he doesn't in fact leave four Liverpool defenders trailing in his wake when he unleashes his curling, goal-bound blunderbuss. He beats only one and it isn't in the final minutes; it is in the 26th, with barely a quarter of the game gone. And yet it is such an important game in the history of Chelsea Football Club that the record books deserve to be tweaked and all footage edited in order to reflect as much. Because the Blues only need to draw the game, Marcel Desailly's equaliser is arguably more important, but history will cast Gronkjaer's goal as the one that not only handed his team victory, but changes Chelsea's destiny. For now, they are back in the Champions League and, as I watch the highlights, I find it difficult not to get all dewy-eyed and lumpy-throated at the final whistle, and at the sight of the players and Claudio Ranieri celebrating as if they've won a hat-trick of trophies in one afternoon. Yes, it was an important game, but it's almost as if they know something that we don't.

Sliding Doors: 1984 to 2003, An Alternative Version

We probably all reflect upon our lives at times and wonder what might have been had we made different choices. If one day it turns out that the theory of the multiverse just happens to be true, and there are indeed parallel universes that are materially similar to our own and governed by the same rules, then somewhere out there is a different version of myself, standing on the platform of life, and pondering alternatives to the following history which, to him, is a reality...

On September 15th 1984, having declined an invitation to hop off the Manchester United Express in order to go to London for the day to see Chelsea play West Ham United, I stay on board, unknowingly bound for the good times. Following their unscrupulous treatment of Brighton & Hove Albion in the FA Cup Final replay in 1983 – the team having teased their opponents to within a whisker of a historic victory in the first game before swatting them aside in the replay – doubts about the credibility of supporting a bunch of bullies that I really have no connection with begin to creep in. The signings of Gordon Strachan and Jesper Olsen lend a more diminutive and pacey look to the team that reminds me of the United side of the mid-1970s that I miss so much, which in turn helps me overcome my doubts and I subsequently discard all thoughts I have recently entertained of switching my allegiance to Oxford United, and continue to wear my replica Sharp shirt with pride at kick-

abouts in the park. My loyalty is rewarded within a year when, as underdog once more, we win the FA Cup again in 1985, beating the new League champions, Everton, 1-0 in the Final, despite having only 10 men, and thanks to a wonder strike in extra-time from Norman Whiteside; a goal that causes me to momentarily forget that I've grown too large to jump on my Dad in celebration without causing him discomfort, but thankfully his discomfort proves only minor.

A run of 10 consecutive wins at the start of the 1985/86 season leads to my thinking that we might finally get to win the League title, but my hopes are left in tatters as a dismal run of form sees the team let me down again, with Liverpool, the bane of my life, winning it to complete the first League and FA Cup double in their history. Due to the attendant distractions of life as a sixth form student, my interest in both football and studying slacken, even more so as United lose their first three games of the new season and, worse still, lose to Chelsea at home, and I subsequently suffer abuse from friends, the likes of which I haven't experienced since primary school.

Ron Atkinson is sacked in November 1986, to be replaced by the former Aberdeen manager, Alex Ferguson, and his first game in charge sees the team lose 2-0 at Oxford United and, with Oxford having won the Milk Cup earlier that year, it appears that my decision not to pledge my allegiance to them in 1984 might, in hindsight, have been a bit hasty. A surprising 1-0 win at Anfield on Boxing Day adds to the Christmas cheer and rekindles my passion momentarily, but it doesn't last, as United finish the season in 11th place and with no trophies. We beat Chelsea three times the following season and finish second in the League behind Liverpool (predictably,) but I barely notice as thoughts of impending A-level exams displace an interest in football completely. Having ditched plans to attend Manchester Polytechnic – which I had chosen to apply to the previous year following a sudden burst of enthusiasm for the music of The Smiths – in favour of a venue closer to London, I leave home for Kingston Polytechnic in September 1988 with a lazy quiff and a lot of apprehension.

Excepting a brief flurry of excitement when millionaire, Michael Knighton, offers to buy United and promises to return them to the top of the English game – an offer that comes to nothing – my interest in United lays dormant for over a year. Until, while at home for the Christmas holidays, my Mum asks me to take a look in the loft to sort through some of my old stuff and put aside anything that I want kept. Whilst doing so, I come across an old Woolworths bag, containing football programmes and other Manchester United memorabilia from my youth, and as I tip the contents onto the loft floor, a football card flutters to one side. Picking it up and turning it over, I am surprised to see the face of Lou Macari staring back at me, assuming that I'd got rid of the card soon after it had cost me my whole collection of Topps football cards in 1978. In a sudden fit of nostalgia, I slide the card into my back pocket and return the rest of the contents from whence they came and add the bag to the pile marked "to be kept".

A couple of days later, Mark Robins heads the winner from a Mark Hughes cross in a surprise away win at Nottingham Forest in the third round of the FA Cup. The night of the win against Forest, I go for a drink with friends to The Castle in Bexhill, and as I reach into my back pocket to remove my wallet, out falls Lou Macari, a little creased but still looking as good as he did in 1978. Immediately, I put two and two together and come to the natural conclusion that the rediscovery of Lou is responsible for United's victory that day and he must therefore be kept inside my wallet, like a genie in a lamp, for the rest of the season. Then begins a sequence of Cup wins that take me all the way to the Final, my first in five years. I watch the match at the flat of a fellow Man United supporter in Putney and, with our team struggling and Crystal Palace looking to be heading for a 3-2 win in extra time, in desperation, I remove Lou from his leathery confines and place him on the coffee table in front of me. A few minutes later, Danny Wallace pokes the ball into the path of Mark Hughes who scores to set up a replay. Five days later, I watch the replay at home in New Malden and place Lou on the floor at my feet for the duration of a game in which Palace never really get started, allowing us to win our first trophy for five years with a goal from Lee Martin, an unlikely hero who then, for several weeks, replaces Steve Coppell as my favourite player of all time.

The following season, United reach the final of the League Cup where they are to meet Sheffield Wednesday, who are a league division below them and who, much to my delight, managed to knock out Chelsea 5-1 on aggregate in the semi-final. But having up until then successfully managed to watch every televised game featuring Manchester United that season, so ignoring my nerves in order to repeat the Lou ritual and ensure success, I am then unable to watch the League Cup Final as I have to attend a family get-together in Sutton, and United lose. Four weeks later, disaster almost strikes once more as an old friend and I, having met in the West End for a drink, frantically search for a pub in which to watch the second half the of the Cup Winners' Cup Final, but seem to have found the only patch of London in which televisions do not exist. Eventually stumbling into a tiny, near-empty wine bar somewhere in Mayfair, we find the barman, who is Spanish, staring at a small TV set perched next to the optics. Reassuring him that, although English, we do not want Manchester United to win, the barman, whose name is Cesc, allows us to watch it with him, and I surreptitiously remove Lou from my wallet, along with a £10 note with which I use to pay for the drinks, flamboyantly motioning for Cesc to keep the change, which, I note when looking at the till, turns out to be only five pence. When Mark Hughes prods me into the lead in the 67th minute, we remain unmoved, while Cesc gesticulates wildly, claiming that it should never have been a free kick in the first place. When Hughes adds the second seven minutes later, I am unable to control myself and let out a cry of "Yes" that is so loud, it wakes up the only other customer in the place, and causes an already-tense Cesc to vent his anger at my reaction and blatant lying by forcing us to leave. As we're walking down the street, I realise that I've left Lou on the bar, and I feel my chest tighten at the thought of what dreadful torture he'll be subjected to at the hands of Cesc when he is discovered. Without explanation, I turn around and sprint back to the bar as one who is being chased by the henchman of a notorious band of East End racketeers to whom I owe a substantial amount of money. Realising that my only hope of saving Lou is to wait until Cesc isn't looking before entering, I wait outside until I can see that the customer whom I had just awoken decides to buy another drink, at which point I burst through the door, lunge toward the part of the bar where we were sat, grab the unharmed Lou, and make my exit, all in one swift and fluid motion. By the time we find another pub with a TV, the game is over and Brian Robson is lifting the European Cup Winners' Cup. Placing Lou on the bar, I turn to my friend and vow not to neglect that totemic little football card ever again, at which he rolls his eyes skyward.

In 1991, having left Kingston after failing my final exams as a consequence of a lack of concentration caused by the tense run-up to, and the joyously hazy aftermath of, the European Cup Winners' Cup triumph in May, I move back to Bexhill-on-Sea to live with my parents and get a job working at a local off-licence. We are also challenging for the League

Championship and looking odds on to finally win the thing when, on Sunday 26th April 1992, I make a decision that proves fatal. As Manchester United are playing at Anfield in the penultimate game of the season – a game that they have to win to be in with a chance of pipping Leeds United to the title – I am playing for a friend's church football team in the semi-final of the Eastbourne and District Evangelists Cup. Deciding that superstition has no place in a changing room occupied by a Christian football team, I choose not to place Lou face up on the floor whilst we play the game, which we manage to win 2-1, but in the meantime, United lose 2-0 and Leeds are crowned champions. I'd already won the League Cup two weeks previously by beating Nottingham Forest 1-0 at Wembley, but this serves as scant consolation because the League Cup just isn't enough anymore.

The newly-formed Premier League kicks off in August 1992 and, as the season progresses, my yearning to win my first League title, and the club's first since 1967, becomes a desperation that is all-consuming and leads to my receiving a severe reprimand from the area manager of Threshers for what is perceived to be a general and prolonged lack of concentration that culminates in the discovery that I have stocked a fridge full of red wine and have filled a shelf with two-litre bottles of Bentley's bitter that are four months past their sell-by date.

Despite the form of Eric Cantona, I become increasingly anxious and more certain than ever that, with Blackburn Rovers having secured the vast financial resources of their owner, Jack Walker, this could be my last chance of winning the League. Anxiety gives way to resignation when, on Saturday 10th April, United draw at home to Sheffield Wednesday and, switching off the radio in disgust, I retire to the bedroom to adopt the foetal position. It is not until an hour or so later, when a fellow United-supporting friend phones me in a minor state of delirium and blathers on about Steve Bruce scoring in the sixth minute of injury time, that I realise I'd turned the radio off too soon and that United had in fact won the game. This appears to break the spirit of my closest challengers, Aston Villa, and when they lose at home to Oldham Athletic on 2nd May, after 19 years of pain, I have won my first ever League Title.

Other than defeats to Chelsea, home and away, there is less cause for anxiety the following season, but much cause for celebration, as the championship is won for the second consecutive season and I exact revenge upon Chelsea by whipping their sorry behinds 4-0 in the FA Cup Final, thus recalling United's victory over Brighton 11 years earlier, only this time I enjoy the bullying because United have won the Double for the first time in their history. At work on the Monday after the Final, I am disappointed to note that the congratulatory words and pats on the back I expect to receive from customers are not forthcoming and, instead, those with the faintest interest seem sympathetic to Chelsea, as if in some way, they were the real heroes.

As the following season unfolds, I begin to feel a sense of disillusionment with the club I've supported from the age of five; a feeling that is compounded by my good friend Chris' decision to abandon United in favour of Coventry City. Having already developed warm feelings for Brighton & Hove Albion following a trip to the Goldstone Ground to see them play Swindon Town in late October 1994, my disillusionment grows still further when Eric Cantona assaults a Crystal Palace supporter in the style of David Carradine and gets himself banned for the rest of the season. By the time Blackburn Rovers are confirmed as Premier League champions on the final day, I've already lost interest and Lou hasn't seen daylight since September. Consequently, United also lose to Everton in the FA Cup Final.

The distance that this fresh antipathy creates allows me to reflect that the desire to see my football team succeed has led to me taking my eye off the ball and neglect any ambitions that I may have had for myself. With this in mind, I see fit to confide in Vanessa that I have, for some time, wished to move closer to London, to which she responds that she has also, and so it is that, in January 1996, we leave Hastings and move to a flat above an off-licence in Cheam, where I now work.

My interest in football quickly resumes as United begin to chip away at Newcastle United's 12-point lead at the top of the Premier League. My team beat Chelsea at the end of March, to reach their third consecutive FA Cup Final, and by the end of the season, Lou has been in constant use and is missing one corner, torn off amid a rapturous display of emotion upon Cantona stroking home United's winner in the last minutes of the Cup Final; a goal that wins us the Double for the second time in three years.

On instruction from the area manager, I am unable to wear a United shirt whilst working in the shop, so I choose to pin an enamel badge to my chest instead; an adornment that leads to customers variously claiming either that I've come out of the woodwork, or that I'm a typical Man United fan, on account of the fact that I live in Surrey. Dismissing such childish remarks to be the products of envy, I hang a United calendar above the counter in defiance.

In August 1996, I see them play in the flesh for the first time as I visit Selhurst Park, where they beat Wimbledon 3-0, although having already left in order to avoid the rush to exit the ground, I miss a late wonder goal by David Beckham – struck from the halfway line – that is to be talked about for years. I am the victim of much light-hearted abuse over the course of the next few months, particularly during a run of three consecutive defeats, with a 5-0 hammering by Newcastle *and an even more painful 2-1 home reverse to Chelsea, bookending a bizarre 6-3 loss at Southampton that renders my recent purchase of what I consider a rather fetching new grey United shirt, to be meaningless. In May, I have the last laugh as, once again, we clinch the Premier League title.*

Despite a decent start to the 1997/98 season, and knocking current holders, Chelsea, out of the FA Cup, panic sets in as the year turns, and it finally dawns on me that, without Eric Cantona, who retired in May, we aren't as good. Both Arsenal and Chelsea are breathing down my neck and Manchester United are knocked out of the FA Cup by Barnsley. By the end of the season, my tattered nerves are reflected in Lou's own increasingly dishevelled appearance, and not even he can prevent Arsenal winning the Double and me ending the season without a trophy.

In complete contrast, the 1998/99 season passes in a dizzying haze as United sweep all before them to win first the League, then the FA Cup and, best of all, the Champions League. Having seen an unprecedented amount of action in this most magnificent of seasons, Lou is in a desperate state, having lost all four corners, leaving only his head, but despite his injuries, I swear that, as Ole Gunnar Solskjær hooks the ball into the roof of the net in injury time in the Champions League Final, and I fall to my knees in disbelief, I look into his eyes and he sheds a tear of joy.

A desperate truth reveals itself over the following days: when looking to remove Lou from my wallet, he isn't there. It then occurs to me that, having left him on the floor on the night of the Final and Vanessa having vacuumed the next day, Lou, or what was left of him, had been sucked into the Dyson. Further realising that the bin men had already taken the rubbish, I am filled with a sense of grief such as would normally be reserved for the loss of a lifelong friend.

As the new season begins, panic sets in as it becomes apparent that, without Peter Schmeichel, who retired in May, we aren't as good. Although we win the Premier League again, with some ease, after the record-breaking heroics of the previous season, the winning of just the one trophy feels like a failure. In 2000/2001, I miss Lou more than ever. As if losing 2-0 to Chelsea in the Charity Shield isn't bad enough, we are knocked out of the FA Cup, League Cup and Champions League far too soon and, again, only manage to win the Premier League.

By February 2002, there is no trace of any Manchester United-related merchandise at the off-licence; United have sold star defender, Jaap Stam, and are out of the FA and League Cups, and Arsenal are looking good to win the Premier League. By the time the Gunners are confirmed as champions and Double winners in May, United have also lost in the semi-final of the Champions League to Bayer Leverkusen, and the memory of Lou is so distant that I give up hope.

There is opportunity to celebrate once again in 2003, as I win the League title, having overturned what seemed to be an unassailable lead from Arsenal. In mid-April 2003, a customer offers me tickets for the quarter-final second leg Champions League match, to be played at Old Trafford against Real Madrid. I turn them down and decide to watch the game at home instead, knowing that, in reality, I would watch little of it because United had no chance of overturning a 3-1 lead. On the night, I manage to watch much of the game whilst pacing up and down the front room, lured as I am by United's brave display, but although they win the game 4-3, the aggregate defeat sees them go out. It has, for some months, been obvious that the scorer of the final goal of that game, David Beckham, would be leaving the club, but when the news is confirmed on 1st July 2003 that he has signed for Real Madrid, it still comes as a shock, and panic sets in as I start to feel that, without his and Lou's talismanic qualities, we really won't be as good. But then, I come to my senses and I realise that this is Manchester United, the biggest club in the world. We'll be dominating the English game for decades, and it'll take something pretty miraculous to stop us...

Part Four

Something Pretty Miraculous

The Golden Ticket — 2003/04

"God bless Mum, God bless Dad, God bless Ian, God bless Andrew, and God bless all my relatives and friends. And please Lord, help Man United to beat Brighton tomorrow. Amen."

I can't remember clearly enough to confirm this, but I can assume, with some confidence, that I would have said a prayer to this effect the night before the 1983 FA Cup Final. I was God-fearing enough as a boy to know that to just pray for a Manchester United victory would not be the done thing and to think that it should be balanced by a far more important request. I might even have begun by asking for an end to Third World famine and the threat of nuclear war, and would have genuinely wanted this, but when it came down to it, and I admit this with a huge dose of shame on behalf of my 13-year-old self, at that precise point, I would have wanted a United victory more. The game was tortuous and, eventually, only Gordon Smith's last gasp miss spared United's blushes and led to the replay four days later. I'm sure the prayer was repeated the night before that game, in which case, in that instance, it was answered emphatically.

"Dear Lord. Please help Chelsea to become a dominant force; one that can compete for all the top honours every season and can consistently attract the biggest names in the footballing world. Amen."

At no point did I ever say a prayer like this. If I had done so at any time during the early days of the summer of 2003, then I would cite it as irrefutable evidence of the existence of God.

On 1st July 2003 comes the news that a Russian billionaire/oligarch named Roman Abramovich has bought Chelsea Football Club. Although many Blues fans might have welcomed the news, it concerns me at first. Immediately, there is talk that Chelsea, with a portion of Mr Abramovich's vast wealth now at their disposal, will come to dominate the game; not just in England but in Europe too. He seemed to appear from nowhere, and the announcement has come completely out of the blue.

The first player they buy to usher in the new and glorious era is Glen Johnson, a young defender bought from West Ham for £6 million. Ordinarily, this would've seemed like an outstanding signing; here is a young player, a potential England international of the future, and he hasn't signed for Manchester United or Arsenal, but for Chelsea. And yet, it isn't quite enough to confirm the new owner's commitment to the footballing domination of which has been spoken. Geremi Sorele Njitap Fotso, or Geremi as he is more commonly known, was then bought from Real Madrid, but has, until recently, been on loan at Middlesbrough.

Again, I remain sceptical. I can remember fanfares sounding at the slightest hint of a big money takeover at other clubs that soon faded to a whimper, and I can't help thinking that it is all too good to be true, and that this was Chelsea's very own Michael Knighton moment. It isn't until the speculation about Damien Duff's £17 million transfer from Blackburn Rovers looks like becoming a reality that I begin to think that it isn't all some sort of cruel joke.

Upon our return from a fortnight's holiday in Normandy, where we had entered a news void, amid the blistering temperatures of this year's heatwave, the first thing I do is to check Soccernet and the Chelsea website to see whether we've bought anyone else whilst I was away. Not only have we completed the signing of Duff, but we have also bought Juan Sebastián Verón from Manchester United for a whopping £15 million, England International left back, Wayne Bridge, from Southampton for £7 million and, the best of the lot, Joe Cole from West Ham for a bargain £6.6 million. Hmm, that's nearly £60 million spent already on just six players. Perhaps it isn't all hot air after all.

Before the season begins in earnest, and with Chelsea spending tens of millions on yet more players, the whole scenario seems as confusing as it does enthralling. Friends have variously warned me that it either won't end happily or that any subsequent achievements would seem hollow and shop-bought, and though I have the same fears about the former, I was quite happy to turn a blind eye to any accusations that Chelsea will be simply buying success and to just sit back and enjoy the ride. And yet, something still doesn't ring true. This sort of thing just doesn't happen. If someone had written a novel featuring a football team who were in the financial mire, but who had suddenly been bailed out by a mysterious billionaire from a foreign land, and who was intent on world domination, it would surely be dismissed as fatuous nonsense in need of a plotline that didn't attempt to combine *From Russia With Love* and *Jossy's Giants* so clumsily. It isn't until the opening League game of the season that I can finally embrace the truth.

On 17th August 2003, Chelsea travel to Anfield to face Liverpool for their first Premier League fixture of the season. It is an ironic piece of scheduling, given that the two clubs had met on the last day of the previous season; a game that cost Liverpool a Champions League place and, in essence, made Chelsea a far more attractive prospect for any potential investors. Ordinarily, it would be the cruellest of opening fixtures for Chelsea, at a ground at which they hadn't won for 11 years. With the fuss being made about Chelsea's windfall, and talk of the game signalling the start of a new era of domination for the club, I am trying not to get too carried away. If Chelsea can beat Liverpool on their own patch, then I might be convinced that it isn't all a dream, designed to help me overcome the recent departure of Gianfranco Zola, and that I won't soon be shaken awake by the news that the club has gone into administration.

The signs are good when Verón scores the first, but when Michael Owen equalises with a re-taken penalty 10 minutes before the end, it's obvious that nothing will ever change. However, a draw at Anfield is still unusual, and ordinarily a cause for mild celebration in itself, but then Jimmy Floyd Hasselbaink weaves his way into the box in the 87th minute to score the winner, and 2-1 wins against a once-dominant Liverpool have closed the old era and opened a new and potentially glorious one. There is further irony in the fact that the winning goal has been scored not by one of the new and expensive stars, but by Jimmy, a player who's been at the club for three years and has scored over 60 times in that period. In the moments after his winning goal, it is apparent that the irony isn't lost on him either, as he wheels away, swinging his shirt above his head, an expression approaching anger on his face as if to question the wisdom of spending over £30 million on two new strikers. There is still a familiarity about the team, but definitely not the result.

In times gone by, a win at Anfield might have provided the season's only highlight. In 2003/04, however, there are others, including a 4-0 win at Lazio, 5-0 wins against Wolves and Newcastle, and a home win against Manchester United.

But the best moment of all is reserved for the first week of April. What has become increasingly apparent as the season has unfolded is that, despite the cash injection, Chelsea aren't going to win a trophy. At least not a domestic one. As if in reaction to both United's title win the previous season, and the new threat posed by Chelsea, Arsenal have stepped up their game. Along with the flair displayed by the likes of Thierry Henry, Robert Pirès and José Antonio Reyes, there is a renewed steel to their performances and a startling level of consistency that will ultimately lead to them remaining unbeaten in the League for the whole season, as they go on to win the Premier League by 11 points. It is an unprecedented achievement that deservedly results in them being labelled "The Invincibles". As well as effectively ending Chelsea's hopes of winning the League by beating them twice, the Gunners also knocked them out of the FA Cup in the fifth round. So, when Chelsea are drawn to play Arsenal in the quarter-final of the Champions League, it seems obvious that the Blues' season has as good as ended.

*

There are certain footballers who, by virtue of one moment of magic, can secure a place in a fan's heart forever, no matter what else they achieve during their careers. These unlikely heroes can prompt misty eyes and a beaming smile at the mere mention of their name. For a Manchester United supporter, I would suggest that Lee Martin is the classic example of this. Martin scored the only goal of the FA Cup Final replay against Crystal Palace in 1990, a victory that secured Alex Ferguson his first trophy for United and arguably acted as the catalyst for the continuous and remarkable success that followed. Otherwise, he had an inauspicious career at United, scored only twice in total, struggled to get into the first team squad for the following few seasons, before leaving the Club in 1994. Roy Essandoh might be just such a name for fans of Wycombe Wanderers too; a player acquired via an advert placed on Ceefax by manager Lawrie Sanchez, looking for a fit striker. Within days, he scored a late-winning goal at Leicester City to send his team into the FA Cup semi-final, and was then released by the Club two months later. He came, he scored, he disappeared. And then, of course, for Southampton fans, there is Bobby Stokes.

Mention the name Wayne Bridge to me and I am immediately transported to April 6th 2004 and a house in Portland, Dorset, where I am sliding on my knees with the TV screen approaching my face at speed. In the first leg at Stamford Bridge a fortnight earlier, Chelsea had taken the lead through Eiður Guðjohnsen, but Pirès had soon equalised to set up a tense return leg at Highbury. With the Gunners in such dominant form, once Reyes had scored for Arsenal at the end of the first half, Chelsea's season was over. When Lampard equalised early in the second period, it was game on once again. But Arsenal knew how to win games, especially against the Blues, whom they hadn't lost to in five years. When left back Bridge surges forward in the 87th minute, plays a one-two with Guðjohnsen and slides the ball beyond Jens Lehmann, after burning my knees in celebration, I perform some mathematical gymnastics involving aggregate scores, permutations and outcomes, to discover that Arsenal now have to score twice more in the last few minutes to win. Even a pessimist like myself knows that even a team as good as Arsenal are unlikely to manage that, although by the time I've done the sums, the game is over. Claudio Ranieri, still manager for the time being, celebrates like a child for whom Christmas has come eight months early, expressing perfectly the way I myself feel as the final whistle brings an end to one of the most surprising results in my 20-year Chelsea history. Ultimately, Ranieri's team will be knocked out in the semi-final by an unfancied Monaco side, and for all the riches bestowed upon them, Chelsea haven't managed to win any silverware, and yet that one, dramatic win at Highbury is more than I could ever have hoped for.

The Man Who Fell To Earth — 2004/05

"Remember those jokes about the pensioners? No more of those now. Watch those boys go... Chelsea, for the first time in their career, are top of the League. And here's the man who did it; Ted Drake, the manager, the unyielding coach, the welder of team spirit." – Pathé News, April 1955

I'd never heard of Roman Abramovich before July 2003, and I had no idea what an oligarch was either. Prior to June 2004, the name of José Mourinho had entered my consciousness only once or twice. Firstly, there was his now infamous victory sprint down the touchline at Old Trafford in March of that year, as his FC Porto side scored a last gasp equaliser to send Manchester United out of the Champions League. Following that, there were increasing rumours that he might be the next manager at Stamford Bridge. As his winners' medal was placed around his neck at the end of the Champions League Final – in which his side had defeated AS Monaco, Chelsea's conquerors, 3-0 – Mourinho was stern-faced and had taken the medal off within seconds. It appeared that the only way to read this was that he knew he was on his way to Chelsea. He might have chosen to eschew a visible display of joy as a mark of respect to his current club and their fans, but it concerned me nonetheless. If he'd just won Europe's top prize for my club, I would want to see some sign that he was enjoying the experience, whether or not he was on his way out. On the other hand, perhaps the man was in fact a managerial machine, programmed to do nothing but win and to show no emotion whilst doing so, in which case, I couldn't wait for him to join my team.

Although I'd followed the latter stages of Celtic's march to the UEFA Cup Final in 2003, and had watched the whole of the Final against Mourinho's Porto, I still hadn't really been aware of him. Perhaps my disappointment with defeat for a British side had obscured his presence, but it is true to say that I never really paid much attention to managers of other teams; decent European teams in particular. There didn't seem to be much point in doing so because, prior to the summer of 2003, they were hardly likely to end up at Chelsea.

When Mourinho finally arrives at the Bridge, he does so with style and purpose, like Aragorn sweeping through the doors of Helm's Deep, and as he makes his first appearances in the media, it is clear that here is no ordinary manager. He is less like the men we are used to seeing, barking orders on the touchline or going through the motions in cliché-ridden press conferences, and more like a Hollywood version of a football manager: he looks good in a suit, has a glint in his eye, and he is handsome enough to make women, and possibly men, interested in a game they once detested. It is as though his forays into the consciousness during Porto's winning of the Champions League had acted as a convenient and hurried backstory to the main feature.

Of all the football managers, I have admired none more than Brian Clough. Apart from the extraordinary success he and Peter Taylor achieved in the 1970s and 1980s with Derby County and Nottingham Forest, both relatively small clubs at the time, he had character in abundance. So, when Clough himself describes Mourinho as being like "a young Brian Clough", I take notice. When, as a young Clough might himself have done, José then declares himself to be "a special one" at one of his first press conferences as Chelsea's new boss, I can see that he's the real deal, and it is then safe to start dreaming of impending success. But can he live up to the hype?

What better way to test his own claim than to start his competitive Chelsea career with a game against Manchester United? As I settle down to watch the match, I do so with an unusual sense of optimism. Although they haven't bought any established international stars, the Club have spent a lot of money on some promising players, including the young Dutch forward, Arjen Robben, and Didier Drogba, a striker from the Ivory Coast who'd been making a name for himself in France whilst playing for Marseille. Mourinho balanced the inexperience of these players by bringing both Ricardo Carvalho and Paulo Ferreira with him from Porto – two defenders who had been an integral part of the Portuguese side's recent successes – along with key members of his backroom staff, including Baltemar Brito, Rui Faria and André Villas-Boas. As far as coaching staff were concerned, the retention of Steve Clarke as assistant manager pleased me most, representing as it did a link between the old and new: a Chelsea that in the 1990s had finally achieved success, and this new, affluent version that seem destined to achieve yet more.

If Chelsea are a team on the ascendancy in 2004, Manchester United appear to be in danger of losing ground. Although they beat First Division Millwall 3-0 to lift the FA Cup in May, United had finished third in the Premier League for the second time in three seasons, which was, by their high standards, disappointing. They have themselves made no significant signings, with the purchase of Everton starlet, Wayne Rooney, still just a rumour. This is, I feel, as good a chance as Chelsea will ever have of not only beating United, but of making a genuine and prolonged challenge for the Premier League title.

When Guðjohnsen ghosts into the penalty area and scrambles the ball into an empty net in the 15th minute, I am out of my seat in celebration, as is José. As the rest of the game passes in an anxious blur and ends in a one-goal victory for the Blues, it seems clear that this might be the start of one truly memorable season.

But then, of course, there is Arsenal. "The Invincibles" have started the new season as they'd finished the last; by winning. And they aren't just winning games; they're scoring goals for fun in the process, beating Everton 4-1 away in the first game of the season, and regularly scoring three or four goals per game. Despite Chelsea enjoying an unusually bright start to the season, having won six and drawn two of the first eight games, they then lose away at Manchester City to a Nicolas Anelka penalty, leaving Arsenal to extend their lead at the top of the table to five points with a 3-1 win at home to Aston Villa. There appears to be little chance that the Gunners will be willing to do the decent thing and stand aside to allow Chelsea to stroll to the finishing line and win their first top flight League title in 50 years in this, their 100th year as a football club. From somewhere, Chelsea need, if not yet a miracle, at the very least, a helping hand.

Next up for Arsenal is Manchester United, at Old Trafford. United are struggling – a whole 11 points adrift of Arsenal – prompting pundits to rule them out of the title race, despite only two months of the season having elapsed. I'm not used to wanting United to win, but at Old Trafford on 24th October 2004, I watch the game, pleading through the TV screen for United to do me a favour, and they do. A typically contentious game ends in a 2-0 victory for the

Manchester Reds, and consigns Arsenal to their first League defeat in 50 games. The game is soon dubbed "The Battle of The Buffet" in honour of the fact that, as the arguments continued to rage between the two sides after the match, an Arsenal player, reputedly Cesc Fàbregas, had thrown some food, reputedly a slice of pizza, at Alex Ferguson. Food fight or no food fight, the result represents a significant turning point in the race for the title, and United, my nemesis, have made it happen.

Arsenal then draw three of their next four games, against Southampton, Crystal Palace and West Bromwich Albion; teams they might have expected to have beaten by two or three goals at the start of the season. Their title hopes are then dented further at the end of November by Neil Mellor, whose stunning injury time strike secures a 2-1 win for Liverpool over Arsenal; a goal that consigns the latter to falling five points behind Chelsea at the top, and me to a short period in the metaphorical doghouse, having scared the cat as I leap off the sofa in jubilation, causing him to leave a couple of unsightly scratches in the leather.

When the Gunners entertain Chelsea on 12th December 2004, it already has the feeling of a title decider, despite there being six months left of the season. As soon as Thierry Henry scores in the second minute, I walk out of the front room. I walk back in upon hearing the increase in volume that meets John Terry's equaliser, only to leave again 10 minutes later as Henry celebrates the scoring of a cheeky free kick, taken as Petr Čech is still lining up his wall. Eiður Guðjohnsen's equaliser at the start of the second half is perfectly timed, and, as far as it is possible to determine these things, the players celebrate with the steely determination of champions elect, as if the goal, and a welcome point at Highbury, are the very least they expected.

Mourinho has already split the previously unbreakable United-Arsenal duopoly. In truth, United are in a transitional stage and have been for a couple of seasons, and yet with Chelsea's newfound wealth, and José at the helm, the bar has been raised. It seems increasingly obvious that other clubs, even Manchester United, might struggle to compete. But this is Chelsea, and United are United: they will always find a way to stop us winning a trophy, given half a chance.

In 2004/05, their chance comes in the semi-final of the Carling Cup. A League win over them was one thing, but to knock them out of a Cup competition has always proved too great a challenge. The first leg, played at Stamford Bridge, finished goalless, and a victory for United at Old Trafford in the second seems inevitable. But things are different now, and the Blues have started to win games even when they aren't playing well. Can Mourinho conjure another victory against previously insurmountable odds? In my opinion, this is to be his biggest test yet. The bigger clubs, particularly Arsenal and United, have, in recent seasons, used the League Cup as a means to give their reserve team players a run out whilst they concentrate their efforts on winning the bigger prizes. From the very start of the competition, Mourinho has declared his intent to take it seriously, and proves true to his word at Old Trafford by recalling first choice keeper Petr Čech to the starting line-up, whilst United also field their strongest team. I am confident enough to watch most of the game and, after a nail-biting last few minutes, Chelsea win it, 2-1. It is the first time Chelsea have ever beaten Manchester United in a Cup competition. The Special One is proving to be just that.

Then comes the Final, to be played at Cardiff's Millennium Stadium, where Liverpool are waiting. Though not the force they once were, Liverpool have maintained a challenge for the top honours since their own glory days of the 1980s and are experiencing a resurgence under new Spanish manager, Rafael Benítez. This is to be the first time the teams have met in a major Cup Final. Having seen the Merseysiders win so many Finals and League championships in my lifetime, to see Chelsea win a trophy at the expense of a club of their stature would further enhance a season that had already taken on a dream-like quality. Within 45 seconds of the game kicking off, I have been rudely awoken by John Arne Riise. I decide that Liverpool taking such an early lead is an indication that I should forego the rest of the game and walk the one-and-a-half miles to our friend's house to feed their cats for them while they're on holiday, instead of waiting until full-time. As I walk, I listen to the game on the radio, which, with Chelsea then missing some clear chances to equalise and Liverpool threatening to extend their lead, is no less stressful, and my hope that it is all part of José's plan, and that Chelsea will eventually equalise, is beginning to look fanciful at best. But by the time I get home and switch the TV on, within minutes, they have indeed equalised, thanks to an unlikely looping header of an own goal from the Liverpool captain and star man, Steven Gerrard. Mourinho's response to the goal is to walk in front of the Liverpool fans and goad them by holding a finger to his lips, a reaction that leads to him being ordered from the dugout and sent to the stands. Unsurprisingly, many see his behaviour as unbefitting of a top manager. On the one hand, his divisive act serves to enhance his reputation as an arrogant character who supporters of other clubs find difficult, if not impossible, to like. But to Chelsea fans, he has endeared himself still further. To me, the gesture is worth, if not a thousand words, then certainly enough for me to resist the temptation to send a mildly gloating text message to the first Liverpool fan I can think of as the final whistle blows at the end of extra-time and Chelsea have secured their first trophy of the Abramovich era with a 3-2 victory.

By Christmas, Chelsea are top of the League and you'd think that I'd be happy, but for some reason I'm not. As the New Year begins, I immediately start to fill my new 2005 diary with thoughts and concerns on a daily basis; something I haven't done for some years. Much of it makes for awkward reading, the entries variously describing a general lack of fulfilment in my work, the state of our new house, and the associated frustration with a variety of tradesmen, comments on how much I miss Vanessa when she works away, concerns that a band called The Murder of Rosa Luxemburg might be splitting up, excitement at having a new boiler installed, fears that I drink too much too soon at the pub on Friday nights, and thoughts about a newly-acquired DVD box set of *The Hammer House of Horror* TV series from the early 1980s that I've just bought and am working my way through, and that I'm finding just as creepy as I did when I'd first watched it at the age of 11. Scattered amongst these ramblings are frequent mentions of Chelsea's progress in the Premier League and Champions League, which, in the second half of the season, involves them winning without exception. In my diary, as the first half of 2005 proceeds, a pattern emerges; for every Chelsea victory, and the obvious pleasure that each brings, there follows, in complete contrast, a darker entry about my general state of mind. The trend increases as April unfolds. For example, the aggregate win over Bayern Munich – clinched despite a 3-2 defeat in Munich on April 12th – means that Chelsea are in the Champions League semi-final for the second successive season, and my diary entry reflects my obvious delight. Jump forward two days and I am writing of feeling depressed, nipping out to buy a packet of Marlboro Lights (despite being a non-smoker), two of which I smoke whilst listening to Pink Floyd's *Dark Side of the Moon*, which apparently seems to help a bit.

Following the Bayern Munich fixture, Chelsea don't have a game for over a week when, on Wednesday 20th April, they are to face Arsenal at Stamford Bridge. In the interim, the diary reveals yet more anxiety. The game ends in an uneventful 0-0 draw, which means that the Blues are only two wins away from claiming the League title. Although Chelsea have sustained a challenge for the Premier League before, they have never been in as strong a position as that in which they find themselves now. This time, barring a capitulation of gargantuan proportions, such that would invite rival managers to draw comparisons with Devon Lock's famous collapse whilst only yards from victory in the Grand National of 1956, the title is theirs to lose. I'm no psychiatrist, but it seems clear to me that, in the final months and weeks of the season, I am finding the pressure far more difficult to handle than José Mourinho and his players. Chelsea's games have been televised on a weekly basis, or so it has seemed, and I've hardly missed one all season – although of those watched, I have obviously missed sizeable chunks of the draws or narrower victories. But this commitment has come at a price. As the impending triumph draws closer, I find it harder to watch. I've been calculating all the possible scenarios, spent far too much time sweating on how we could cope without the injured Arjen Robben, and have greeted each draw or defeat for either Arsenal or a resurgent Manchester United with the cheerful ebullience of a Chelsea victory, which, in effect, it is.

As Saturday 23rd April arrives, and Fulham visit the Bridge, it all seems to be set up perfectly. If Chelsea win and Arsenal lose to Tottenham, then Chelsea will win the League, exactly 50 years to the day since they'd won it for the first and only time. But sadly, due to the TV scheduling that now dictates the timing of all major football fixtures, Arsenal aren't playing Spurs for another two days, so an impossibly poetic ending to the season will prove just that; impossible. Chelsea labour to a 3-1 victory, meaning that, should Spurs get a draw at Highbury on Monday night, the Premier League is Chelsea's; five words that I thought I would never get to hear.

As Arsenal and Tottenham kick off, I sit in excited anticipation, with a Chelsea Cup Winners' Cup baseball cap that Ian bought me from Stockholm in 1998 sitting on one arm of the sofa, wrapped in the Chelsea scarf that I had owned since 1984, perhaps hoping that the presence of both will somehow provide the extra impetus Spurs need to ensure that they get the draw required to hand Chelsea the title – as if beating their bitter rivals isn't impetus enough. Ultimately, the hat and scarf prove useless, as a first-half Reyes goal is enough to give Arsenal the three points, but had Robbie Keane made the most of a glaring opportunity at the end of the game, chaos would have ensued, with the cat scratching the sofa as I leapt to fulfil a promise I had once made by running naked up my street with my arms held aloft, hailing the new champions. Keane is a great striker, but all the top marksmen have their off days, and perhaps it's just as well that this has been one of his.

We Are The Champions — April 2005

"...and Dalglish is in here... yes! The player-manager scores the goal that may edge Liverpool closer to their 16th championship." – John Motson, Stamford Bridge, 3rd May 1986

*

In a way, I'm relieved that Arsenal beat Spurs. I've long had it in mind that, should Chelsea win the hallowed League title, I want to be amongst other Blues fans, to prolong the moment for as long as possible, and to be held aloft and carried along the Fulham Road on a wave of celebration as if it was all a movie. I'd seen Liverpool win the League at the Bridge in 1986, and I was at Highbury in 1991 on the night that Arsenal won it, and having witnessed the subsequent celebrations of both sets of fans, I thought I might never get to experience that level of happiness myself. It's the 30th April 2005, five days after Arsenal played Tottenham, and Chelsea have travelled north to play Bolton Wanderers, and they need to win to clinch the title.

Coventry Chris has agreed to meet me at Stamford Bridge. I want to sit down to watch the game – for comfort primarily, but also to force myself to stay for the duration for fear of losing my seat if I vacated under pressure – so we make our way along Fulham Road until we find a pub that's showing it. We commandeer a table that is the perfect viewing distance from the TV and settle in as the venue quickly fills up around us; Chris in a state of complete relaxation, whilst I nurse my beer like a security blanket. I cling on for a first half made uncomfortably tense by a strong Bolton side that threaten to spoil Chelsea's day. In the second half, things don't improve greatly and, with away games at Manchester United and Newcastle still to come, I am already contemplating the possibility that, if they fail to beat Charlton Athletic next week, the chance for the Club to win their first League title in 50 years, and my first ever, will be gone. As the ball falls to Frank Lampard in the 60th minute, reality distorts; and time slows to a crawl.

I lurch forward. My beer glass is knocked from the table.

The pensive soundtrack to *28 Days Later* seeps through the loudspeakers.

The glass falling.

Lampard cuts inside a defender.

The glass still falling.

Lampard hammers the ball past Jääskeläinen.

The glass smashes to the floor: a momentary silence.

Then, as time regains its natural momentum and the music hits crescendo, the pub erupts.

That much does happen; the pub roars as one, but the goal itself occurs at normal speed to no soundtrack and my beer remains unmoved. With half an hour of Bolton pressure still to suffer, the celebrations soon dwindle. But then, 15 minutes later, Geremi... No! Čech tips round the post to prevent an embarrassing moment for the Chelsea player. Bolton have a corner. It's cleared by Guðjohnsen to Claude Makélélé, he's lost it – no he hasn't... he plays a long ball to Frank Lampard, *and he's through.*

Lampard breaks clear.

He's unchallenged. He has an option to square it – but he doesn't.

He knocks it past Jääskeläinen... slides it goalwards...

It's there!

The celebrations resume; and this time, they don't stop.

I see the Liverpool fans in '86 and the Arsenal fans in '91, and I feel their joy.

Chris and I stay at the pub for a while after the game and, as we eventually leave and make our way toward the ground, the scene that unfolds before us is unlike anything I've ever seen. Fulham Road, which just three hours earlier had been as quiet as any normal non-match day, is completely engulfed in a sea of blue; flags, shirts and scarves as far as the eye can see. It is exactly the party atmosphere I'd imagined and, although I'm not being carried aloft by a random bunch of ecstatic strangers, I make my way through the crowds of people in a reverie, out of which I am momentarily lifted in disbelief as four young and well-spoken boys and girls ask me what's going on, and have Chelsea just won a game or something? It's hard to believe that anyone won't have known that Chelsea have just won the Premier League. This is the epicentre of all that is right with the world, surely. I will be eternally grateful to Chris; not just for spending his Saturday watching a team he doesn't care about, but also for being the voice of reason and preventing me from buying a blue and white jester's hat to add to the collection of flags, t-shirts and badges that I've already bought from the string of roadside vendors that have sprung up outside the ground. We then go for a curry at the Blue Spice, and I keep the complimentary chocolate as a further memento, and can say with some confidence that I will never part with it.

The magic of the evening extends into my journey home as, with my flags fluttering proudly, I receive knowing nods from other fans, witter incoherently to a taxi driver, who I suspect is less than interested, and, as I arrive at Carolyn and Stuart's house, where Vanessa had been spending the afternoon, I am met with the sight of their garden shed wrapped in a string of lights, glowing blue. *We are The Champions* is played to death once we get home, as I reflect upon the fact that, yes, I've paid my dues, time after time, and I've had sand kicked in my face, but I really have come through.

When I wake the next morning and it quickly dawns on me that Chelsea are the League champions, I ignore a headache, get up and dressed, and walk jauntily to the newsagents to buy as many Sunday papers as I can carry. I even flash a cheery smile and a good morning nod to every passer-by, so happy am I. The one thing I haven't done is run naked up my street, but then again, I'd never thought that I'd have to, and I am feeling far too amenable to do anything that might upset the neighbours.

The Bottle had travelled with us when we moved from our old flat to our new house in Carshalton in 2004, and now sits in a cupboard, awaiting an occasion fitting for it to be released. Until midway through the 2004/05 season, I'd intended to open it as and when Chelsea won the League title, but as that achievement became increasingly likely, instead, I decided to save it for the day they won the Champions League; the ultimate prize, which will surely happen before too long, won't it?

The Great Divide — 2005/06

I have a handful of friends who suffer at the hands of the game the way I do, and over the years, we've developed an understanding whereby we won't gloat if our team beats theirs, and if their team get walloped by some part-timers who wash their own kit, we keep quiet about it. Even sympathetic text messages are out of the question because we respect the fact that, following a bad result, we're all in denial, and it's best to pretend that football doesn't exist. I once sent a text message to Mel minutes after Chelsea had beaten Arsenal, in the form of a genuinely consolatory sad face, i.e. :-(, which, thanks to the delights of predictive text and inter-network miscommunication, was translated as a smiley when it appeared on her phone. I was given the cold shoulder for a week. I don't think that was long enough.

*

Over the course of the first year in our new house, we got to know our new next-door neighbours, Kevin and Clare, and it soon became apparent that, in some ways, Kevin and I are kindred spirits. We have similar tastes in music, we enjoy the same TV programmes, and we both like football. That we share interests in this way not only made the potentially awkward first meetings a pleasure, but came as a great relief as it meant that our initial concerns – that by moving we might be swapping neighbours who we loved for neighbours who would make our lives a living nightmare – were completely unfounded. It's also become clear that Kevin and I have the same attitude to football; that being one of an irrationality informed by what might seem from the outside to be a combination of immaturity and paranoia. If our team loses one afternoon, we will tread carefully and change the subject as soon as possible, and because of the unspoken understanding that we have, it hasn't once been suggested by either of us that we should watch a match between our teams together. Ordinarily, this level of symbiosis would be idyllic, if it wasn't for the fact that Kevin supports Manchester United. I've swapped a situation in which I was living above a passionate Arsenal supporter for one in which I am living in a house adjoining that of an equally zealous United fan. Kevin's Mancunian revelation had initially come as a disappointment to me, although it was hardly surprising. A lot of people support Manchester United. No matter where in the country you live, if not the world, the probability is that there will be a greater chance that your next-door neighbour supports Manchester United than any other football club that aren't within 50 miles of your house. What's more, I have actually met him at a perfect time: for the first time in several decades, Chelsea are officially a better team than United. Whether or not they are a better club is another matter but, on the pitch, where bragging rights between friends and neighbours are determined, they are superior.

In the weeks and months following Chelsea's title triumph in April, my general state of unhappiness didn't improve. The diary entries stopped two days after the game against Bolton, but it was clear that I had a problem that required more than a historic and convincing Chelsea triumph to solve. By the start of the new season, I'd sought the advice of a doctor and my head was soon clear enough to have concluded that my working situation needed to change – not as a result of working relationships but for reasons of practicality – and I am now working from home. Although self-employed, I had previously been sharing an office, but my working environment now comprises of an office at the bottom of the garden and a radio tuned to either TalkSport, BBC London or BBC Five Live, so I have effectively swapped my old three-dimensional colleagues for new ones, who include Alan Brazil, Adrian Durham, Robert Elms and Danny Baker, and who exist only as voices. In those first months, listening to football-related programmes had never been more pleasurable. Not only were Chelsea constantly referred to as The Champions, but they'd had a tremendous start to the season, beating Arsenal 2-1 to claim the Charity Shield, and winning their first nine League games, and their momentum was such that I rarely had cause to turn the radio off. Any negative comments about Chelsea from presenters or pundits amounted to office banter (albeit banter that I was unable to involve myself in), and even with the increasing amount of criticism levelled at the team for their boring, workmanlike performances, I can dismiss such talk as simply being the kind of jealous heckling that comes with being the League champions.

The first occasion I have to avoid all forms of media comes as late in the season as November 6th. Unbeaten after 11 games, Chelsea meet Manchester United at Old Trafford for a Ford Super Sunday Premier League clash to be shown live on Sky Sports. Despite the Blues' recent form, and thoughts that they might go one better than the previous season by this time remaining unbeaten on the way to claiming a successive League title, I am as pessimistic as ever. They may be in something of a transitional period, and are only seventh in the League, following a 4-1 defeat at Middlesbrough the previous week, but this is still Manchester United. They still have dangerous players; namely Ruud Van Nistelrooy, Wayne Rooney, and a blossoming Cristiano Ronaldo, and having signed Edwin van der Sar pre-season, they now have a world-class goalkeeper. They also have a point to prove: Chelsea had not only won the title the previous season but they had subsequently won 3-1 at Old Trafford, with the United players sportingly forming a guard of honour to hail the new champions before kick-off. That must have hurt, and now my concern is that the Reds have become a wounded animal with revenge on their minds: that Chelsea might have inadvertently awoken the beast. I watch the game alone, but once Darren Fletcher's looping header finally deduces that it can't just hang in the air all day and needs to land somewhere – and chooses the Chelsea net in which to do so – only half an hour of the game has passed, and I decide that I can't watch much more. The game finishes 1-0, and my team has lost a League game for the first time in just over a year.

I was half expecting to hear a cry of delight from next-door when Fletcher scored, but I heard nothing, which was a small blessing. The chances of me asking Kevin round to watch the game were zero, and the chances that he would have accepted the invitation were equally small. I'd once made a premature attempt to prove that, since the FA Cup nightmare of '94, I'd grown enough as a person to sit through a match with an opposing supporter, as I watched Arsenal beat Chelsea with an Arsenal-supporting friend. Though they hid their pleasure well, I summoned enough maturity to realise then that it's unfair to rob anyone of the chance to celebrate a victory in a normal and relaxed manner, particularly in the comfort of their own home, so I left immediately after the final whistle had blown, vowing that I would never put myself nor anyone else in that position again. That he suffers the same angst about his team's fortunes makes Kevin the perfect neighbour in many ways; gloating is virtually non-existent and only occurs at moments of extreme stress. For those occasions when our teams are to play each other, there is the briefest, tight-lipped mention in the days or hours beforehand, and very little said afterwards, other than a few words of grudging yet well-intentioned congratulation. Had that understanding not existed right now, in light of United's win, I would've succumbed to the temptation to erect one of the large flags bought to celebrate the League championship win in 2005 on the roof of the tool shed, to flap mockingly in the breeze.

*

The gulf between Chelsea and United, if it could ever be described as such, has narrowed alarmingly. Following their win at Old Trafford, within three weeks, United had climbed from seventh in the Premier League to second, and by the end of November, they had cut the gap between themselves and Chelsea from 18 points to just 10. Now 10 points might seem like a huge gap to some but, as the old cliché goes, a week is a long time in football and fortunes can quickly change: two dodgy performances from the Blues, combined with two United wins, and that 10-point gap could be reduced to 4.

Sure enough, in February, the Reds began a run of nine consecutive wins to leave them just seven points behind Chelsea by the first week of April, and with the game between the two – to be played at Stamford Bridge on Saturday 29th April – drawing ever closer, I am starting to worry. This is unknown territory for a Chelsea fan. A year spent hearing your team referred to as The Champions proves addictive. I want another year of that and am willing to forego any of the other prizes on offer to ensure it. The Champions League dream has already been put on hold for another year, courtesy of Chelsea's aggregate defeat to Barcelona in the first knockout stage, and expectation and ambition has now inflated to the extent that the League Cup defeat to Charlton Athletic in October, far from being the tragedy it might once have been, now seems a mere inconvenience. There is still a good chance that the Club might make more history by winning the Double for the first time, but that dream ends on 22nd April with a 2-1 FA Cup semi-final defeat to Liverpool.

As another old cliché has it, you should take one game at a time. In practice, as a fan, that just isn't feasible. It's fine to say that you only need three more wins and the title is yours, but when those upcoming fixtures include games against West Ham United, Bolton Wanderers and Everton, all of whom have, in the recent past, proved they are more than capable of beating your team, and your team have just drawn 0-0 at home with Birmingham City, Devon Lock once again rears its ghostly head and the Fat Lady abandons the gig with a sore throat. When James Collins heads West Ham into a 1-0 lead inside the first 10 minutes and your team have a man sent off soon afterwards, the season is over. But then, improbably, the Fat Lady finds her voice again and, thanks to Drogba, Crespo, Terry and Gallas, your team actually end up winning the game 4-1. Another 2-0 win at Bolton and an impressive 3-0 victory at home to Everton follow and, with Chelsea nine points clear of Manchester United, the game between the two on 29th April is set up beautifully: if Chelsea avoid defeat, they will be crowned champions once again.

Since United's mauling of them in the Cup Final of '94, Chelsea have beaten United seven times; enough, one might assume, to consider that revenge has been exacted. But even the 5-0 League victory in 1999, the Charity Shield win in

2000, nor either of the three wins the previous season has really satisfied me or served to prove that, on balance, Chelsea have come close to proving themselves the equal of United over the course of the 22 years since I swapped the Reds for the Blues. It shouldn't really be that important. Supporting a football team can be just as rewarding, whether your team are constantly challenging for the top honours or striving for great things in the lower divisions – just a quick look across at the progress that AFC Wimbledon were making would have proved that. Had Chelsea not attracted the attention of Roman Abramovich and secured the resources and opportunities that he could provide, then perhaps I would've been quite content with the occasional Cup victory. But now the potential is so much greater; to continue living this dream within which Chelsea fans are caught, to win the Premier League title at Stamford Bridge against Manchester United – their closest rivals and the destroyers of so many former dreams – is essential. In the end, the match is everything the fans could have hoped for; an early goal from William Gallas to calm the nerves, a wonder goal from Joe Cole on the hour, and a third from Ricardo Carvalho seals a 3-0 victory and the title is Chelsea's, and won in style. The elation isn't quite on the same level as the previous season, and though I might have felt sympathy for Kevin as a friend, I celebrate the win quietly in the front room, as much in relief that I would be the one who would have to keep my joy in check.

The Empire Strikes Back — 2006/07

"Can Manchester United score? They always score."
– Clive Tyldesley

Any hope of a bright start to the 2006/07 season to rival that of the previous one is soon dashed when first, Chelsea lose the Charity Shield to Liverpool in August and are then beaten by a 90th minute Mark Viduka goal at Middlesbrough in the second fixture of the League campaign. The premature level of panic that these two early defeats cause is prompted by the pre-season optimism having been so high, with the Club having made some major new signings, including the £30 million purchase of the highly rated Ukrainian striker, Andriy Shevchenko from AC Milan, German international, Michael Ballack from Bayern Munich, and Ashley Cole from Arsenal, and it was beginning to look as though they might become unbeatable. Meanwhile, back at fortress Old Trafford, Emperor Palpatine, aka Sir Alex Ferguson, is plotting Chelsea's downfall. The United manager has made only one major pre-season signing, paying Tottenham £13 million for Michael Carrick, but his defence is now bolstered by Nemanja Vidić and Patrice Evra; both signed midway through the previous campaign. Perhaps more significantly, Wayne Rooney and Cristiano Ronaldo are beginning to forge a striking partnership more fearsome than any.

In 2003, when Chelsea had embarked upon this glorious adventure, once I'd overcome my initial scepticism, I'd been determined to enjoy the impending victories and conquests unconditionally and without question. What I hadn't prepared myself for was the level of self-doubt and anxiety that these successes would bring: when you reach the top, the only way is down. I'm sure most fans would agree that when your team achieve success, though you want that success to continue, deep down, you're convinced that, sooner rather than later, it will all come to an embarrassing end. In 2005, I had every reason to believe that a new dawn was upon us and that, as long as the funding remained, Chelsea would dominate for years to come. The Invincibles of Arsenal were now less so and Manchester United faced capitulation. In a move that echoed that made by the fans of Wimbledon three years earlier, a group of United supporters had formed a new club, to be named FC United, as a reaction to the takeover of Manchester United by American businessman, Malcolm Glazer. This desertion of their team by a portion of the Club's most ardent fans was sure to undermine them. Add to that the fact that not only might Sir Alex himself decide that the new ownership would prove too disagreeable for him to remain at the Club, but that surely, at the age of 64, he would be due to retire soon, and then Chelsea's tenure at the top of the English game would be secure. And yet this assumption would turn out to be nothing but a pipedream.

*

I'd be lying if I said that criticisms of Chelsea since the Abramovich takeover haven't started to bother me. They bother me, mostly because I know that they contain some truth. The one prevailing criticism has been that the Club is buying success. In effect, that much is true, in that, without the substantial funds now at their disposal, they wouldn't have been in a position to ever win the League the way they had, if at all, and especially not in consecutive seasons.

On 25th November 2006, on the eve of the first League meeting of the season between Chelsea and United, TalkSport presenter, Terry Christian – a Mancunian and a United fan – has just intimated that Chelsea's cash means that no other club have a chance of winning anything anymore and that, in his words, *"filthy lucre sort of devalues everything"*. This annoys me but I can understand the point he's making. I felt exactly the same way when Jack Walker appeared from nowhere in 1991 and funded Blackburn Rovers, who won the Premier League three years later, so to denounce such remarks entirely would be complete hypocrisy. I would challenge any fan claiming that, given the choice, they would not prefer their club to achieve success without selling out. Had Chelsea managed to win the title in 1999 it may not have felt any better for a fan, but they might have received less begrudging congratulations from fans of other clubs, due to the perception that their success had been achieved by purer means, despite the level of debt the Club was supposedly operating under at the time. Manchester United were often perceived as being a club who went about things in the right manner, as were Arsenal and Liverpool, and these proclamations were often accompanied by the phrases "illustrious history", "marble halls", "fine institution" and "honourable tradition". Perhaps Chelsea couldn't lay claim to any of those things, but these were clubs whose successes over the decades had helped their fan bases to grow, allowing them to take their place among the world's elite. This gives them the moral high ground, whereas Chelsea, a club who are often accused of having no history, were perceived as the new kids: the brash, young pretenders, formed only 100 years before. I should, of course, have phoned Terry Christian to tell him all this while he's still on air and to make my point, both to him and to the nation, but that was never likely to happen.

*

There isn't as much praise for the Blues now as there had been at the beginning of the previous season, due, in large part, to the pragmatic and efficient style of play that Mourinho's team had adopted in the 2005/06 campaign; one which generally involved them getting their noses in front and killing the game to secure three points. It was a style that many deemed dull, but one that I was quite happy with, as long as it meant winning. Similar criticisms to those of the Arsenal team that won the League in 1990/91 – criticisms that led to the familiar, ironic chants of "1-0 to the Arsenal" and "Boring, boring Arsenal" from their own fans – always seemed unfair and born of pure envy. Nevertheless, it would be nice to see Chelsea win it in a more flamboyant style this time around, if just to silence the critics. But that wish is to remain unfulfilled.

The game on 26th November ends 1-1, but United have been top of the League since the beginning of October, and Ronaldo and Rooney are scoring for fun. Chelsea are still managing to win most games by the odd goal, and are pushing United in second, but ultimately, they are undone by three 2-2 home draws against sides they would be expected to beat; Reading, Fulham and, finally, Bolton Wanderers. The draw with Bolton late in April is a gift for United. The image of Alex Ferguson skipping jubilantly from the Goodison Park dugout to signal to his players that the game at Stamford Bridge had just finished 2-2 will, I fear, be forever etched on my memory. Effectively, Chelsea's draw, coupled with United's 4-2 win at Everton, means that, should Chelsea fail to beat Arsenal at the shiny, new Emirates stadium the following week, Ferguson's men would win the title.

Chelsea are more than capable of beating Arsenal, and have recently beaten them in the League Cup Final to claim Mourinho's fifth trophy for the Blues. Ironically, we are at our house in Portland that weekend with Kevin, Clare and their son, Charlie. Having no access to Sky TV or the Internet, our only way of finding the result is via trusty old Ceefax. As both Kevin and I wait an agonisingly long time for page 302 to unfold, I have already resigned myself to the fact that, with only two games left to play, even a win against Arsenal won't be enough, whereas I'm sure that Kevin is feeling equally pessimistic about his team's ability to hold onto a five-point lead at the top. As we glare at the television screen and 302 finally appears, with the headline at the top reading "Chelsea Draw Hands United Title" or some such, Kevin graciously stands up and walks away, to take his celebrations elsewhere, leaving me to mourn alone. I read the report and learn that Michael Essien equalised for Chelsea but, despite a valiant attempt to win it whilst reduced to 10 men for half the game, they couldn't find a winner and the game ended 1-1 – meaning that the red half of Manchester can celebrate winning the title for the first time in four years. As I switch the TV off and sit staring at a blank wall, it occurs to me that not only would Chelsea no longer be referred to as The Champions, but United are back, and the dominance of the domestic game that I've enjoyed thus far is under threat; and I'm not ready for that.

The Red Mist

It's autumn 2006 and I am alone in the house. Outside, it's dark, and all the lights indoors are switched off. I'm sat in the back room whilst a projector fills a wall with the opening credits for *The Descent*, a film that I know to be scary, firstly, because a friend has told me so and, secondly, because the cover to the DVD is predominantly black and shows the partially illuminated and blood-speckled face of a woman who is clearly in some distress. I also know that the film is set in a network of caves and I'm not a fan of enclosed spaces, particularly ones in which there is little or no chance of escape. One hour later, every light at the back of the house is switched on and I am standing by the back door, only peering at the screen fleetingly when a lull in the soundtrack indicates that it is safe to do so. The horror ends: of the six who descended – spoiler alert – there are no survivors, and I am left wondering exactly why I have just spent the best part of two hours of my life allowing my head to be filled with images of subterranean beings whose sole purpose is to hunt down intrepid but defenceless cavers.

Fast forward six months and I am sat in the same room, in the same chair, looking at the same wall, knowing that I am about to spend the next two hours being scared witless once again. To watch those players in blue take to the field prior to the 2007 Champions League semi-final, second leg at Anfield, is akin to watching those six poor women assembling at the mouth of the cave within which they are about to meet their doom. Chelsea are 1-0 up after the first leg, but with the intensity of the Anfield atmosphere projecting a climate of fear and foreboding into my own small space, with 20 minutes gone, I am already struggling with claustrophobia. As John Obi Mikel charges toward Boudewijn Zenden, I scream at him, pleading for him not to go down there because it's dark and bad things will happen, but, ignoring both my own warnings and those of some imaginary and sinister cellists, he carries on running and gives away a free kick, from which Daniel Agger scores. For the remainder of this so-called entertainment, the Chelsea players look increasingly trapped, not knowing which way to turn or why they even thought to come here in the first place. As extra-time passes, and the dreaded penalty shoot-out looms large, the lights are on and the chair is empty. Having sought refuge in the front room, a consolatory text message from a friend informs me that the game is over and that there are no survivors; Chelsea have lost in the semi-final yet again.

Given that I don't claim to be a big fan of horror movies – and often find them hard to watch, even with the safety of a cushion – it's hard to explain why I bother watching them at all. If I've heard recommendations or read a good review of one then I'll give it a chance and, as with all films, I feel that I have to watch it to the end, whether I'm enjoying it or not. It's similar with football; if I'm watching a Chelsea game, the effect it has on my mind and body is exactly like that of watching a horror film, even to the point that I'll hold my fingers in my ears or leave the room if I think something bad is about to happen, such as a hairless, carnivorous fiend jumping out of a tunnel, or Dirk Kuyt appearing on the edge of the six-yard box while the Chelsea defence is nowhere to be seen. In contrast, watching a game that doesn't involve Chelsea is like sitting through a rom-com; it's innocuous, not particularly challenging, I won't be too concerned about the outcome, and I might even laugh a few times.

*

According to Chinese culture, the colour red represents integrity and good fortune, and I have little reason to dispute this. It shouldn't be a consideration when picking a football club but if you want a better chance of your team winning then it follows that you should pick one who play in red, and the more red the better. Whoever it was who, at the end of the 1960s, decided that Liverpool FC should swap white shorts and socks for red ones to match their existing red shirts might, in doing so, have laid claim to sole responsibility for ushering in the most successful period in the Club's history. Similarly, Manchester United won nothing until they switched to wearing red shirts in the early 1900s. I've suffered more at the hands of teams in red than those in any other colour over the years. Even when I supported United, Liverpool were the immovable object that prevented my team from winning the League, and when it wasn't Liverpool, it was either Nottingham Forest, who wear red, or Aston Villa, who wear claret, which is itself a shade of red. Between 1975 and 2007, the League title was won by teams in red, or shades thereof, on 26 occasions.

This fear of redness is probably highly irrational, but experience dictates that my team's chances of winning a match will be marginally smaller if they are facing a team in red. Although it's been far from unusual for Chelsea to lose to teams from the lower divisions in cup competitions over the years, as they lined up to face non-League Scarborough in the FA Cup in January 2004, despite the fact that their opponents were clad entirely in red and had beaten them in their last meeting, I was confident that a newly-affluent and star-studded Chelsea would beat them easily. As it turned out, the performance of both teams was hardly reflective of the chasm between the clubs and, in the end, I was relieved that we managed to get away with a 1-0 victory. Four years later, I was less than surprised to hear that the Blues had been knocked out of the FA Cup by the Reds of Barnsley. But, of all the so-called "smaller" teams-in-red, for a couple of seasons, it was Charlton Athletic that antagonised me the most. Prior to 2003. I'd always quite liked Charlton, to the point where I had even considered buying a season ticket at The Valley in 1998, before I'd opted for one at Wimbledon instead. But from 2003 onwards, Chelsea's wealth led to them becoming the team to beat and, to a smaller club, to beat them represented a symbolic scalp with which to hold up as an example of the ills of the modern game, and this was often made clear by the Charlton fans, who would phone in to TalkSport or BBC Five Live following wins over Chelsea. My resentment at this perceived attitude was directly linked to my prior inexperience of supporting a club that could be described as either successful or rich, and would lead directly to an ill-tempered outburst in front of friends one evening, caused by one of them suggesting that Charlton Athletic were a better club to support because there was a nice family atmosphere at the ground. So, having literally seen red the night before, in the morning, as I walked to the shops, the first person I saw walk toward me was a young man, proudly sporting a Charlton shirt. I wanted to shake his hand and apologise to him and his club for my behaviour, and to explain that I was new to this game and just couldn't handle the pressure or the banter that supporting a rich club entailed, but instead I chose to walk on sheepishly, with my head bowed in shame.

When Chelsea lost to Liverpool in the Champions League semi-final of 2005, the second leg had been played only four days after we had clinched the Premier League title at Bolton. Although it was disappointing, I wasn't devastated. By the time the two clubs were drawn to play each other two years later, the need to win the Champions League had become an obsession for Chelsea and their fans. For all their on-field successes, both post and pre-Abramovich, it was the one trophy they wanted to win, and if they couldn't do so soon, with the advantage that all their wealth and resources gave them, perhaps they never would. In the second leg at Anfield in 2005, it was felt that Chelsea had been unlucky because it seemed clear that Luis García's shot hadn't crossed the line. Had that goal not been awarded, Liverpool might have considered themselves equally hard done by, having been denied a penalty immediately prior to the ball falling to Garcia. But it seemed that it was Liverpool's fate to make it to the Final that year, not least when, three weeks later, they managed to pull off one of the greatest comebacks of all time in a game soon to be dubbed "The Miracle of Istanbul". Liverpool were playing in their familiar red strip, whereas AC Milan were forced to change from their usual red and black striped shirts to an all-white kit. The luck, therefore, would all be with the Merseysiders. But, by half-time, it appeared that nothing could be further from the truth, as the Reds of Liverpool headed to the dressing room, 3-0 down, and with the fans playing the role of extras in their very own horror film. But what happened next has made for what is now widely considered to be the best Champions League Final of all time.

When Steven Gerrard headed past Milan keeper, Dida, in the 54th minute, I assumed it would just be a consolation goal and that the Italians would reinforce their dominance to win even more comfortably. But the goal had the opposite effect, and players in red who had previously been playing as if they weren't quite sure what they were doing in a major European Final, started to play like champions, and players whose abilities had, in the past, been bought into question, suddenly sprang to life. When two minutes after Gerrard's goal the ball fell to Vladimír Šmicer, 25 yards from goal, and he shaped to shoot, it was reasonable to assume that Dida would be taking a goal kick 20 seconds later, so as the ball found the back of the net, the most unlikely of outcomes now seemed anything but. Within three minutes, Liverpool had drawn level at 3-3. Gerrard was bought down in the Milan box when through on goal and, although Dida saved his first attempt from the penalty spot, Xabi Alonso scored from the rebound. As the game reached the lottery of the penalty shoot-out, it was left to Andrey Shevchenko to score his spot kick to keep Milan in contention. His attempt was saved by Dudek and Liverpool were the champions of Europe for the fifth time. Although I was still slightly begrudging of their place in the Final, as I watched the match unfold, I was in absolute awe of their achievement. I envied the fans their storybook ending and now I wanted one for myself.

*

The European Cup had a magical and mystical aura to me when I was a boy, when year after year I would watch in fascination as either Emlyn Hughes, John McGovern or Dennis Mortimer walked up steps to lift a trophy that looked as big as they were, having beaten teams with glamorous and superior-sounding names. It appeared to me that Liverpool, Nottingham Forest or Aston Villa were the only English sides who would ever be able to win the competition in the 1970s and '80s, and following the ban from European competition for English clubs between 1985 and 1990, it began to seem increasingly unlikely that a team from this country might win it again. That ended in 1999, with Manchester United's win against Bayern Munich, and, although Leeds had a great run in 2001, from then on, it seemed that it might only be United or Arsenal that would ever be capable of winning it.

Chelsea were favourites to get to the final in 2005, and probably 2007 as well, particularly given that they went to Anfield for the second leg with a one-goal advantage from the first. Throughout both ties, I once again clung to the hope that what goes around had to come around sooner or later for Chelsea, and that the fates would this time align themselves with the Blues in order to balance the books. But instead, I spent the game hiding like a child in fear of the Daleks, as Rafa "Davros" Benitez became the architect of Chelsea's demise once more. And yet it had all seemed so different in February 2005 when, with Chelsea on course to win the League, and having just beaten Liverpool in the Carling Cup Final, it really felt as though we were entering a new Blue age. Manchester United and Arsenal would end the season scrapping for the FA Cup, and it appeared that Liverpool were but a shadow of their 1980's selves. As it was, semi-final victories for the Reds of Merseyside over Chelsea in the Champions League and FA Cup in 2005, 2006 and 2007 amounted to a cautionary cuff round the ear for a precocious child, and a reminder that, no matter how rich the Club became, there will always be a gremlin hiding in the wardrobe, and it will probably be wearing red.

Fuzzy Logic
— May 2007

"Here's Irwin. Keane. Giggs. They're just starting to build something here, United, it would seem. Irwin... Oh! Oh! Eddie Newton on Dennis Irwin! A penalty in the Cup Final." – John Motson, Wembley, 1994

Dennis Irwin is cartwheeling over Eddie Newton's outstretched right leg on the edge of the penalty area: it's May 14th 1994. Chelsea have managed to keep United out for an hour and it's approaching the stage in the game when, if they can continue to do so for another 10 minutes, anything could happen; United might panic, leave a little gap at the back somewhere, and John Spencer might nip in unseen to win the Cup for the Blues in the final minutes. That United should score when they did wasn't a surprise in itself, but it was made more heartbreaking by the manner in which the penalty was conceded and the subsequent onslaught that ensued. It was clearly the right decision, but it was a tragedy for Newton; a hero at the Club he'd been at since a boy. Ultimately, he would come to balance that memory with a happier one by scoring at Wembley three years later, and although the FA Cup win in '97 had in turn helped ease the pain of the defeat in '94, there was a swagger and a cockiness about that particular United team that made the 4-0 score line even harder to stomach. Players like Eric Cantona, Roy Keane and Paul Ince were all supremely talented footballers, and no doubt loved by United fans, but they were each the type of player that were difficult for fans of other clubs to like. Victory over Middlesbrough in '97 was wonderful, but it hadn't fully redressed the balance. There was still a score to settle.

But as Michael Ballack swept the ball home in the second half of extra-time at Wembley in the 2007 FA Cup semi-final to put Chelsea 2-1 up against Blackburn Rovers, my delight quickly gave way to trepidation as I realised that it would be Manchester United that they'd be facing in the Final.

*

19th May 2007 is the day upon which the FA Cup Final is to be played at the new Wembley Stadium for the first time. We are visiting Vanessa's parents in Bexhill. My Mum is on holiday, so I've decided to nip down the road to watch the match at her house; alone. The solitude is essential. I am so nervous about the game that I would rather not watch it at all if the only alternative is that, for some reason, I will have to watch it with someone else, no matter who they are. And yet that is exactly the choice I am to be faced with. Knowing what my reaction will be, Vanessa takes me to one side, out of earshot, before asking me whether it would be okay if her dad, Vernon, came with me to watch the match at my Mum's house. A discourse follows that largely involves me repeating the questions: "Doesn't he understand?" and "Can't he stay here and watch it?" Both reasonable questions I think, although both voiced with a frustration informed by the knowledge that I know full well how ridiculous my attitude appears to other people; especially people who really don't understand. We decide that I should explain to Vernon myself exactly why it is that he can't watch the game with me, and as I do so, his expression is one of confusion and hurt. As I dig deeper in an attempt to clarify the reasons why

I have to be alone, I struggle, purely because I'm not really sure myself. He is a neutral, but comes from London, so will always support a London team over and above any other; he doesn't like Manchester United; he is unlikely to say much throughout the game, even less so if Chelsea should lose; and above all, he is a nice man. The more I struggle to explain myself, the more hurt he looks, and in his face, I see my own childishness reflected back at me. Why shouldn't I spend a bit of quality time watching a football match with my future father-in-law? Can't I just control my emotions and show a bit of maturity for one afternoon? What's the worst that can happen? The worst that can happen will be that United score at least four goals and humiliate Chelsea like no other team has ever been humiliated at Wembley before, forcing me to descend into the mother of all sulks, upsetting Vernon in the process and alienating him for good. Finally, I relent and drive round to Mum's house, with Vernon by my side.

As we arrive and make ourselves comfortable in front of the TV, I cannot recall ever feeling as tense as I do now. Before the final in '94, I'd felt fine because I didn't really expect Chelsea to win. But there's nothing to choose between Chelsea and United now, so Chelsea have a chance of winning, and I allow myself to believe this, which makes me feel worse. To compound my nervousness, Kevin and Clare have kindly invited us around to their house for dinner tomorrow evening and, by some miscalculation, we have gratefully accepted. I know that Kevin won't gloat if United win, but the problem is that their son, Charlie, has a far healthier attitude toward the sport and most definitely will; and he supports United too.

As the game gets underway, barely a word is exchanged between Vernon and I, and as the match progresses, both teams seem to have forgotten that the object of the game is to score goals, meaning that the commentators, John Motson and Mark Lawrenson, don't have a lot to comment on either, which is perfect. The conversational vacuum and the lack of excitable commentary allows my mind to drift in an attempt to distract myself from my team's plight. Vernon, on the other hand, is no doubt hoping that the game will liven up, and that there'll be plenty of goalmouth action, and that Chelsea might win by the odd goal in seven. If United win, he'll tell me that he's disappointed, but I know that, deep down, he won't really care, and I then start to wonder what it might be like to be that way.

"*Scholes... Looking for Ronaldo! Something here perhaps...? No,*" John Motson says hopefully.

It must be wonderful and strange, and I envy Vernon his neutrality, but I am rarely more envious of anyone than on those occasions when Chelsea have lost a crucial game, and I walk into another room where Vanessa is sitting, cheerfully watching something else. When she sees how far my shoulders have dropped, she always instinctively knows to drop the tone of her voice down to a sympathetic level. This helps because I know that she understands what I'm feeling in some way, but ultimately, she doesn't really care about the result at all. She's happy when Chelsea win simply because I'll be happy too.

"*Brown... Scholes... Carrick... and again, oh it's Ryan Giggs here! Chelsea had to hurry there.*"

Both Vanessa and her father are moved by important things like the General Election results – things that really affect the way that people live their lives – and I would love to share their relaxed and realistic attitude to football. But I would also love for them, and other disinterested friends, to be able to experience the feeling of elation that watching your team win a big game can provide. On the other hand, I crave their lack of understanding when my team lose.

"*Here's Rooney... it may not be 0-0, he's got Giggs to his left... and it's Rooney's shot! Beaten out by... and... offside flag is up.*"

My old Kingston Polytechnic housemate, Katharine, is famed for her unique perspective on football, which results from a total disinterest in it, and is best illustrated by her reaction to the announcement that, following a televised FA Cup tie between Norwich City and Liverpool in 1990 that finished 0-0, the game would be replayed the following Wednesday night, at which she commented that a replay would be pointless because the same two teams playing each other so soon would obviously result in another 0-0 draw. Now, the logic behind that statement might at first seem unfathomable, but if you care to meditate upon it further, which I have often, it begins to make some sense. Take away a basic understanding of the machinations of the game, leaving it stripped of all potential for randomness, then it might follow that 22 grown men kicking a ball around a field would perform like crudely programmed robots, with no potential to think for themselves or react to new instructions, and that a 0-0 draw would be repeated ad infinitum.

The 90 minutes are nearly up, the game is still goalless, and I would be quite happy for the match to finish 0-0, and for Katharine's law to come into full effect, with no prospect of a replay or a penalty shoot-out. Up to this point, the FA Cup Final has, to some, been dull and entirely unbefitting of such a historic occasion, but to me, the lack of any real action has made it far easier to bear. Because Vernon is here, I have been determined not to leave the room for prolonged periods and, although I've been to the bathroom several times, I've spent the majority of the match actually sitting down, watching the TV.

As it reaches full-time, still goalless, I become anxious, and increasingly so as extra-time looks destined not to yield any goals either. There is no way that I'm going to sit through penalties: I've been brave; I've proved that I can hold my nerve and watch a Chelsea game in a civilised manner, so surely I've earned the right to vacate the front room for the duration of the shoot-out lottery. I am petrified. Chelsea aren't good at penalties; they haven't won a shoot-out for nearly 10 years. With four minutes of extra-time still to play, I'm planning my exit. Then, as Drogba plays a little one-two with Lampard and lopes into the box, I jump to my feet. As he pokes the ball past the advancing Edwin van der Sar, before it has even reached the net, I'm charging through the dining room, kitchen-bound, and leaving a bemused Vernon in my wake. As the game ends, the players receive their medals and José Mourinho holds six fingers up to the Chelsea fans to indicate how many trophies he's now won for them. In the warm afterglow of victory, I feel that this has been the best of the lot. Although winning the FA Cup is enjoyable whoever it's against, it's all the sweeter when it's Manchester United, and although it was hardly the drubbing that had been meted out to them by the same club 13 years before, it feels as though the cycle is now complete. In three years, Chelsea have beaten United to the title, twice, knocked them out of a major cup competition for the first time ever, and now beaten them in an FA Cup Final at Wembley.

*

I make little mention of the previous day's game to Kevin. He congratulates me, which is as much as I expect, and I want no more than that. Winning is enough and I feel it right to point out that it is a good thing that Chelsea and United have shared the three domestic trophies between them: at the end of the day, we are all winners. As a consolatory remark, it may seem disingenuous, and it may or may not be appreciated, but if I was in Kevin's place, it would have helped to remind me that United had won the League. But quietly, I am thinking that yes, revenge is ours; not only for United's re-claiming of the League title a few weeks earlier, but also for 1994 and for every year in between.

But The Bottle remains unopened.

Do You Know The Way To Keep José? — 2007/08

"Something's happened to Mourinho..."

It is with these words on the morning of Thursday 20th September 2007 that I learn the news that all hope of Chelsea winning the Champions League in 2008 has gone. It's one of those bleary, dizzying moments in which you're awoken from a deep and satisfying sleep by some awful news that you aren't quite sure whether is real or not. As Vanessa whispers that sentence, I am unable to spring forward violently as my brain feels I should, with a maniacal yelp, caught somewhere between a giggle and a scream – in a manner reminiscent of one of the demon-possessed girls in *The Evil Dead* – so I simply lie there, staring at the ceiling, feeling certain that some dreadful accident must have befallen José.

"What happened to him?" I croak.

"Don't know. They've been talking about him on the radio."

Joanne Good, the host of BBC London's breakfast show, has mentioned his name so yes, something has happened to him, and the wait for the news to find out exactly what his fate had been seems to last, if not an eternity, then long enough to forge a variety of bleary-eyed fantasy scenarios. The most ridiculous of these is that he's either bought Roman Abramovich out, or that he's been arrested and put in the cells for dog smuggling. For some reason, him actually leaving the

Club is the last thing on my mind. It just seems too obvious and insignificant an event to have prompted a mention on a show that usually shows no interest in sport at all.

But I discover that José Mourinho has indeed left the Club, two days after a 1-1 draw at home to Norwegian side, Rosenborg, in the first Champions League game of the season and, as I make my daily commute to the end of the garden, I have already shut my mind to all thoughts of football and prepared myself for a day without TalkSport or Five Live, safe in the knowledge that the one great thing about working from home is that, on black days such as these, nobody can take the mickey.

But I've neglected the fact that our friend, Portland Bill, a Nottingham Forest fan, is staying with us, and before long, he is knocking at the shed door and pointing to an advertisement in the paper for tickets to Arsenal vs Newcastle in the Carling Cup for only £10, suggesting that I should switch allegiance now that Mourinho has gone. I try not to rise to it.

Later, he returns, fired by rumours that José might be on his way to Tottenham Hotspur and further suggesting that I should support someone else because Mourinho *was* Chelsea. This time I rise to it, asking whether if the late, great Brian Clough came back to life *and* he was then given the job as manager of Notts County, would he support them instead of Forest? Bill replies no and walks away, his work here done. The goading continues, despite my being alone, as Danny Baker later quips, "Everyone will remember where they were when they heard that, all of a sudden, Chelsea were in the mire…" before going on to suggest that Chelsea "… will do a Leeds".

Throughout Mourinho's time at the Bridge, although I hoped otherwise, it has been obvious that he wouldn't stay longer than a few seasons. He was a young manager who obviously had ambitions in the game that extended beyond the confines of a club like Chelsea. Other clubs would be courting him; clubs with histories and traditions more illustrious than ours; clubs from cities like Madrid, Milan and Manchester, for example. My concerns weren't based on any concrete evidence; it just seemed obvious that he'd move on, sooner rather than later, and his own attitude had done much to strengthen this assumption. In interviews, he spoke in terms of his coaching team's success as opposed to the Club's. As an example, when commenting upon Chelsea's second Premier League win in 2006, as well as stating that he hadn't enjoyed winning it as much as the previous season, he made clear his pleasure that he and his team had won four League titles in succession; in other words, referring to the continued success of the coaching team that had previously won two Portuguese titles with Porto, in addition to those with Chelsea, as opposed to the club he was currently working for. That one comment may have been innocuous enough, and he was clearly only stating facts, but to me, it spoke volumes. Fans want to hear the manager speak in terms of being one of them; that they are themselves a part of a greater whole; that theirs is the only team that matters, the only team in the manager's thoughts. In the immediate aftermath of the Premier League win in 2006, as the players and staff were presented with their winners' medals and the celebrations at Stamford Bridge began, José threw his own medal into the crowd. A nice gesture perhaps, but I immediately recalled the prompt removal of his winners' medal following Porto's Champions League win two years earlier, and took it as a sign that he was no longer happy at the Club and might soon be on his way.

The following season, there were rumours that at least one of the new signings – Shevchenko in particular – may not have been Mourinho's choice; leading to talk of an increasingly-strained relationship between himself and the Club. The professional relationship between the two had apparently come under further pressure upon the appointment by Abramovich of his friend, Avram Grant, as the Club's "Director of football" – a position that is becoming increasingly fashionable among football clubs. But beyond the boardroom, the Director of football appeared to exist as a patriarchal mentor to the manager, watching over him like a supervisor on the factory floor. How true this is in Chelsea's case is unclear, but it's easy to see how Mourinho might have felt undermined. I just wanted to see him happy, at one with himself and the Club that we all cared about, enjoying every victory the way he had when we'd beaten Barcelona at the Bridge in 2005, invading the pitch and celebrating like a fan. The English media will miss his grey overcoat, the glint in his eye, the cutting sound bites, and I will miss all of those and more.

Grant is quickly confirmed as manager and, within the blink of an eye, the most charismatic man in world football is replaced by someone I know nothing about, and this is particularly concerning because his first fixture in charge is to be an away game at Manchester United.

All thoughts immediately turn to anything other than football. Is it time to get the loft converted? Should I start taking my work seriously enough to deem it a career? Should we buy a shack in some remote and desolate corner of these islands and learn to live off the land just like Hugh Fearnley-Whittingstall? The answer to all these questions is yes, if it means that I can limit my exposure to Chelsea's certain demise significantly enough for it not to matter. But then again, the owner hasn't left, and the players haven't either, so maybe, just maybe it will all work out fine.

Chelsea's 2-0 defeat at Old Trafford on Sunday 23rd September 2007 confirms my worst fears: Chelsea are doomed, and Manchester United have overseen their downfall. That brief and glorious era of domestic domination had ended with the 1-0 victory over United in the FA Cup Final. Players who were driven to tears at José's departure would soon leave the Club, and Roman Abramovich would follow, ruing the day he let the Portuguese maestro go.

More bad news follows in December when it's announced that Christmas had come early for Queens Park Rangers with the arrival at the Club of Lakshmi Mittal, a multi-billionaire who has just bought a stake in the Club. The ensuing media excitement is alive with talk of QPR now being the wealthiest club in the world, and how the imminent arrival of players such as Luis Figo and Zinedine Zidane will see them immediately clinch promotion back to the Premier League and swipe Chelsea, their closest rivals, swiftly aside. Fanciful speculation perhaps, but it is enough to confirm to me that the party would now be moving away from Stamford Bridge. The opportunity for Rangers to put one over the Blues then comes much sooner than expected when they are drawn to play each other in the third round of the FA Cup.

*

On 5th January 2008, I visit the Bridge with QPR Chris and his two boys. We sit in the West Stand, close to the Shed End, in which the buoyant Rangers fans sit waving wads of cash in the air in mocking tribute to their newly-acquired wealth and position as the richest club on the planet, and not even a dull 1-0 victory for Chelsea can shut them up.

Amidst all the upheaval, Grant has actually managed to steer the team to a run of good form. Since the defeat at

United, Chelsea have only lost once in the League – away at Arsenal. They are winning the games against mid-table teams that they might have drawn with in the previous season, and by April, they are neck and neck with United. Better still, they've managed to put the disappointment of the draw at home to Rosenborg behind them to embark upon an impressive run in the Champions League that saw them go on to win their group, then beat Olympiakos and Fenerbahce in the knockout stages to earn themselves yet another appearance in the semi-final; their fourth in five seasons. But that is where their luck appears to have run out. To have faced Liverpool in two semi-finals had seemed coincidental, but now, by some twisted manipulation of fate, they are drawn to play each other again. Liverpool is a team that knows how to beat Chelsea better than any and, more significantly, are a team in red, so I fear the worst. And yet there is still the faintest glimmer of hope, offered by the fact that, this time around, the second leg is to be played at Stamford Bridge, so avoiding the horrors that a hostile Anfield would provide for the decisive final game of the tie.

What concerns me as much as anything is that perhaps, when it comes to the big games – the title deciders, semi-finals and finals – Grant might just be too nice. In interviews, he comes across as an affable chap, more a kindly uncle in character than an authoritarian leader of highly-paid footballers, and as such is more Claudio Ranieri than José Mourinho. He led the team to another League Cup Final, having beaten Everton in a tough semi, but prior to the Final itself, the press had made much of the fact that his success rate in Cup Finals wasn't good, and the subsequent 2-1 defeat to Spurs at Wembley confirms as much. The loss is the first time Chelsea have failed to win a Cup Final in the Abramovich era, but by the time of the Champions League semi-final first leg at the end of April, I am hopeful that Avram's luck might change. Dutifully, I watch the first half develop, and as Chelsea avoid conceding an early goal and slowly find their feet, I recline slightly. Anfield now seems a less intimidating place, until, in the 43rd minute, the cellists awake, the Blues defence stutters, Mascherano hooks the ball forward, and Dirk Kuyt pounces to put Liverpool ahead. There will be no third time lucky – the Reds are about to dump Chelsea out of the competition they are so desperate to win yet again. The sense of déjà vu has become so strong that I'd almost forgotten that there was still the second leg at Stamford Bridge to come. I give up on watching the game the moment Kuyt scores, but switch to *Sky Sports News*, just in case there might be some positive news from Anfield – namely that Liverpool haven't managed to extend their lead. But, when it comes, the news is far more positive than I could have hoped. John Arne Riise has headed the ball into his own net in the fourth minute of injury time to equalise for Chelsea and, more importantly, given them a precious away goal, so handing them the best imaginable chance of reaching the Final.

I spend the first hour of the second leg hovering in the doorway to the front room, from where I see Didier Drogba fire Chelsea ahead in the first half, and from where I disappear following Fernando Torres' 64th minute equaliser, only to return as extra-time looms. When Frank Lampard, in his first game back since his mother's death earlier in the month, has the courage and composure to take a penalty kick in extra-time and score, it proves to be the single most poignant moment of the season. He celebrates by pointing to the sky and kissing a black armband worn in his mother's memory, which serves as a sobering reminder that of all the football-related news surrounding Chelsea Football Club this season, in comparison, none of it really matters. All the hyperbole that football, or any sport, encourages is exposed for its puerility at such times. A defeat isn't "tragic", an own goal isn't a "calamity", and a poor refereeing decision might not be the "travesty" it briefly appears to be. In the back of our minds. we football supporters realise this, but it stays rooted deep within our subconscious. In light of this sobering reality check, I remain in my seat and watch the rest of the game virtually unmoved as Chelsea grind out a 3-2 victory on the night, and I applaud Avram Grant as, at the final whistle, he sinks to his knees and reaches for the sky, perhaps in prayer, but undoubtedly in celebration. He has managed something that José couldn't: he's defeated Liverpool in a Champions League semi-final and, in doing so, the Club are in the Final of Europe's premier competition for the first time ever.

Part Five

The Impossible
Dream

The Wrong Ending, Part 2: The Final Cut — 21st May 2008

"You've got no history."

This song echoed around Stamford Bridge on the night of Wednesday, November 8th 2006 as Aston Villa fans proudly mocked their hosts for, above all, never having won the European Cup. As some of them waved their inflatable European Cups in our direction, Portland Bill muttered, "But we have, we've won it twice." He was right. Nottingham Forest had indeed won the European Cup twice before, and Villa once, Liverpool five times, and Manchester United twice. Chelsea's quest to join that exclusive club had become an obsession, of which they would hopefully soon be cured.

*

21st May 2008. This is it. This will be my chance to experience just how it feels to see the captain of my team lift that enormous cup with the oversized handles – the "trophy with the big ears" – having won a game on foreign soil against one of the best teams in Europe. The Final is to be played in Moscow, so the soil is indeed foreign, but I just wish it wasn't Manchester United that we have to play. For one thing, they are an English club who we are more than used to playing against, which makes the Final seem less glamorous. In addition, they've just beaten Chelsea to the Premier League title for the second year in succession, and Alex Ferguson has the experience of these occasions, whereas Avram Grant and many of his players don't. The temporary epiphany that I experienced during the semi-final win over Liverpool has, in the three weeks since, predictably given way to anxiety and the returning belief that football is all that really matters.

Having arranged to watch the game at Mel and Dave's, Vanessa and I walk there; me with The Bottle in hand and the peculiar certainty that in three-and-a-half hours' time, I will either be feeling ecstatic or despondent, and she with a carefree nonchalance that I can only dream of. I'm taking The Bottle – more in hope than expectation – and the possibility that, by remaining unopened for at least another year, the wine might therefore become corked is, quite frankly, not at the top of my list of concerns. What has immediately risen to the top of that list is the fact that, upon our arrival, I discover that Dave's friend, Steve, is also here, and I know that he doesn't like Chelsea. Having assured myself that watching the game with my friends will be a good thing to do – on the dual basis that they don't like Manchester United and that their presence will force me to sit through the majority of the game – I am now quite ready to turn around and go back home. But I am reassured to hear that Steve, a Prestonian, dislikes United even more than Chelsea, so I duly take my place on the sofa and brace myself.

I'm quietly confident that we might actually win: I've thought about all the signs and indicators and have concluded that, what with having just lost out in the League to United and having come so close, and having never before reached the Final, Chelsea will want it more than United and will seize their chance. For one thing, I am sat in the Lucky Lounge, but I feel that we have the stronger team anyway. We beat United just a month ago, and the Blues' starting line-up is the strongest possible, albeit with Michael Essien playing in an unfamiliar right back position. Perhaps history might have a say too; in 1955, when the competition first started, Chelsea had qualified as England's sole representatives, having won the League championship that year, so becoming the first English club ever to qualify to play in the European Cup. They were subsequently advised by England's own Football Association not to enter, so dutifully relinquished their place. The following season, Manchester United qualified, received similar advice, but chose to ignore it. Maybe it would be Chelsea's destiny to re-right that wrong. And then, of course, there is the added poetry that the Final being played in Russia, Abramovich's homeland, lends to the story. But above all, I feel that, with all the ups, downs and drama that Chelsea have experienced during the season, the only conclusion that could provide the romance befitting such a prestigious and upstanding competition will be for Chelsea to end an arduous year by crossing the finishing line - in slow motion, and to the strains of Vangelis - as winners.

All such optimistic thoughts are cast aside in a first half in which United batter Chelsea, who are lucky to have conceded just the one goal - a header scored by Cristiano Ronaldo. But when, at the end of the half, Essien tries his luck and the ball breaks free to Lampard, who lifts it over Edwin van der Sar for the equaliser, that romantic ending is once again possible. Chelsea are a different team in the second period and look the more likely to win, particularly when Drogba hits the post with a tremendous effort from outside the box. This game can surely only go one way now. Full-time is drawing nearer but Chelsea seems to be getting stronger. Just as it was in the FA Cup Final last year, a goal in extra-time will win it for the Blues. We're into the extra half-hour but, as Lampard's shot hits the bar, the game now seems destined to end in a penalty shoot-out. I'm experiencing a new form of anxiety. As both sides look to win the game in the final minutes, tensions reach boiling point, and Drogba is sent off for slapping Nemanja Vidić across the cheek. I choose the moment to leave the room and find a safer seat elsewhere in which to assume the crash position. When I reach the dining room, Mel is already sitting there, and through either sympathy or osmosis, she is as anxious as I am. And we talk about the weather, or music, or anything but football in a futile attempt to take our minds off the game.

The rain in Moscow has been unrelenting; conditions that, in a shoot-out, are sure to favour the goalkeepers. As it proceeds, I pop my head through the doorway intermittently and can see that Chelsea are doing okay: Michael Ballack and Juiliano Belletti have both scored and the shoot-out stands at 2-2. When Ronaldo steps up to take his kick, his body shape looks all wrong; he begins his run-up, then he hesitates in an attempt to wrong-foot Petr Čech, but the Chelsea keeper stands firm, wrong-footing Ronaldo, whose weak kick is saved.

I leave the room again, far too nervous to sit through the remaining penalties, but still able to hear what is going on. Lampard scores, then Hargreaves, then Ashley Cole, and then Nani. The score is 4-4 after nine penalties, meaning that should John Terry, the captain, score with the very next kick, Chelsea would be the new European champions. What happens next is that Alex Ferguson disappears into a quiet corner of the dugout and says a short prayer and does a little dance; the rain subsequently begins to fall twice as heavily as before – mainly concentrating itself on the area around the penalty spot – but nobody has noticed. As John Terry slips in the process of trying to make history, I can only hear the roars from the TV, accompanied by groans from the front room.

"No, he's missed it!"

But it's okay, because we're still in it. Terry's miss doesn't have to prove that costly, but by the time Nicolas Anelka's attempt is saved by van der Sar, it has long been obvious who would win.

It's "tragic", a "calamity", and the result is a "travesty". I don't really know what to do. Normally, I would've wanted to go home the moment Anelka had missed, but the preceding events have introduced me to a new level of despondency and I need the support of friends. A few text messages of condolence follow, along with a genuinely helpful recorded message from Kevin who, masking his obvious and understandable delight, offers the line that a penalty shoot-out is no way to win a Champions League Final and that he hopes we can still have a beer sometime. In contrast to this, a friend of ours, who also supports Chelsea and has watched the game with us, asks me why I'm taking it so badly. This isn't helping me in the slightest, but she repeats the question, going on to proclaim that it was enough that Chelsea had made it to the Final and that I should be happy they did so. But I'm hardly in the mood to concede that she might have a point, and as I grow increasingly frustrated with this line of thinking, and having become tired of saying that she doesn't understand, this isn't 1994 anymore, and that only winning is enough these days, I ask Vanessa if she'd mind if we left.

When I wake up the following day, my first thoughts are for John Terry. I can't grasp the enormity of what happened and I am simply struck by that feeling you get when you shake away sleep and slowly come to the realisation that something terrible and irreversible happened yesterday and that all you want to do now is go back to sleep, to return to a state of blissful ignorance. It's hard to understand how the game had ended that way. To be within the width of a post from seeing Terry take his place alongside Hughes, Bowyer and Mortimer by lifting the world's most prestigious trophy for it then to be taken away and handed to Chelsea's, and my, greatest nemesis seems cruel in the extreme. It was an ending that made little sense. United had won it before so why give it to them again?

*

Alex Ferguson will soon allude to the fact that, as soon as he saw that it was raining in Moscow, he felt confident that his team would win. He will also point out that the day of United's previous Champions League Final victory in 1999 had fallen on the birthday of the late Sir Matt Busby, the Club's legendary former manager, and that perhaps he'd been looking down on United – both on that night and in Moscow – to influence the results. Maybe that had been the case, and Ferguson's right in saying that fate plays a part in football. As such, United had a 12th man on both occasions, and both times Sir Alex had seen his side handed victory from the clutches of defeat. Whatever the case, Chelsea's victory over United in the FA Cup Final the previous year now seemed a trifling irrelevance and, in Moscow, on the biggest stage of all, Alex Ferguson and Manchester United had the final word.

Are We The Baddies?
— 2008/09

"Hans, I've just noticed something. Have you looked at our caps recently? The badges on our caps. Have you looked at them? They've got skulls on them. Have you noticed that our caps have actually got little pictures of skulls on them? Hans, are we the baddies?" – from *That Mitchell and Webb Look*, 2006

The first purchase of the 2008/09 season was a revolving door to be installed in the manager's office. Avram Grant was sacked in the aftermath of the Moscow Final. It seemed a harsh step to take for a man who had come so desperately close to winning the Club the one trophy they coveted, and with a tad more luck, he could have won them a treble. Yet it wasn't a surprise. Although I had my reservations about him when he was first appointed, he seemed like a nice man and I'd grown to like him, just as I had Claudio Ranieri. But, as had been the case with Ranieri in 2003/04, it had appeared obvious that Grant would be replaced at the end of the season, and no amount of success would ensure that he would keep the manager's job. When it came to finding a longer-term replacement for José Mourinho, the owner, and the fans, would want a big name, a "marquee signing", someone with a global reputation who had tasted success at the highest level; and the level doesn't come much higher than the World Cup. Luiz Felipe Scolari, a World Cup-winning manager with Brazil in 2002, was named as the new Chelsea boss on 11th June 2008.

By February 2009, he too had left the Club. Scolari's dismissal resulted from a sequence of poor results that included defeats at Manchester United and Liverpool, with the manager's fate finally sealed by a goalless draw at home to Hull City. It appeared that Scolari, who had been in charge of the Portuguese national team prior to his arrival at Stamford Bridge, hadn't got to grips with either the rigours of club football – and in particular, the rigours of the Premier League – or the English language, and, in particular, the correct pronunciation of the word Chelsea, which from his lips became "*Chel-see-aah*" in the style of The Fall's Mark E. Smith.

With the Blues lying fourth in the Premier League, and having been knocked out of the League Cup by Burnley after another penalty shoot-out, Guus Hiddink, the vastly experienced Dutchman, was appointed interim manager until the end of the season, whilst still remaining in his full-time job as manager of the Russian national team. He was tasked with ensuring that the Club finished high enough in the Premier League to secure Champions League football the following season, and to try to win one of the two trophies that were still realistically obtainable. Ray Wilkins had, earlier in the season, replaced Steve Clarke as assistant manager; a fine appointment that further strengthened the link with the Club's past, and it was he who, prior to the arrival of Hiddink, took charge for a 3-1 victory at Watford that booked the Club a place in the FA Cup quarter-final. Hiddink then oversaw wins against Coventry City and Arsenal to reach the Final, which was set to be played later in the season than usual, on May 30th.

But Hiddink had also arrived in time to mastermind another impressive run in the Champions League, although his job was possibly made easier by the tide of determination triggered by the Moscow nightmare. It's easy to imagine the desperation the Chelsea players must have felt to win the competition after that defeat – it has borne an obsession in myself that is already becoming a burden. There was a time when merely qualifying for the Champions League group stages was satisfying enough, but one quarter-final, one Final and three semi-final defeats later and those innocent times are consigned to a past that I can no longer connect with. This year's run included a quarter-final fixture with Liverpool, which was the fifth time the teams had been drawn against each other in as many seasons. The first leg was again to be played at Anfield, as it was the previous season, and it turned out to be a glorious night for Chelsea, who survived the customary early Liverpool goal to win 3-1 on the night, so virtually guaranteeing their passage to the semi-final. Or so we thought. Most people wouldn't have given Liverpool a hope of overcoming the deficit in the return leg at Stamford Bridge, and even one as pessimistic as I couldn't have foretold the ludicrous drama that was about to unfold.

If ever a film director needs guidance on how not to structure a plot, they only need to watch the full 90 minutes of Chelsea versus Liverpool, 14th April 2009 version, and he or she will instantly learn that sometimes, one well-executed twist in a story is enough. Also, contrary to prior perceived wisdom, anyone watching the game on the night will have learned that a hatful of goals does not necessarily make for a good game.

It started as a simple survival tale: could Liverpool somehow find a way out of this mess? As the game kicked off, it then switched genres and became a slasher movie as Liverpool scored twice in the first half an hour and Chelsea ran for their lives as the Red hordes threatened to wipe them out. It then took on the tone of a melodrama as these characters whom we'd come to know so well squabbled and bickered in the face of extreme external pressures, before it settled on a classic good versus evil action spectacular that saw Chelsea battle their way back into the game by scoring three goals of their own to restore order and see them into the semi-final for the logical sequel that would follow. And there it should have ended, but instead, we were subjected to a Keystone Cops-style farce as Liverpool scored two late goals that had everyone hastily attempting to work out exactly how many more goals they needed to win the tie on aggregate. A last-minute goal from Frank Lampard eased the nerves, made it 4-4 on the night and 7-5 to Chelsea on aggregate, and bought the curtain down on one of the most ridiculous games of football ever to be played at the top level.

In the pre-Abramovich era, a local derby for Chelsea could either mean a trip to Queens Park Rangers or a meeting with Fulham at the Bridge. With Champions League football now such a regular part of the season, a game against Liverpool is so commonplace it has itself taken on the feel of a derby, redefining the word "local" to cover the whole of the country. Having played each other six times between 2005 and 2008 – in addition to the Champions League quarter-final meeting in 2000 – a meeting with Barcelona is now more common than with Chelsea's more traditional rivals, QPR. Of those Champions League ties, honours are more or less even, but with Barcelona having won the competition in 2006, I was hopeful that, prior to the first leg of the semi-final in Barcelona on 28th April, the fates, in whatever form they might take, would check the record books thoroughly enough to deduce that, this time around, Chelsea should emerge victorious.

*

All is going to plan, with Chelsea defending heroically to draw the first leg 0-0. Barcelona are by now gaining a reputation as the greatest footballing side in the world, playing in a style that many find to be wholly entertaining and that is, at times, mesmerising. Players such as Andrés Iniesta and Xavier "Xavi" Hernández can torment teams with their passing and movement and, in the Argentine boy-wizard, Lionel Messi, the Spanish side can boast of having the world's best player on their side. The purists love them, and I'm sure I would too, had they not so frequently represented such a barrier to my team's aspirations. Last night, Manchester United secured their place in the Champions League Final with an impressive 3-1 win at Arsenal, winning the tie 4-1 on aggregate. The scene is now set for Chelsea to overcome Barcelona tonight, May 6th 2009, and make it to the Final themselves, where they will exact the most perfect revenge over their Manchester foes. I've made mental notes over the years about how these things pan out, and have noticed that a balancing of fortunes usually occurs, or in other words what goes around does indeed tend to then come back around. United had recovered from FA Cup Final defeat in 1976 to win it a year later. Chelsea had also bounced back from defeat in the same competition in 1994 to win it three years on. Bayern Munich's last gasp defeat to United in the 1999 Champions League Final only made them stronger, and they returned two years later to lift the trophy. Although that is the only example I can think of in the Champions League, I cling to it because it gives me hope – I have conveniently ignored the fact that when Bayern won in 2001, they beat Valencia in the Final; a team who had also lost in the Final the previous season and have never been back since. I also remember the biblical paraphrase that, if you keep knocking, the door will be opened, and Chelsea have knocked at the door of the Champions League trophy cabinet so often that their knuckles are raw. This year, it will surely happen: we are the good guys, the nearly men whose time has come.

I am hopeful enough of a victory to revisit the crime scene of the previous year, so I've made my way around to Mel and Dave's to watch the game. Knowing that I'm not exactly cheerful or engaging company when I'm watching Chelsea, it was nice of them to have asked me, but they understand because Mel finds it as hard to watch Arsenal as I do Chelsea. The Lucky Lounge isn't quite so lucky anymore, but it's yet to prove unlucky enough for me to refuse their kind invitation. It couldn't really have started any better, as Michael Essien's stunning left foot volley in the ninth minute looks as though it might have set Chelsea on the way to a convincing victory. More chances follow but aren't converted, but the Blues don't appear to be under too much pressure. In fact, they seem to have everything under control, and the threat of Lionel Messi is being well-contained. But the signs begin to take an alarming form. Referee, Tom Henning Øvrebø, turns down three clear penalty claims for the Blues, and it's hard to see why he's not awarded at least one of them. But when Barcelona defender, Éric Abidal, is sent off in the 66th minute, it feels as though Chelsea will cruise through the rest of the game regardless, still 1-0 up, and without having to dwell too much on the missed chances and bizarre decisions. And cruise they do.

We're into the third minute of stoppage time and it all looks comfortable for them. Only a couple of minutes left now and we're in another Final. The ball is lumped into the Chelsea penalty area as a last throw of the dice by the Catalans – no danger. It's miss-controlled by a Barcelona player – still no danger. An opportunity to clear the ball isn't taken by a Chelsea player – a bit of danger. The ball falls to

Messi – lots of danger. He lays it off to Iniesta on the edge of the box, and I perform an odd telepathic ritual that I've become used to using at times of extreme pressure that basically involves me willing a force field into existence to envelope the six-yard box and repel the ball, just in case a Chelsea defender can't get there to clear the danger first. It seems to have worked in the past, but this time, Iniesta finds a hole in it and the ball flies past a despairing Petr Čech and into the top corner. Even as the Barcelona players and staff go wild in celebration, I'm still not sure whether or not there will be extra-time. Do away goals count? Amid all the shock and confusion, I've forgotten the rules, but when I see the dejection on the Chelsea players' faces, I know that we are out. There's still time for another clear penalty claim – for an obvious handball from a Michael Ballack shot – but the referee once again ignores it. This time it matters and I am incensed. To rub salt in the wound, former Chelsea favourite, Eiður Guðjohnsen, is brought on for Barcelona with seconds remaining, and someone in the room quips that he will probably score now too.

*

Soon after the game had ended I left, not wanting to hang around for the post-match comments because there never seemed to be any point in doing so, and, as usual, nobody tried to stop me; either because they knew that there was no point in doing so, or because they were relieved not to have me moping around the flat. No matter how many people agreed that Chelsea had been robbed of their place in the Final as the result of inexplicable refereeing decisions, it wouldn't change anything. Once again, the script was poor, unrealistic, and cheating the punter of the ending they required. In the first *Rocky*, the hero, like Chelsea in 2008, finished as the unlucky loser, having taken the current heavyweight champion, Apollo Creed – the bad guy – the full 15 rounds. In *Rocky 2*, however, Rocky Balboa – the good guy – won the rematch. But at Stamford Bridge, the good guys had lost. We were the good guys, weren't we? To the majority of football fans, we were probably nothing of the sort, especially when pitted against the skill and tradition of Barcelona. In so many ways, they are the ideal club; owned and controlled by the fans, and refusing shirt sponsorship in favour of wearing the name of Unicef on their shirts, in return for which, the Club pay the charity a sizeable donation. They have a gigantic and iconic amphitheatre of a stadium – Camp Nou – and, with the classic blue and red-striped shirts, they have one of the best strips. They play attractive football, have the world's best footballer, and half the soon-to-be World Cup-winning Spanish national side in their ranks, and in Pep Guardiola, they also have a young and, some say, attractive manager, which, in Hollywood terms, is a must. Chelsea, on the other hand, are owned and controlled by one man, aren't currently known for playing attractive football, and have a handful of players who opposing fans love to hate. In effect, they are the team with the skulls on their caps.

Thanks to a myopic view of the club I support, I've always assumed that, on the whole, people quite liked Chelsea. In 1994, I wasn't aware of anyone who wasn't a fan of Manchester United that didn't want Chelsea to beat them in the FA Cup Final. They were the underdogs, for one thing, but I also suspect that fans of most clubs considered them to be mostly harmless. Occasionally, we'd beat the big teams, but we were never likely to threaten them on a long-term basis. The Blues could also boast a playing squad that was predominately British – 26 out of the 35 – which, over the coming years, was to become increasingly crucial in garnering the support of the wider public. A friend once told me that he hated Chelsea, and when I asked him why he felt that strongly, he said that it was because they'd been the first club to field a starting 11 that consisted entirely of non-British players. Indeed, they had been, at Southampton on Boxing Day, 1999, and it's true to say that, in the mid-1990s, Chelsea had been one of the first clubs to start signing foreign players en masse. I've defended the policy many, many times over the years, and the one counter-argument I've frequently used is to say that British players of the top standard commanded a premium and were therefore too expensive. As an example, in 1998, Sol Campbell, a young English centre back of some promise, would reputedly have cost a club upwards of £10 million to buy from Tottenham Hotspur, whereas Marcel Desailly, an older, but far more experienced centre back, who had just won the World Cup with France, cost Chelsea around £5 million. If a club wants success, they have to improve their squad, and to improve a squad costs money, and if money is short then they will be forced to look overseas.

But thanks to Manchester United, this argument frequently fails to make an impression. Throughout the 1990s, United had consistently proved that it was possible to bring British players through the youth system to become regulars in the first team, whilst still achieving success. Most notably, Paul Scholes, Ryan Giggs, Nicky Butt, Gary and Phil Neville and David Beckham, now known as the "Class of '92", who were all a part of the team that won the FA Youth Cup in 1992 and were integral to the senior side's successes that followed, not least as part of the treble winning team of 1998/99, and in the meantime, they had all become full internationals. I was envious of this, of course, because, although Chelsea had good young players of their own, they were rarely given a chance in the senior squad. Ian Pearce and Muzzy Izzet were possibly the best examples: Pearce made a handful of appearances for the first team before being sold to Blackburn Rovers in 1993, where he helped them win the Premier League, and Izzet, for whom great things were expected, never played in the first team and moved to Leicester City in 1996, where he was instrumental in helping them cement their place in the Premier League and win the League Cup on two occasions. Other players from the youth system had become regulars but were then sold to Premier League rivals, namely Graham Stuart, Graeme Le Saux and Jason Cundy. There were a few who made it into the first team to play regularly throughout the 90s, such as Frank Sinclair, Eddie Newton, Andy Myers and Jody Morris, but by the turn of the decade, most of them had gone. The only way that I could think to explain the success of United's youth system was to say that, clearly, they were the equivalent of that one Little League team in every district that cherry-picks the best players from their competitors; either by luring them with promises of a bar of chocolate and a can of pop after every game, or by charming the parents. So, even before 2003 and the Abramovich takeover, any good reputation that Chelsea might once have had was slowly being eroded. Ironically, from 2003 onwards, the Club could afford to buy young British players, and at one point, could boast of having six players in the England team. But by then, they were the wealthiest Club in the land, and to most football fans, that was an even greater crime.

*

I watched the 2009 Champions League Final, hoping that Barcelona would beat Manchester United. It was the first time that I'd actively supported a non-English team playing an English one in a European Final. I'd sided with the purists, recognising that Barcelona were a truly great club and one whose universal admiration was wholly justified – they were the good guys. It was a peculiar view, given that the Catalans had dealt Chelsea such a cruel blow three weeks earlier, but since the final of 2008, my grudge against United had grown to such a size that I'd gone way beyond feeling bitter and twisted. I applauded the Barcelona players as they collected their winners' medals, overjoyed that Manchester United, the champions of England, but to my mind still the bad guys, had been toppled.

*

Three days later, Vanessa and I are in Bexhill, visiting our parents, and I am alone at my Mum's house – because she is out, and presumably, Vernon, Vanessa's dad, has decided that watching the game with me again might be too much like hard work – to see Chelsea line up against Everton at Wembley and attempt to win the FA Cup for the second time in three seasons. A frantic start sees Everton passing the ball around comfortably, Chelsea looking uneasy under the early pressure and the ball falling to Louis Saha after 25 seconds. As the Everton striker volleys past Petr Čech to score the fastest goal in FA Cup Final history and steal Roberto Di Matteo's record, there are two stabs from a brass section, a silhouette of James Bond, a single gunshot, and the outline of a dancing lady. Within a minute, I'm lying on a spare bed – the same bed upon which I'd taken refuge in 1983 – wondering how on earth Chelsea are going to overcome this latest predicament and put a stop to Everton's evil plan, whilst simultaneously hoping that I might fall asleep for the next hour-and-a-half and miss the whole thing. Being alone in the house, I could have got away with it, but I quickly come to my senses and decide that I should do the honourable thing and support my team by watching the rest of the game from the comfort of the sofa. Fortunately, the fact that Chelsea are wearing yellow (and that I'd so ungraciously celebrated United's Champions League defeat) doesn't affect the team's performance after all, and goals from Drogba and Lampard win me my first piece of silverware for two years.

The Green, Green Grass of Home — 2009/10

"...but it's Messi... IT'S INIESTA! ... And the Chelsea fans cover their eyes in horror! Two minutes from time and it's heartbreak at Stamford Bridge. Iniesta rattles one in and suddenly, in the minute-and-a-half that remains, Chelsea find themselves needing a goal." – Rob Hawthorne, Stamford Bridge, 6th May 2009

What this? No, this is nothing. We're just good friends, that's all. It's an escape. I had to get away – it's been stressful y'know?

It's like a scene from a strange but colourful dream. It's the end of April 2010. I'm in a place that is familiar and yet unfamiliar all at once. It's red versus blue. I'm watching my team, in red, winning a game that they have to win at all costs, and then a gang of superheroes invade the pitch. But this isn't a dream, it's real and it's one of many highlights from an odd but memorable season.

*

It may not be a significant date to most people, but for my old non-League companion, Barry, the 10th day of May 2008 signalled the end of a 24-year habit. That was the period of time that had elapsed since he'd last missed a Crystal Palace home game. The reason he was missing their game that day was that he was one of 27,000 part-owners of Ebbsfleet United Football Club, and they were playing Torquay United in the FA Trophy Final, which Ebbsfleet went on to win 1-0. As we watched live footage of Crystal Palace's Championship play-off semi-final first leg fixture against Bristol City on a small screen within the bowels of Wembley Stadium, he announced that he felt funny, as you would, had you just broken the habit of what for some prisoners is a lifetime. During those two-and-a-half decades, he'd missed important family occasions, and fallen out with relatives as a result, but he had always found his way to Selhurst Park, even for friendlies.

There have been others whom I've similarly admired for the level of commitment that they've shown their teams over the years. I know a Brighton fan who was once selected to present the Fans' Player of the Year award to the winning player prior to a Brighton & Hove Albion home game, having earned the right to do so by attending every first team match that season, home and away. I have a friend who has been a season ticket holder at Bayern Munich for many years and rarely misses a game, despite being English and living in Surrey; and I know a fan of Aldershot Town FC who supported Aldershot FC from a young age and continued to make the 170-mile trip from Hastings to see Aldershot play when the Club was forced out of the Football League and re-emerged at the foot of the Isthmian, and still does so.

I missed going to the football. Being able to watch games on TV is great, and necessary when watching Chelsea for the presence of an easy escape route, but I missed actually visiting a football ground on a regular basis to see a team that I cared about, but not quite enough for it to ruin my weekend if they lost. It would be nice to be able to show a level of physical commitment that could equal even a fraction of that shown by people I know. I was missing live football for social reasons too. As is the way with football (and is partly the point of it), people don't all support the same team. Among friends who live locally, there are supporters of Tottenham Hotspur, Arsenal, Preston North End, Manchester United, Crystal Palace, Raith Rovers, Bayern Munich, Liverpool, Woking and Norwich City. At one time or another, I've been to see most of those teams play, purely because I like watching football, whoever is playing, and because, unless it's Chelsea, I find it more enjoyable to watch a game with someone else. Kevin and I were never likely to go to see a match together, which was a shame, particularly given our similar attitudes toward the game. Though I'd tried to lure both him and his son Charlie to a Chelsea match once, in the hope that they might succumb to the magic of Stamford Bridge and turn their backs on Man United, it had been a pointless exercise. We both felt trapped by the need for our teams to constantly win games; a pressure that, with Man United having always had that expectation, Kevin was more used to than I. We'd discussed our reasons for supporting our teams on several occasions and had usually concluded that it didn't really matter whether or not you were born in the same half of the country as your club, or rarely paid to go and see them; if their results had the potential to either upset you or make you feel like a child on Christmas morning then your emotional attachment meant that you were entitled to call yourself a fan. We'd also agreed that everyone should support their local team, whether to the exclusion of their existing team of choice or not, and any rule that said otherwise should be adapted to make allowances. More importantly, I needed something to take my mind off Chelsea.

*

One Saturday afternoon, toward the end of August 2009, I found myself at a loose end so I decided to go and watch our local team, Carshalton Athletic. I'd been to see them play a few times before and always looked out for their results, which had encouraged larger match reports than usual the previous season, and they'd even been mentioned on national radio, having reached the play-off final that would have seen them promoted to the Conference South, the second tier of non-League football. Unfortunately, they'd lost that game to Staines Town after extra-time in agonising circumstances, having missed a penalty with only four minutes of normal time remaining. But, although they clearly had a good side, I wasn't expecting the quality of football to be quite as good as it was. The passing was fluid, the ball control was admirable, and the defending was solid. From my days as a rookie Traveller, I knew that the standard at Ryman League Premier Division level was good, but I hadn't expected Carshalton to be playing in such an attractive style – although when I'd last seen them play, they wore white shorts and socks, whereas now they were entirely in red, which obviously helped. Poor old Ashford Town struggled to cope for long periods and, on occasion, it was tempting to think that it was a little like watching Barcelona. I'd always liked the ground – compact but with a vast, covered swathe of concrete terracing along one side of the pitch, and a decent club bar – but now there was the added bonus of a tea bar that claimed to be selling the best burgers at any football ground in the country. I was hooked.

We then went on holiday for three weeks and, when I got back, having told friends how enjoyable the experience was and how good the team were in an attempt to convince them that we should all start going, Stuart came with me to see Carshalton entertain Dartford and they were rotten. The team had changed completely. It transpired that the manager had left two weeks earlier and some of the players had followed. From being top of the League when I'd last seen them, they'd now plummeted to mid-table, and it was easy to see how. The game ended in a 4-0 defeat, but surprisingly, Stuart had enjoyed it enough to want to go again. Despite the dip in quality of the home side's play, it was still a proper football experience that harked back to the days when, at any ground in the country, you could stand whilst watching the game and enjoy a drink at half-time. They even had a glossy, full-colour, professionally-printed programme – that was professional enough to call itself a match day magazine – that had all the features of a Premier League programme; the player profiles, the stats pages, reserve team results, the words from the manager. The only thing it lacked was that feature in which a grinning fan is pictured in a remote and exotic part of the world, wearing a replica team shirt, which was a shame because the image of a middle-aged man standing in the ruins of Machu Picchu sporting a Carshalton Athletic shirt with the words "Walkers, The Builders' Merchants" emblazoned on it would've worked wonders as an artistic statement.

There was much to like about the team too. There was a star striker – Richard Jolly; a gutsy, attacking midfielder – Barry Stevens; a captain and defender who led by example – David Ray; a tricky winger – Rashid Kamara; and, in Nick Hamann, a gifted goalkeeper who had just signed from Hamburg SV of the German Bundesliga, having spent time in the youth team at Chelsea. These were players who ably filled the boots of Drogba, Lampard, Terry, Cole and Čech in my affections on a Saturday afternoon or Tuesday evening. So, for £15 per game, you got to see a team you could believe in and who had a fierce local rivalry (with Sutton United), a small but passionate crowd who sang their hearts out, win or lose, a "match day magazine", a coffee, a large KitKat, *and* an award-winning burger.

Within weeks, I was going regularly, with a revolving cast of friends, for midweek games in particular, for which the skill of players of the calibre of Jolly and Kamara were further enhanced by the glare of the floodlights. Surprisingly, given the delights that were on offer, the average attendance was such that you could wind your way through the gaping holes on the terrace and take your time to pick a spot from where to watch the game, and the most die-hard fans would swap ends at half-time so that they could give their team their fullest support by deafening the opposing goalkeeper for the full 90 minutes.

A character known as Fred, whose legend was well-known, would often be seen to walk among the crowd during the game, conducting a head count, and when he'd finished, would announce to whoever was standing closest what his own unofficial attendance figure was, and with mixed results.

During one match, Bill took a call from his son, who was on a visit to Barcelona and had rung to excitedly report that he was at Camp Nou, among a crowd of 80,000, to which his dad replied, less excitedly, that he was at Colston Avenue, among a crowd of 150. And at an evening match at home to Badshot Lea in the Surrey Senior Cup in December, there had been a crowd of just 81, and I was rather proud of the fact that I was the one.

∗

At the turn of the year, rather than being in the thick of a battle for promotion, The Robins were facing four months embroiled in a relegation dogfight, whereas, back in the glamorous world of the Premier League, the garden was rosy and, at Christmas, Chelsea were top of the League. I've often looked to other teams' results as some form of compensation for a Chelsea defeat, and over the years, the list of these compensatory teams has been shaped by places I've visited or have some form of connection with, and has included Oxford United, Wimbledon, Vancouver Whitecaps, Kingstonian, Brighton & Hove Albion, Helsingborgs, Hastings Town, Haugesund, and Haverfordwest County. However, as much as I enjoy seeing that Haverfordwest have beaten Afan Lido, there is no chance that it could ever compensate for a defeat for Chelsea at West Bromwich Albion on the same day. But for the 2009/10 season, Carshalton Athletic and Chelsea are often effective foils for each other. As Chelsea were heading for a 2-1 defeat at Aston Villa, Carshalton were hitting five past Aveley. While Carshalton toiled at home to Tonbridge Angels, courtesy of the *Sky Sports News* app, I could take heart in the fact that Chelsea were winning at Wolves, and as the season progressed, the contrasting plight of both teams became clearer.

When Carshalton's dream of a day out at Wembley for the FA Trophy Final is ended by Worcester City, Chelsea's march to the FA Cup Final continues, and as the Blues score freely and make a strong challenge for the title, The Robins leak goals and slip further toward the relegation zone.

*

Francis Vines had replaced Hayden Bird as Carshalton Athletic's manager in September, and subsequent results had been inconsistent at best. A run of poor form early in 2010 lead to the departure of Vines, who was replaced by Ian Hazel in February 2010, and it appeared that the manager's office had been fitted with a revolving door, identical to the one at Stamford Bridge. Hazel's arrival triggered a slight improvement in form, but by the end of April, with just one fixture remaining, the Club are still in danger of being relegated.

I've been to over 20 games this season, including a few away games, and though that level of physical commitment is a drop in the ocean compared to that shown by the likes of Barry, I am quite proud of it nonetheless. Kevin and I now both own Carshalton Athletic scarves, and at last we have one club in common that we can talk football over without fear of causing offence, whilst still secretly fretting over Chelsea and Manchester United as much as ever. The last match of the season is at Wealdstone; a team who are aiming for a place in the promotion play-offs, whereas Carshalton have to win to stay in the division. It transpires that of those who've been to games with me during the season, I am the only one committed enough to The Robins' cause to want to travel to North London to support the team in their hour of need, although in reality, I'm more than happy to go alone if the alternative had been sitting at home, sweating about Chelsea's progress against Stoke City.

As it turns out, I witness one of Carshalton's best performances of the campaign, played amid a carnival atmosphere, created by a crowd of over 700, including a sizeable contingent of Robins' fans, some of whom are dressed as superheroes. Any pre-match tension is quickly dispelled as Carshalton find themselves 4-1 up after half-an-hour; a score line that remains unchanged for the rest of the game. As the final whistle blows, The Robins are mobbed by a jubilant Batman and his crime-fighting friends, and a chaotic season has been bought to a close by one special game of football. I've needed my local team this year and I'm grateful to them; they've helped divert my attention away from Stamford Bridge. When I've been with them, I've checked the Premier League scores frequently, but at least I've had something else to concern me. But now their season is over, and in that sense they've gone; and now I have no option but to focus my anxieties elsewhere.

We've Got Some History — 2009/10

"*We've played nearly 45 seconds of time added on. They're squirming and screaming on the bench. And he's done it! Villa have won the European Cup! Peter Withe's goal has bought the European Cup to England again.*" – Brian Moore, Rotterdam, 26th May 1982

Mr C Ancelotti
c/o Chelsea Football Club
Stamford Bridge
Fulham Road
London
SW6 1HS
August 4, 2009

Dear Carlo,

First of all, welcome to London. I really hope you enjoy it here and settle in quickly. I'm really pleased that you've joined us at last. It's been tough here at Chelsea for the last couple of years. Since José left us, we've been finding it difficult to cope. We just haven't been able to find anyone else who compares. No doubt you know about what happened in Moscow, and realise how painful it must have been for us, losing to Barcelona last season in that way. You know how much we want the Champions League now, but I think you can do it. You've got the experience we need. You won twice as a player and you've won it twice as a manager. But the worry I have is that, on each occasion, you won it with AC Milan, so you obviously share a chemistry with them that might not transfer to a different club, particularly one in a different country. Football's different here. It's faster, and more physical, and players don't get away with things the way that they might do in Italy. And I worry that you might not be given much time to prove your worth; we need a bit of stability but you know how quickly we change managers here. I hate to worry you too much when you've only just arrived, but the squad is getting old now so time's running out. But I'm sure you'll do well. And Carlo, I know it's only the FA Community Shield and doesn't really mean that much, but please beat Manchester United this Sunday.

Yours sincerely,
Concerned, of Carshalton

Carlo Ancelotti arrives at Chelsea in the summer of 2009 and, as is frequently the case with Chelsea managers, for his first competitive game in charge, he is to pit his wits against Sir Alex Ferguson; this time in the traditional showcase opening to the new season, the Charity Shield, or the FA Community Shield, as it is now known. The game finishes 2-2 after extratime, so the teams are forced into another penalty shoot-out, just 15 months after Moscow. It is now 11 years since Chelsea last won on penalties, and yet again, they are to be taken at the end of the stadium where the Manchester United fans are sitting, meaning that the Chelsea players are forced to take their kicks to a hostile backdrop, with the fans in red, gurning and gesticulating at the players in blue in an attempt to put them off. Yet it appears that the United players are the more distracted and, thanks to misses from Ryan Giggs and Patrice Evra, Chelsea win, and Ancelotti has his first trophy after only two months in charge.

Although the shoot-out victory over United was enjoyable, as a compensation for the defeat in Moscow, it fails miserably, and begs the question as to why we couldn't have won that one instead. But the winning of any trophy is nice, however insignificant, especially when it's won at the expense of the Red Menace of Manchester. But another threat has now emerged from that very same city. Despite their new-found wealth, to my relief, the purported emergence of Queens Park Rangers as a new footballing superpower hasn't happened, but on 1st September 2008, Manchester City were bought by an Abu-Dhabi-based investment company, led by billionaire, Sheikh Mansour bin Zayed bin Sultan bin Zayed bin Khalifa Al Nahyan (quickly to become known simply as Sheikh Mansour). Amid an increasingly familiar fanfare, proclamations that City would soon come to dominate English football, and rumours linking the Club to every one of the world's top footballers – Lionel Messi included – were difficult to take seriously. Until, that is, on 2nd September 2008, I awoke to the news that Robinho, the Brazilian whizz-kid whom Chelsea had looked certain to sign, had instead been bought by Manchester City for £32.5 million late the previous day. My team had been gazumped, and I had become so used to Chelsea having the greatest purchasing power of any team in England, if not the world, that it felt as if Robinho himself had just scored the decisive penalty for the opposition in a major Cup Final at our expense. As a wake-up call, it was suitably alarming; enough to make it obvious that, if Chelsea didn't win the Champions League soon, they might never get another chance.

*

Progress in the Champions League has been efficient, if not wholly impressive, and the Blues win their qualifying group, despite a disappointing 2-2 draw at home to APOEL of Cyprus in the final game. There are certainties in football that belie its random nature: that Dennis Law would be the player to score the goal for Manchester City that beat Manchester United – a club at which he had spent 11 years as a player – and doom them to relegation in 1974 obviously hadn't been planned, but the irony was startling. On such occasions, it seems clear that football is governed by the laws of determinism and that these events are somehow inevitable, and this is especially so in the Champions League. In 2009, when Chelsea were drawn to play Liverpool for the fifth consecutive season, coincidence seemed an inadequate explanation. In the same year, when Claudio Ranieri returned to Stamford Bridge as manager of Juventus, it was a happy coincidence that allowed the former Chelsea boss to enjoy a warm welcome from the home fans in recognition of the fondness felt for him during his four years at the Club. In 2010, when Chelsea are drawn to play José Mourinho's Inter Milan in the first knock-out stage, it again seems as though destiny has once again demanded it be so.

Though the draw is a gift for the media, it is the cause of some distress for me. I feel as though dark clouds are gathering over Stamford Bridge, and that events are now conspiring against Chelsea with such weight that an imminent collapse is unavoidable. These miserable musings are inspired by Manchester City's win at the Bridge and Inter's 2-1 first-leg victory over Chelsea having occurred within four days of each other. When Mourinho makes his return to London for the second leg in March, he pokes a finger in the ribs of his former club in a pre-match press conference – although wittily so – praising the Club for their continued success since his departure, and listing those successes – one FA Cup – with a sarcastic and knowing roll of the eyes. His team then finishes the job on the pitch, winning 1-0 on the night, thanks to a late goal from Samuel Eto'o, thus making sure that, when José leaves Stamford Bridge this time, Chelsea definitely won't be taking any further part in the Champions League. With that defeat, I become a nervous wreck. My attentions turn to the Premier League and I am now certain that Arsenal – who are having an unusually consistent season, and whose remaining fixtures, on paper, pose less of a problem to them than those of either Chelsea or Manchester United – are going to nick the title.

*

After a tricky start to the League campaign – in which Hull City threatened to earn a point at Stamford Bridge until Didier Drogba's late and lucky winner – Chelsea won their next five games to lead Manchester United by three points at the top of the table. There then followed defeats at Wigan Athletic and Aston Villa, and my concerns for Ancelotti were already growing. Had he lost the next game, at home to Blackburn Rovers, it would not have come as a surprise if he'd been shown the revolving door with the season less than three months old.

But rather than extending a blip into a calamitous run of bad form, Chelsea beat Rovers 5-0, won 4-0 away at Bolton, beat Man United 1-0 at Stamford Bridge, put four past Wolves, and ended November by winning 3-0 at Arsenal to put themselves five points clear at the top. It appears that, at last, the owner has found a manager who can give him what he wants; namely a team who can, not just win, but can win whilst playing attractive football – a style that was exemplified by the fourth goal at Bolton, with Drogba finishing a four-man move in which the ball didn't touch the ground once. Ancelotti is coolness personified, and to support a club that has a manager who seems impossible not to like is a source of great pride.

And then came Manchester City. For me, the 2-1 defeat at the City of Manchester Stadium was not only three points lost, but also indicated that a change in the natural order of the Premier League will not be far away. The loss also began a run of three draws from the next four matches, followed by four wins, including a 7-2 home win against Sunderland, a draw at Hull, another win over Arsenal, defeat at Everton, and then a win at home to Wolves, and it appeared that, along with an on-field swagger, the team had re-discovered a level of inconsistency that the Club hadn't known for several years. And then came Manchester City. Again. When they arrived at Stamford Bridge at the end of February 2010, recent revelations concerning the private lives of John Terry and Wayne Bridge – following which Terry momentarily became public enemy number one – were still fresh in the mind and lent added spice to the contest. Forget the game itself, what people really wanted to know is whether or not Bridge – who'd left Chelsea for City in January 2009, whilst the Manchester club were enjoying the first flush of wealth – would shake Terry's hand in the customary round of pre-match flesh-pressing. He didn't, and his team went on to win 4-2. It is now clearer than ever that, for Chelsea, time is short.

A draw at Blackburn Rovers on 21st March 2010 saw Chelsea drop to third in the League, having led since October, and means that the destiny of the Premier League crown was now out of their hands. I had to look away. I start avoiding all radio stations that might feature bulletins that contain any suggestion of football, and flick through newspapers, wincing the way you do when you watch a TV programme featuring candid footage of a surgical operation.

Although Carshalton Athletic's fight for survival helps provide a distraction, the next two months prove so tense that any morbid thoughts of Chelsea's elimination from the Champions League, in what I've been convinced will be the last season in which we might win it, were put on hold. A surprising draw for Arsenal at Birmingham, combined with a resounding 5-0 win for Chelsea at Portsmouth, meant that we were now second – just one point behind Manchester United – and that, when the two sides meet at Old Trafford on Saturday 3rd April, it effectively amounts to a Cup Final. Put simply, Chelsea have to win to stand any chance of ending the season as champions.

*

I spend the duration of the game checking *Sky Sports News* on my phone and then, for the second half, sitting in the car, listening to BBC Five Live's commentary on the radio, whilst waiting for Vanessa, who is shopping in town. The full-time whistle blows and Chelsea have won 2-1, and I am consumed by happiness, but I don't really know how to show it. I've got no one to share it with.

On the evening of 23rd January 1991, Chelsea had travelled to White Hart Lane for a Rumbelows Cup (otherwise known as the League Cup) quarter-final replay, and had beaten Tottenham 3-0 to reach the semi. I'd been out in Kingston that night, and as I walked home through the town centre, I bumped into a Tottenham supporter I knew who was on his way back from the game. As he hurriedly made his way home, shoulders slumped dejectedly, I was, as he immediately confessed, the last person he'd wanted to see, particularly as I was eager to know the score. As I gleefully trotted away into the night to buy a celebratory kebab, a thought was spared for my Tottenham-supporting friend and the biggest risk we all take when attending any game, let alone a game of such importance; we still have to get home afterwards. When watching a match in your own living room, the chances of encountering an opposing fan are significantly reduced. But right now, with my team just having beaten Manchester United in a game that might turn out to be the one that wins them the League title at the end of the season, I'm in a different position entirely; I'm sat in a car, and all I want to do is to talk to another football fan, or someone, anyone, who might understand what I might be feeling.

*

But, as joyous as it is, Chelsea's 2-1 win only really means that their job is made a little easier. They still have five games left to play and will need to win them all; and that will involve winning at Anfield on 2nd May. On Tuesday 13th April, as I sit in The Hope in Carshalton with Dave, having just seen Carshalton Athletic lose at home to Horsham, technology is both a friend and a frustration. My thoughts are at Stamford Bridge, where Chelsea lead Bolton Wanderers 1-0, thanks to a first-half goal from Nicolas Anelka. I'm following the Sky Sports commentary on my phone, which involves waiting for a couple of lines of text to flash up every minute or so, or whenever there's been an incident deemed worthy of a mention. As miraculous as mobile telephone and wireless Internet technology is, there's always a delay with these things when you least need one, and the game has probably already ended. I am effectively following it from sometime in the past. In the final minute, Bolton are apparently awarded a corner, but then no news appears for the next 10 minutes, and I am still none the wiser and growing increasingly certain that Bolton must have equalised. Then, and without any fuss or warning, the score line at the top of the screen turns red, indicating that the game has ended. Chelsea have managed to survive intact, and the title dream is still alive.

*

Four days later, Chelsea lose at Tottenham and, although they still remain top, it means that victory at Liverpool is now imperative. A 7-0 thrashing of Stoke City follows, on the day that Carshalton Athletic escape relegation at Wealdstone, and then, to Anfield…

I spend the afternoon of Sunday 2nd May visiting my brother, Ian, who now lives in Germany. We are being driven around some incredibly picturesque parts of southern Germany with Vanessa, Mum, Ian, my sister-in-law, Lisbeth, and niece, Maia. I have no idea what the score might be but am thinking of nothing else as I walk around a traditional German fishing village that I'm sure would have given me a fascinating insight into the history of the industry, had I been paying attention. When Ian finally manages to get news of the game, we are standing outside what is without doubt the most magnificent church I have ever seen, and it seems even more so once my brother excitedly informs me that Chelsea are 2-0 up.

Watching the highlights with him that evening, I love Liverpool in a way that I never believed possible. Such is the rivalry between themselves and Manchester United, the

Anfield crowd appear to want a Chelsea win as much as I do, and when Steven Gerrard hits a poor back-pass to Pepe Reina, which Drogba intercepts to score the first, I love him like he's one of the family.

When, at the start of the year, I'd booked tickets to see Brian Eno perform at Brighton on 9th May, I hadn't realised that it was on the final day of the Premier League season, nor had I realised that it was a matinee performance. I should have checked both of course, but, as it is, although I go along and enjoy the show, I spend large parts of it wondering what is happening 60 miles away in London SW6. Quite rightly, the audience are under strict instructions not to be seen using mobile telephones, firstly to avoid taking photographs and, more importantly, not to annoy other people. As Vanessa and I emerge from the darkness to be engulfed in the bright Sussex sunshine, I reach for my phone, which seems to take an age to boot up. For it to reveal that Chelsea are 2-0 up against Wigan would be plenty good enough, but to see that the score is 6-0 makes a good day perfect. I listen to the last minutes of the game as we drive home, to hear Didier Drogba and Ashley Cole complete an 8-0 rout and secure Chelsea their first Premier League title in four years, finishing one point ahead of Manchester United.

*

Unlike the Champions League, Chelsea had benefited from a kind draw in the FA Cup, and having beaten Watford, Preston, Cardiff and Stoke, they were next to meet Aston Villa at Wembley in the semi-final. The game was to be played on 10th April, a week after the win at United, meaning that, in the space of just eight days, there was the potential for the

Club to either end the season as also-rans, or as League and Cup Double winners for the first time in their history.

Chelsea beat Villa 3-0 to reach the FA Cup Final for the third time in four years, and, surprisingly, Portsmouth beat Tottenham in the other semi to book their own place at Wembley. The Portsmouth manager at this time is one Avram Grant, so, yet again, as if it has been pre-determined, a former manager is waiting to exact his revenge on the club that had once let them go.

*

On 15th May 2010, I watch the Cup Final with Stuart, who has an easy-going approach to football that I would give anything to experience, just for a short time at least. If his team, Tottenham, lose a game then he can laugh it off and get on with life as if football was, well as if it was just a game, and I admire that attitude in the same way that I admire astrophysics: I'm wholly impressed, and often awestruck, but I will never fully understand it. He says he wants Chelsea to win and, as usual, I believe him, in the knowledge that, even if he doesn't, he won't let on. It's not that I'm confident as such; more hopeful that Portsmouth, who have just suffered relegation from the Premier League, might not be able to pick themselves up from that disappointment enough to stop Chelsea making history. As chance after chance goes begging, the aforementioned hope becomes fear that the Blues might now pay for their wastefulness. I have a sudden flashback to 1985, and to Everton, who then had the exact same opportunity at their mercy. Having just won the League title, they too were faced with the chance of winning the Double for the first time in their history, but on the day, they seemed to freeze. Even once Manchester United had been reduced to 10 men – when Kevin Moran had become the first player in history to be sent off in an FA Cup Final – Everton struggled, and eventually lost to a superlative curler from Norman Whiteside in extra-time.

When Juliano Belletti concedes a penalty early in the second half, it seems certain that history is repeating itself, but Petr Čech's save from Kevin-Prince Boateng's spot kick turns fortune in Chelsea's favour. Minutes later, Drogba fires in a free kick to score his customary Cup Final goal, and Chelsea begin to look comfortable again, even affording themselves the opportunity to miss a penalty of their own, as Lampard does the gentlemanly thing and fires wide from the spot, just to make Boateng feel better. The game ends, Chelsea have retained the FA Cup and, more importantly, have become only the seventh club in England to win the Double; a fact that I can now add to their being the last club to win the Cup at the old Wembley, the first club to win it at the new Wembley, and the first English club ever to qualify for the European Cup, should anyone dare argue that they had no history.

Ancelotti's achievement in his first season has arguably eclipsed anything that José Mourinho achieved during his, and I am delighted for him. But, like all good forces of nature, a week after Chelsea clinch the Double, Mourinho goes one better by winning the Champions League for Inter Milan, thus securing a remarkable Treble with a team that was assembled with the skill and tenacity of an alchemical grand master, but that was hardly given a chance at the start of the campaign. Like the cartoon depiction of God in *Monty Python and the Holy Grail*, it's as if José has found a cloud over Stamford Bridge through which to poke his head, to remind us that there can only ever be one Special One.

Jules Rimet's Still Dreaming — June 2010

"What a responsibility for Chris Waddle now. Illgner knows that if he keeps Waddle out here, Germany are in the Final, and England are out. Would you want to be Chris Waddle now?... And England are out of the World Cup! West Germany are through to the Final on penalty kicks." – John Motson, Turin, 4th July 1990

How many more times are they going to do this? We've just had to sit through England's humbling at the hands of Germany and now I have to sit here and have my nose rubbed in it like this. Given the USA's supposed lack of interest in football, I thought it would be a lot easier to ignore the fact that my football team have just lost an important game. Big mistake. It's a glorious June day in 2010, and Vanessa, Katharine, Eric and I have just been sitting in a bar in New York, watching England being dismantled by Germany in the World Cup, in the company of just a small collection of fellow England supporters and a couple of disinterested bar staff. As the game finished, my disappointment was tinged with relief; firstly, because Germany had only managed to score four times, and also, because we could now get on with the day's sightseeing activities without being reminded that England have just been humiliated and that the chance of winning another World Cup has passed us by again.

But here we are, waiting for our tour bus to arrive whilst sitting outside the United Nations building, where

10 minutes ago, a BMW drove past with its roof down and a large German flag draped over the boot. The driver and his passenger were beaming from ear to ear, and shouting something in German that clearly indicated that they'd just watched the match and had been quite pleased with what they'd seen. As if that wasn't bad enough, it then became apparent, as they drove past for a second, third and then fourth time, that they'll be spending the next couple of hours just driving around the block in celebration.

Our bus takes 20 minutes to arrive, but it feels like longer. When we finally board and take our seats on the top deck, it quickly transpires that our tour guide is German, as are some of our fellow tourists, who are proudly decked out in replica Germany shirts and jabbering excitedly about Podolski and Müller.

But it hasn't always been this way. When we visited Washington DC in October 2001 with my brother, Ian, it had taken us two days to discover that England had qualified for the following year's World Cup, and even then, we only managed to find out because I'd scoured a copy of *USA Today* and found a list of nations who'd qualified for the finals in tiny print in the back pages. England's name was there so we assumed that they'd beaten Greece two days earlier, as everyone had expected them to, and had no clue as to the drama that had actually occurred. Ian and I naturally wanted to celebrate somehow and, if possible, watch the highlights of the game somewhere. Yet, in an age before Internet access was commonplace and smart phones were but a twinkle in Apple's eye, it was as though America's capital, and the world in general, was closing in around us, quashing any ounce of joy that we wanted to feel. It was another two weeks before I finally learned that England hadn't beaten Greece at all, and that David Beckham had equalised in the dying seconds of injury time but, because Germany had surprisingly only drawn with Finland, we'd qualified anyway.

I'm surprised by the level of enthusiasm shown by the US media for football during the 2010 World Cup. Whilst their team is still in the competition, their zeal as a nation is a lot greater than I'd expected, with their fortunes becoming headline news on most networks. However, once they're knocked out by Ghana, the uncertainty about the future of basketball star, LeBron James, swiftly takes the limelight and normal service resumes. The games are still featured, if you care to look for them, and the coverage is reassuringly familiar, with Martin Tyler having been employed by ESPN to commentate, and with Efan Ekoku, Steve McManaman and Roberto Martinez chipping in as pundits. The James saga is, at first, mildly compelling, then becomes amusing, and then agonising in its longevity, although I do find myself willing him to re-sign for the Cleveland Cavaliers for no obvious reason other than the fact that I'd once spent an enjoyable afternoon in that city.

I envy the fact that Americans appear to have an endless supply of sports to choose from. I'm sure that people have their favourites, be it American football, baseball, basketball or ice hockey, but it's also possible to happily immerse oneself in all four. As such, you could support the Boston Celtics, the New England Patriots, the Boston Bruins, and the Red Sox, thus spreading your bets across all four major sports. If the Celtics lose and you're mocked at work, you can laugh it off by legitimately pointing out that you're not bothered because the Patriots won at the Jets the day before and are heading for the playoffs. Having tried this ploy with other English football teams, I've learned that intra-sport multiple team supporting doesn't work because you will always care about one team above all others, and that other people will realise this.

In 2007, when the pressure of Chelsea having to win each and every game threatened to become unbearable, I entertained the possibility of immersing myself in the fortunes of the England football team as a distraction by joining the England Supporter's Club. One futile thought was that this might enable me to happily watch *Match of the Day*, irrespective of Chelsea's result that afternoon, because I would need to check the progress of any potential England squad players featured in the other matches. Another greater advantage of following England is that supporters of Liverpool, Everton, Tottenham, Arsenal, or whoever, will be united in their support for the national team, and even a Chelsea or Manchester United player can become a hero to all, temporarily at least. Before we discovered the sanctuary that is Carshalton Athletic, the only time that Kevin and I shared the same levels of joy or pain was following an England match.

The whole England supporting idea lasted a few weeks at most, failing at an early stage when, following a defeat for Chelsea at Manchester United, and a disappointing 0-0 draw at home to Fulham, my dejection was deepened by an equally disappointing 0-0 draw for England at home to Macedonia, and a 2-0 defeat in Croatia four days later. There then followed a five-week period during which I dwelt upon those two poor results before England played again, and it was that agonising hiatus that reminded me why I'd tried not to think about England too much in the first place.

Ultimately, they failed to qualify for the European Championship Finals of 2008, meaning that, for the first time since 1994, I was able to enjoy an international tournament, free of the expectation that England might actually win it this time, and the fear of yet another defeat to Germany or Portugal on penalties. In some ways, over the years, I'd suffered the same raising of expectations with England as I had with Chelsea. I was amazed when they reached the World Cup quarter-final in 1986, and not too disappointed that they were beaten by Argentina, particularly because they were both plucky and unlucky, and could quite legitimately claim to have been cheated out of a place in the semi-final by Maradonna's left hand. But their fantastic performance in 1990 had forged an unrealistic expectation that England could and would go on to win the World Cup sometime soon, so leading to two decades' worth of penalty shoot-outs and disappointments.

I've even thought about embracing other sports but, unlike in the USA, the options seem limited. I've been to see rugby matches, both League and Union, but although I found the experiences enjoyable – partly due to the madcap antics of some hapless streakers – I've failed to make the connection with the game necessary for it to compete with football in my thoughts. The one cricket match I've been to raised more questions than answers, and, though I'd love to say otherwise, I still can't quite see the attraction. Formula One holds similar mysteries: if every season yielded the same level of drama as the famous duel between James Hunt and Niki Lauda in 1976, I would have no hesitation in getting up in the early hours of the morning to watch the Australian Grand Prix, but these days, it often seems that the World Championship was as good as over by half-time. I've tried, but nothing has ever threatened to replace football as a sporting obsession.

Although Chelsea won the Double in May, and although I'd been delighted that they did so, I still felt disappointed that they hadn't won the Champions League instead, and my obsession with football was now concentrating itself on the winning of that one enormous trophy. I'd made a conscious decision to try and wean myself off football; starting by cancelling my subscription to Sky Sports.

The Bermuda Triangle — 2010/11

"Andrey Shevchenko... must score. He must score... The weight of the world on his shoulders. There will be no second chances... if Shevchenko misses. He's saved it! The European Cup is returning to England, and to Anfield! Liverpool are champions of Europe again." – Clive Tyldesley, Istanbul, 25th May 2005

In 1992, having been a highly-respected goal-scorer at Norwich City, and being bought for a club record transfer fee, Robert Fleck disappeared in mysterious circumstances while travelling on a deserted and misty A11, en-route to Stamford Bridge. This was far from being an unusual occurrence: strikers are often bought by Chelsea, only to simply disappear. What actually arrives is a replicant; a highly-convincing one, faithful to the original in almost every detail, but something is not quite right. Centre forwards come to the Club with highly impressive records then somehow just don't live up to expectations, or in some cases, don't even get close. Occasionally, a player will transcend this hoodoo – most notably, Didier Drogba and Gianfranco Zola – but for this to happen, superhuman qualities are required. More often, a striker will consistently perform like a Subbuteo player; when running to meet a cross, it's as if they are being controlled by an enthusiastic but inexperienced amateur who flicks the player with such force that they topple over as the ball sails out for a throw-in. Eventually, one presumes that whichever white-coated boffin is responsible for producing these inadequate clones will have a re-think and opt to create a new and perfect machine that looks human in every way, but is not based on any existing template. This new creation will have no pre-conceived ideas about what makes a perfect striker; it will simply have an in-built confidence to know that it just is one, and it will have no option but to prove it. It will not just avoid falling over when meeting a cross; it will meet the ball head-on and with such force that you'll hear the net rip, and it will probably have a futuristic and techie name like *The Dr0gba-X1*.

The list of the disappeared is long and noteworthy and includes: Fleck, Sutton, Furlong, Vialli, Kezman, and Schevchenko. Other casualties – Pierluigi Casiraghi and Adrian Mutu – have turned up, looked great, but then been snatched from us, either by freak injury or unprescribed drug-taking. The trend isn't confined to the last two decades either; it stretches back to at least the 1960s and the arrival of Tony Hateley's doppelganger. As with the latter, there will be times when the Club's style of play won't suit the player, or they will be virtually paralysed by the pressure imposed upon them by a high transfer fee. With some players, particularly Chris Sutton, it appeared that both were true. Gianluca Vialli bought him from Blackburn Rovers for £10 million (a whopping amount of money in 1999), where he'd been instrumental in winning the Premier League title in 1995 and was one of the League's top scorers in '98. But all that arrived at the Club was his shadow. He didn't look confident and didn't seem to want the ball very often. I was at the Bridge to see him score his first goal for Chelsea, against Skonto Riga in August 1999, and it was hoped that the floodgates would then open but, as it was, they stayed rusted shut for much of the remainder of the season, and he was sold to Celtic before the start of the next. He scored just three goals in 29 appearances at Chelsea, but at Celtic, he was an immediate success, and as such, his is probably the most spectacular case of striker abduction of them all.

*

When Fernando Torres was signed for Chelsea from Liverpool on 27th January 2011, my resolute determination not to renew my subscription to Sky Sports crumbled. Not having access to live games and rolling 24-hour football news had made the attempt to overcome my Champions League obsession a lot easier, and I didn't appear to have suffered any serious withdrawal symptoms either. I'd been doing okay. I'd started to resign myself to the fact that Chelsea would never win Europe's top prize. But Torres' signing has ruined it. His £50 million fee set a new British transfer record, but for me, it seemed a small price to pay for a player who always seemed to score against us. His first appearance for the Blues was to be against his former club at Stamford Bridge on Sunday, February 6th, and the drama and irony surrounding the game had filled the sports pages and airwaves for a week beforehand. "Will he celebrate if he scores?" they asked. I hoped not. I like seeing players refuse to celebrate a goal against a previous club, out of respect for their former fans and employers. I remember how disappointing it had been to see Eiður Guðjohnsen celebrate his goal against Chelsea during his first season at Barcelona, and much as I thought it likely that Torres would add to the irony of the occasion by scoring against Liverpool, it would be enough that he scored, and I hoped that he wouldn't do an Eiður.

But he didn't need to, because he didn't score, in that game or in any of the next eight, and once again, it would appear that the striker the Club had bought had simply disappeared.

I was desperate for Torres to start scoring. I'd thought that the days when Chelsea bought big name players were gone and that all the stars would now go to Man City, so his signing had come as a pleasant surprise. Like any new player, particularly the better ones, I wanted him to be happy at my club, but he didn't look it.

Last year, Joe Cole hadn't seemed happy and I'd spent nearly as much time fretting about the possibility that he might leave the Club at the end of the season as I had about their upcoming fixtures. Whenever he wasn't in the starting line-up, I worried that he might want to go elsewhere, and if that was to be the case, I worried that elsewhere might mean Manchester United, Arsenal or Tottenham.

On 16th May 2010, as Vanessa and I watched the squad parade their trophies through the streets of Fulham at the end of the season, as soon as I saw a stick of celery sail through the air and bounce off Joe's head, I knew that the moment was too symbolic for him to be staying; and I was right. He left and signed for Liverpool.

I wanted Torres to win trophies with Chelsea because that's why he'd signed for us, leaving behind a club where he'd been revered in the search for material success. When Liverpool won at Stamford Bridge on his Blues debut, I thought that it might become one of those tragic scenarios where a player, such as Michael Owen, leaves a club he'd been at for years, such as Liverpool, for a supposedly bigger one with more potential for success, such as Real Madrid, only for his old club to win the Champions League the next season. Perhaps Fernando thought that too. His body language and his form on the pitch suggested that something wasn't right, so maybe he already regretted signing for us, or, more likely, he'd fallen foul of the curse that had befallen so many before him and would soon be consigned to the strikers' graveyard at the

Bridge. He had chances, and made chances for himself, but for whatever reason, he'd just lost his touch, and suddenly, £50 million seemed like an awful lot of money.

Chelsea were suffering their worst run of form in the Abramovich era when they bought Torres. Ray Wilkins had been sacked as assistant manager in November – a decision that defied logic. The team had continued the form that had clinched the title the previous season, winning their first five games, scoring 21 goals, and conceding only one in the process. It already seemed as though they might be unstoppable, and that Ancelotti would be matching Mourinho's feat of winning back-to-back Premier League titles in his first two years in England. The 1-0 defeat at Manchester City at the end of September was merely a blip. Even when Torres scored twice for Liverpool in a 2-0 reverse at Anfield, we were still top. But then, after a 1-0 home win over Fulham, Wilkins was given his orders and it all went wrong. Following three defeats and three draws in the next six games, Chelsea fell to fourth in the League and, from a position of total control, were now a club in crisis, with the all-important Champions League qualification for next season looking increasingly unlikely. But Chelsea signed another player in the January transfer window who'd given me reason to believe.

Although we had lost the Liverpool match, I was upbeat afterwards. The level of hype surrounding a fixture is rarely matched by the subsequent on-field action, and to lose was no great surprise. It was a miserable performance and I was already regretting the impetuous decision to renew my Sky Sports subscription, until David Luiz took to the pitch in the second half. My mood changed as soon as he made his first foray up field, bringing the ball out of defence calmly and with not one hint of panic; the way that Glen Hoddle might have done all those years before. Not only was he clearly a talented player, but he had big hair too. Some might think that such a large mop of curls has no place on the head of a footballer, but for some reason, I've always thought that a team looks more complete with an afro hairstyle among them. Everton had one – Marouane Fellaini – and I felt sure that the presence of a player with such a dominant pate made them a better side. Perhaps with the exception of Ruud Gullit, the Blues hadn't really had a player with big hair since 1982, when Ian Britton left the Club. Maybe it's the child in me, hankering after the football of the 1970s – a time when, for me, the game was still a form of entertainment in the way that films and cartoons also were – and, as such, a part of me still wants my football team to be like a theatrical version; the cartoon version of the Harlem Globetrotters had a character with an afro and look how good they were.

Although a player's physical appearance shouldn't really matter as long as they do what they're paid to, I'd rather my team had more in common with the *X-Men* than *The Munsters*; to see someone as physically imposing as Didier Drogba take to the field instils confidence in a fan. In contrast, when Peter Crouch was first picked to play for England, I worried about it for the simple reason that his appearance in the side would raise the confidence of the opponents, and when he was cruelly booed by England supporters after coming on as a substitute against Poland in 2005, it was clear that other fans felt the same. Common sense might suggest that a player who is over six-and-a-half feet tall and built like a bean pole wouldn't have the physical attributes necessary to play football, but my own opinion had been shaped by two separate comedic incidents involving the player.

I was once at a Chelsea reserves match at Kingsmeadow and Crouch was a substitute for Tottenham. When the manager told him to warm up, he got up off the subs bench and, in an attempt to extend himself to full height, cracked his head on the roof of the dugout. Raucous laughter ensued. In February 2001, Queens Park Rangers were behind against Wimbledon at Selhurst Park and the sight of poor Peter Crouch forlornly lumbering out for the second half as the theme tune to *Steptoe & Son* was played through the PA – in a humorous nod to Rangers' Shepherds Bush roots – is one of the most comically-tragic things I have ever seen at a football match.

And yet, over the years, Crouch has proved time and again that he is exactly the right build to be a top striker. He has telescopic legs that can extend at will, he towers above every defender he plays against, and he has ball skills that most could only dream of. Where others have failed, he adapted to the international stage without a problem, his goal-scoring record for England is impressive, and the sight of him playing for the opposition now fills me with dread.

*

Within weeks of that first substitute appearance, Luiz scored in wins against both Manchester United and Manchester City, helping turn Chelsea's season around, and he could now look to any portion of the Stamford Bridge crowd to see fans wearing afro wigs in his honour. But, unfortunately, Luiz and Torres could do nothing to prevent Chelsea being knocked out of the FA Cup for the first time in three years, because neither of them played. Everton arrived at the Bridge on February 19th for a fourth round replay and left, having beaten the Blues in a penalty shoot-out. It was the one and only time that my brothers, my now sixteen-year-old nephew, Ben, and I had gone to see Chelsea together, so it was a day of mixed feelings: we'd missed out on the chance of a season-saving trophy, but on the other hand, it was nice that we were all together to share the experience. I wasn't terribly disappointed that we'd lost – the FA Cup is one thing, the Champions League is entirely another – although I'd rather we'd won the shoot-out for the simple reason that it would've proved to me and the players that they had the ability to win one when it really mattered, giving us all the confidence that they'd be able to do it in future, and the knowledge that the Club weren't in fact the subject of a major competition penalty curse.

*

The summer of 2010 had seen several of the more experienced players leave the Club, including Joe Cole, Michael Ballack, Juliano Belletti, Ricardo Carvalho and Deco; each of whom had years of European experience and whose departures left the squad looking a little flimsy. What had become known as the core of the side – Čech, Ashley Cole, John Terry, Frank Lampard and Didier Drogba – remained – all of whom were now over 30 – and, in the summer, only Luiz's fellow Brazilian, Ramires, had joined them. It already looked as though a major rebuilding exercise was in progress, which could take years before the high standards of recent times could be reached again. As much as Ramires added energy to the side, his addition wasn't enough to reassure me that the big-eared trophy would be arriving within the next nine months. But the arrival of Luiz and Torres, whose magic surely wouldn't desert him forever, added sufficient new blood to renew hope that they might still be in with a chance. In mid-March they drew 0-0 at home to Copenhagen to win 2-0 on aggregate and reach the Champions League quarter-finals. I felt certain we'd be drawn to play Tottenham Hotspur, purely because we always seem to be drawn to play English opposition in the latter stages, and that irony itself seems to be a seasonal certainty. But though that particular fixture would prove tense, I wasn't too worried who we had to play, as long as we avoided Real Madrid and Barcelona. And Manchester United.

*

Chelsea faced Manchester United at Stamford Bridge on 6th April and lost to a single Wayne Rooney goal. No goals scored and an away goal against leaves the team with a mountain to climb at Old Trafford tonight, 12th April 2011. We're just not organised enough to get through. Ramires is sent off in the first half and now the mountain has grown to insurmountable proportions. Giggs breaks down the right, there are plenty of defenders in the box, but he's in behind them: 1-0 United – Hernandez with a tap-in, 2-0 on aggregate. Game over, surely. Carlo Ancelotti took a major gamble by not selecting Didier Drogba to start the game, opting to play Fernando Torres instead. Perhaps he was hoping that Torres would suddenly come to life on the big stage and become a hero in the style of Jimmy Grimble, but he's only lasted the first half and now he's been subbed. His replacement, Drogba, was always the more likely to turn in a Grimble-esque performance. With all the disappointments and near misses of recent years, Drogba is a man on a mission. He always rises to the occasion for the big games, and on Champions League nights in particular. It looks as though tonight might be no different, but he only has 45 minutes to save his team.

It's the 76th minute, Drogba races clear on the left and smacks the ball so hard that it looks as though it's passed straight through van der Saar's midriff. One more goal will do it... but no. Rather than spark a glorious comeback, Drogba's strike only serves to wake United up and Park Ji-sung scores a minute later to put the game out of Chelsea's reach. The Champions League dream has vanished once more, and this time, there is no big mystery involved. There's been no bad luck, no phantom goal, no avant-garde refereeing performance and no penalty shoot-out. The Blues have just imploded, through nobody's fault but their own. Ray Wilkins has gone and the team hasn't been the same since. Man City are about to qualify for the Champions League for the first time, Bayern are improving, as are Real Madrid, and Barcelona just look unbeatable. The competition is as strong as it has ever been, and with Chelsea having failed to reach the semi-finals for two consecutive seasons, all momentum is lost.

*

With thoughts now once again turning to the Premier League, rather than struggling to finish in the top four and qualify for the Champions League the following season, it transpires that, following a run of eight wins and a draw, we still have a shot at winning the title. It's May 8th and, as was the case last season, the team have travelled to Old Trafford, knowing that only a win will leave them with any chance at all. The usual media hype in the build-up to today's game would have us believe that it is the most important game of football to be played this season, and that Chelsea have a very real chance of getting a result, just as they did last year. It's not the same team though. I know they don't really have a chance, but nevertheless, I've made the mistake of being seduced by the fanciful speculation and, as I sit down to watch the match, I fully concur with the pundit who predicts that whoever scores the first goal will go on to win the game.

I know that if Chelsea can hold out for 30 minutes without conceding, they might very well come away with all three points. They hold out for 36 seconds.

As the game is about to kick off, Javier Hernández kneels in the centre circle in prayer, and trying to gain an advantage in this way doesn't seem at all fair. Less than a minute later, and fuelled by a higher power, he is sliding the ball past Petr Čech and the game, and Chelsea's season, is as good as over.

I've recently created my first Twitter account, and Hernández's goal inspires me to send one of my first tweets; "All over inside a minute!" I'm not really sure what I thought this might achieve. I only have three followers so I'm really just shouting into the wind. I don't think it's going to help Chelsea's cause in the slightest.

Twenty-three minutes later, United score again, and although Lampard pulls a goal back, it is but a consolation. Chelsea lose at Everton on the last day of the season and, despite leading his team to a second place finish in the table, Ancelotti is sacked in a corridor at Goodison Park immediately after the game. It's a shameful end to a shambolic season, and one that Carlo doesn't deserve. He has carried himself with dignity throughout, but has ultimately paid the price for the Club's stellar expectations. Sir Alex has done it again; whatever Faustian pact he had entered into at the dawn of the Abramovich era has paid off and, with the Blues in disarray, United can once again look forward to an appearance in the Champions League Final with another Premier League title safely locked away.

Remember You're a Womble — May 2011

"Chelsea have missed two of their three. The simple maths tells you they can score no more than three. Liverpool already have three. All that adds up to this. Twelve yards from glory. Dirk Kuyt denied by a linesman's flag during the game... has done it! Liverpool's love affair with the European Cup continues." – Clive Tyldesley, Anfield, 1st May 2007

I've got a problem. I realise that now. I need to sit down and talk it through. Are there people you can see about this sort of thing?

For some, this day – 21st May 2011 – is notable for being the date upon which Harold Camping has predicted that the world will end. More specifically, Camping, a well-known American Christian radio host, has actually foretold that today the "Biblical prophecy of The Rapture" will be fulfilled, and those with a faith in Christ will ascend to heaven, in what will amount to a mass promotion of the righteous, at approximately 6p.m. Greenwich Mean Time. 6p.m. has come and gone and it appears that nothing has happened. As I sit on a coach, full of AFC Wimbledon supporters, driving through Manchester in the early evening, I can't help musing that perhaps Mr Camping had misunderstood the message, and that the prediction had actually referred to the promotion of Wimbledon, that most righteous of football clubs, from the Conference to the Football League. I keep my thoughts to myself for fear of surrounding puerile or offensive, neither of which is intended. The world hasn't ended, but the first chapter of AFC Wimbledon's nine-year history has.

Unusually, the Conference play-off final was to be played at a venue other than Wembley because the National Stadium had been booked to stage the final of the Champions League the following week. That is how it came to be that Barry, Skip, myself and several coachloads of AFC supporters found themselves heading up the M6 to the City of Manchester Stadium, instead of on a short ride around the North Circular. It was to be the first time I'd seen them play in six years, but the moment they'd secured their place in the Final, I'd made my mind up that I wanted to go: having missed out on their first ever game at Sutton United in 2002, I didn't want to miss the next biggest game in their short but remarkable history.

In the intervening years, the Club had won promotion four times to bring themselves within one game of making it back to the big leagues. As was to be expected, Skip was far more nervous than Barry or I; the Club's achievement in actually earning themselves the opportunity of gaining promotion back to the Football League in just nine years was remarkable enough, and I was just excited at the possibility that they might actually do it. As we drove through Manchester, the signs were increasingly promising, literally: every block seemed to contain a shop or superstore with a blue and yellow logo – Lidl, Focus and Jewson seemed to dominate the area, far outnumbering the orange of J. Sainsbury and Luton Town, and I felt sure that this must be a good omen. Better still, an old superstition from the Selhurst Park days appeared to have followed us through time and up the M6, as we arrived late and, in the rush to get to our seats, the turnstile stuck for each of us in turn. To convince us that Wimbledon were sure to win, all that was missing now was the sight of Mister Wimbledon, but despite a *"Where's Wally"* style scan of the crowd, he was nowhere to be seen.

We made it to our seats with minutes to spare, and it was clear that fans of AFC were in the unfamiliar situation of being outnumbered, with Luton supporters making up at least two-thirds of the crowd. Both clubs have reason to feel aggrieved by their treatment at the hands of the football authorities in recent years, and as such, both might believe it to be their destiny to win this afternoon. The Dons could reclaim their rightful place in the Football League; a place that was snatched from them by an unfathomable decision from a three-man committee. Luton, on the other hand, had been deducted 30 points by the FA for financial irregularities in 2008/09; an unprecedented and harsh penalty that cost them their own place in the Football League, so they too had a point to prove.

I've heard arguments against the play-off system over the years, proclaiming it to be unfair on those teams who finish second or third in their League but who then go on to lose to a team who finished sixth, so missing out on a promotion that would've been theirs in the "good old days". The problem with this argument is that it neglects the fact that football is, or at least is supposed to be, a form of entertainment, although usually it resembles anything but. A football match should be infused with drama from the start, and pressure creates that drama, and there can be no greater pressure than to end the season with a game that can secure either side a windfall of millions. I should probably detest the play-offs, given that Chelsea were relegated through them the second season they came into effect in the old First and Second Divisions, in 1988. But the system is different now; there is no relegation, only promotion. Fans and managers alike agree that it's the best way to win promotion, and some of the best games I have ever seen have been in the play-offs. But this one did not prove to be one of them.

The match itself was, in all honesty, quite dull, which illustrates the potential pitfall of a game of such importance: both teams were so driven to win that they seemed frightened to lose. Normal-time ended goalless and with little incident, other than Luton hitting the post and a couple of missed chances from Wimbledon. Extra-time was little different and the sides still couldn't be separated, so at last it was time for the real drama to unfold. The penalties were to be taken at our end of the stadium and, as a result, as the players filled the centre circle, I had an increasing sense that a hero would emerge wearing blue and yellow. In this case, there were two, but the first was wearing green: Wimbledon keeper, Seb Brown, saved Luton's first and fourth penalties, and The Dons were one kick away from winning back their place in the Football League.

I have come to loathe penalty shoot-outs over the years. I'd actually known my teams to win on very few occasions. Chelsea hadn't come out on top in well over a decade, and as for England, one success in six attempts left me praying for an alternative solution to decide a stalemate – reverting to the age-old flip of a coin would be far less painful. Moscow, still too fresh in the mind, had taught me that fate doesn't always take the side you think it will on such occasions, but this time, surely, it was clear what would make for the happier ending. Wimbledon were the smaller club, but their collective effort in just nine years had been massive. It was time for them to claim their rightful place as the club of the people, and as a shining example of what can be achieved with the backing of a focused collective with one single goal. That happy ending beckoned. Danny Kedwell stepped up, held his nerve and, with one kick, destroyed the Death Star.

That's not to say that Luton Town are the epitome of evil in any way (although Watford fans may beg to differ), but more so that football, as a corporate tool, might represent the Dark Side, and on this day, the Rebellion had scored a huge moral victory. The fairy-tale was complete.

I was swept along by the romance of everything I'd just witnessed, and it seemed immediately obvious that the path of true footballing righteousness lead to Kingsmeadow Stadium. This was the story I had always been looking for, and I wanted to be a part of it. Wimbledon were the club I should've supported all along, and had been tapping me on the shoulder for the past 22 years to tell me as much. A few weeks after the play-off final, a letter appeared in *When Saturday Comes* magazine that summed up most of my thoughts perfectly. Written by a Chelsea fan who had become as disillusioned as I had with the Club's behaviour – the irreverent sacking of managers and management staff, and the resultant lack of stability in particular – he'd been as impressed as I and others around the world at the achievement of Wimbledon fans in taking matters into their own hands and starting from scratch to control the destiny of their own club, and questioned whether Chelsea fans might ever do the same. The reality is that he's probably not alone in his opinion and, as such, if it came to it, there would be enough Chelsea fans around the world who feel strongly enough about their club to start again, just as fans of Manchester United had a few years earlier.

*

As is my nature, in a fit of spontaneity and zeal, within weeks of the victory, I have joined The Dons Trust – the fans group that owns AFC Wimbledon – and, jointly with Skip, bought a personalised brick to be installed at a new section of the ground at Kingsmeadow. As soon as the new League Two fixtures are released, I begin mapping out the coming months so as to attend as many fixtures as possible, embracing my City of Manchester Stadium epiphany completely, and with little thought of compromise. But soon afterwards, during a tennis match, I have a conversation with another Wimbledon fan that makes it obvious what a charlatan I have become. He comments on the fact that I am an AFC Wimbledon supporter – a completely reasonable assumption to make, based on the fact that he's seen my Facebook profile and noticed that I've listed AFC Wimbledon as my favourite sports team – and remarked that he is a fan too. The conversation then centres on the club and, more particularly, the play-off final a few weeks previously, but inwardly the walls around my allegiance begin to collapse from the moment I reply "yes" to his question: "So I see you're an AFC fan?" He is a season ticket holder and has been a regular attendee since the Plough Lane days. When asked how often I get to home games, I admit that I haven't been since 2005. Immediately, I feel exposed; as fraudulent as *The Fast Show* character who goes to Arsenal matches in his replica shirt, knows nothing about the sport or the team, randomly shouts "soccer" for no apparent reason, and then mistakenly cheers when the opposition score. Much of the ensuing conversation is true on my part; I had rarely been as happy inside a football ground as I had been at the play-off final, but tempting as it is to mangle the truth, fill in the yawning gaps in my Wimbledon backstory and pretend that I've made even sporadic appearances at Kingsmeadow during the previous six seasons, I just cannot lie.

A New Hope? — 2011/12

"And Nicolas Anelka... a Champions League winner with Real Madrid... who must score. A former Liverpool and Manchester City player, with the responsibility of taking this key penalty. VAN DER SAR SAVED IT! United again!! The newly-crowned champions of England are the new champions of Europe." – Clive Tyldesley, Moscow, 21st May 2008

I begin the 2011/12 season under the cloud of realisation that I will never be able to relinquish my attachment to Chelsea Football Club. I will forever be chained to their fortunes and there is nothing I can do to change that. No matter how frustrated I become with the way the Club is being run, how desperate I am to break free of the obsession I have with them having to win the Champions League, and my conviction that the fairy-tales are all happening elsewhere, I can never break free for long. I'm supporting Wile E. Coyote – the team who will never quite claim their prize.

The relationship between a football fan and their football team being akin to that of a marriage is an oft-used metaphor. Although it's not entirely accurate, in many ways, it is true. Vanessa and I had finally got married in August 2009, having been engaged for 17 years. With Chelsea and myself, there has never been an exchanging of vows as such, and I have never had reason to be annoyed with Vanessa for sacking any of our staff, because we don't live in a *Downton Abbey* universe, so we've never had any. But if we did, and she had done, I would have been duty-bound to find it in myself to understand why she had done so, no matter how much I'd respected the butler or the housekeeper and admired their work, and no matter how rash I thought Vanessa had been in dispensing with their services. I'm still annoyed that Chelsea sacked Ancelotti, but I have to find a way to accept it and, although it's difficult, I have to learn to trust the Club, because ultimately, we both want the same thing.

And then, predictably, as pre-season takes flight, my mood begins to lighten. It's as if the close season is designed to lure the weak of will back from their well-earned holidays and to crush any adulterous thoughts, and Chelsea FC have become the masters of this. Typically, it begins with the announcement of a new manager, which will usually be enough to pique the interest, and the inevitable rumours of impending transfers will further seduce – the bigger the names, the greater the seduction (in the early '90s, the signing of Robert Fleck was enough to get the blood flowing).

In the summer of 2011, the arrival of André Villas-Boas is interesting, and all the previously acquired wisdom is once again dispelled. Here is a young manager, aged only 33, who had once worked at Chelsea as part of José Mourinho's management team, and in 2010/11, had attracted much attention by winning the Portuguese League title – with the team remaining unbeaten all season – the Portuguese Cup, and the UEFA Cup at FC Porto, whilst in his first full season in management. This led to him being dubbed "Mini Mourinho" in honour of his former mentor's similar achievements at the same club. Could this signal a change in attitude from the board and owner? Perhaps so. This might be the dawn of a new, exciting era, with the new man still at the helm well into his 40s or even 50s, thus becoming our very own Sir Alex. Then, just to ensure that I'm in the bag, I'm further weakened by the news that the new manager has chosen Roberto Di Matteo to be his assistant. No other appointment could have pleased me more. It is an inspired decision and plays to my weakness perfectly. For Chelsea fans, the man is a hero, bordering on the status of a demi-god, having proved himself an uncanny talisman during his playing days at Stamford Bridge. Once again, I entertain the possibility that my own fortunes might be cosmically linked to the football club and, as if to further reinforce that thought, as I am writing a diary entry to that effect, a Club representative phones me to explain the benefits of their new foundation lottery, and to proclaim an evening with Ashley Cole as being one of the most attractive prizes. But, as tempting as that might be, I manage to summon enough restraint to resist their thinly-veiled charitable scheme.

The season starts well enough, with a goalless draw with Stoke City at The Britannia Stadium – a ground that was increasingly becoming a thorn in the side of the Premier League's bigger clubs, being followed by wins over West Bromwich Albion, Sunderland and Norwich City. Villas-Boas' new signing, Spanish playmaker, Juan Mata, looks to be a good acquisition, and he is soon joined by Portuguese midfielder, Raul Meireles; a player who'd become known for scoring important and spectacular goals in his short spell at Liverpool, including the only goal at Stamford Bridge the previous season, in Fernando Torres' over-hyped debut. Young striker, Daniel Sturridge, and David Luiz are becoming prominent fixtures in the starting line-up and it seems as though the players are beginning to gel as a team, but to continue their development, a game against Manchester United at Old Trafford on 18th September is, in truth, the last thing they need. The second-half performance shows that the spirit is still there, but the fact that Chelsea had slipped to a 3-0 deficit by half-time, albeit to the reigning champions, makes it obvious that something isn't quite right. To make matters worse, having already scored once to bring the Blues back into contention, Torres then misses an open goal right in front of the United fans, who are unforgiving in their subsequent mocking of the Chelsea striker, and their team end the day, 3-1 victors.

Torres played well at the start of the season and was beginning to show flashes of the form that persuaded the Club to pay £50 million for him in the first place. But the United game has sparked a return to the unconfident Torres that had first arrived at The Bridge. In the next fixture, at home to Swansea City, although he scores the first goal of the game after 29 minutes, he is shown a straight red card 10 minutes later for a rash challenge on a Swansea player. He won't score another League goal for six months.

Aside from Torres' lack of confidence, other cracks have begun to appear in the new managerial regime. For a start, Villas-Boas' frequent referral to his role as Chelsea manager as being a "project" doesn't instil confidence, and he consequently comes across as though he is treating the job more like a school assignment than as the custodian of the hopes and dreams of a major football club and its legion of fans. In addition, he lacks both the humour and passion of Mourinho, and the calmness, charm and expressive eyebrow of Ancelotti. Instead, he seems dour and defensive in interviews, making it even harder to endear himself to fans. It also appears that he's been given a brief to deconstruct the first team squad by replacing the older players far quicker than is necessary, which means that core players such as Didier Drogba, Frank Lampard and Ashley Cole are increasingly side-lined.

To make things worse, the new manager prefers to play with a high defensive line; a system that clearly isn't working with the players he has – a fact that is never more apparent than during the 5-3 home defeat to Arsenal on 29th October 2011. I check my phone and see that Chelsea are 2-1 up at half-time and heading for victory. I then nip out to the shops and, by the time I get back in the car and turn the radio on, Arsenal are winning 3-2. In fear that my switching on the radio has triggered a collapse and a subsequent onslaught from the Gunners, I immediately turn it off again. By the time I've recovered my sense of logic and switched it back on 10 minutes later, Juan Mata has just scored to make it 3-3, and I then conclude that my actions have in fact instigated a glorious Chelsea comeback. As Robin van Persie scores a fourth for Arsenal five minutes later, the radio is back off, which inspires Van Persie to score again.

To play a system that allows so much space between defence and goalkeeper requires players with enough pace to cover an opposition attack, and for all their skill and experience, that's the one thing that the Chelsea defence lacked, until the arrival of Gary Cahill three months later, by which time, Villas-Boas' days are already numbered.

I'd had a go at football management myself for a couple of years in the mid-1990s, whilst running a side that played in the Hastings and District Sunday League. Although I wasn't particularly good at it, I'd learned enough to know that if your centre-backs and goalkeeper aren't the quickest, then you need to dispense with any form of offside trap and ensure that your defenders don't go anywhere near the halfway line. Although I felt certain that I could have helped André by telling him this, I'm not sure that he would've taken me seriously.

Signs of a rift between the manager and players become more apparent as the season draws on. Nicolas Anelka and Alex – two of the most experienced players – requested transfers toward the end of 2011, and were immediately ostracised by Villas-Boas and banned from training with the first team. At the turn of the year, during a match with Wolverhampton Wanderers, Ramires' opening goal was met with a bizarre celebration that featured a few Chelsea players running to the bench to celebrate with the manager and his staff, whilst motioning for others, who were celebrating elsewhere on the pitch, to join in the dugout lovefest. It transpired that this performance had been insisted upon by the manager in a bid to force a sense of unity upon the players and management that was clearly missing. The newer players adhered to his wishes, whereas the old guard declined the opportunity, making it obvious to all that the new manager was dividing the dressing room.

Although they went on to win the game at Wolves, there followed a crippling run of results that included three draws and then a 2-0 defeat at Everton. The third draw of the sequence was the hardest to bear. Though seemingly cruising to victory whilst 3-0 up at home to Manchester United, the Reds scored three times in the last half an hour to draw 3-3.

A week after the Everton loss, Chelsea laboured to a 1-1 draw at home to championship side, Birmingham City, in the fifth round of the FA Cup, and had Daniel Sturridge to thank for keeping them in the competition. They then travel to Naples to face Napoli three days later in the first leg of their last 16 Champions League fixtures. Villas-Boas has decided to start with Ashley Cole and Frank Lampard – two players with a wealth of Champions League experience between them – on the subs' bench. Juan Mata puts the Blues ahead after 27 minutes but Napoli go in at half-time, 2-1 up, thanks to strikes from Ezequiel Lavezzi and Edinson Cavani. Midway through the second half, Chelsea fall further behind as Lavezzi takes advantage of a shambolically-choreographed defensive sequence that sees Čech switch to midfield and David Luiz to goalkeeper, whilst poor old Gary Cahill is probably left wondering whether he's signed for a football club in the January transfer window or a circus act. And then comes the moment that, as much as any other, will alter Chelsea's destiny.

Something's Happening — 2012

"Robbie Mustoe battling with Dennis Wise, now the first sign of Chelsea on the attack with Di Matteo. Oh, and a good run up front by Hughes and DI MATTEO SHOOTS. Oh what about this?! What about this? It's possibly the quickest ever goal in a Wembley Cup Final! It's Roberto Di Matteo inside 45 seconds." – John Motson, Wembley, 17th May 1997

In the Champions League, everything had gone to plan at first, with home wins against Bayer Leverkusen and Genk, sandwiching a draw at Valencia, but then a disappointing draw at Genk, followed by a last gasp 2-1 defeat at Leverkusen, left Chelsea's hopes of progressing to the knockout stages hanging by a thread. Heading into the last game of the group stage, Chelsea had to beat Valencia at Stamford Bridge to finish as runners-up, as it had to be assumed that Leverkusen would win at Genk (who had struggled in the competition thus far), and would therefore win the group. On the night of the Valencia game, Villas-Boas had once again snubbed one of his older stars by leaving Lampard out of the starting line-up, but could be grateful for the big game heroics of Didier Drogba for helping his side to a 3-0 victory. Then the first real slice of luck in Chelsea's campaign occurred, in Belgium. Bayer Leverkusen only managed a 1-1 draw at Genk, meaning that not only had Chelsea secured qualification for the knockout stages, but they'd also finished as group winners. As the winners of each group were to be drawn to play the runners-up from any one of the other groups, Chelsea would therefore avoid having to face either of the favourites; namely Real Madrid, Barcelona or Bayern Munich. Whereas the Blues were drawn to play Italian side, Napoli, poor Leverkusen had to play the reigning champions, Barcelona, in the first knockout stage, and ended up losing 10-2 on aggregate, having succumbed 7-1 in the second leg at Camp Nou.

The first leg in Napoli had ended in a 3-1 defeat for Chelsea, but it could have been even worse. With 10 minutes left to play, up stepped Ashley Cole for his moment of glory. Although it may not have seemed significant at the time, Cole's goal line clearance in the 80th minute prevented Napoli taking a three-goal lead back to Stamford Bridge, which would have left Chelsea with no chance of progressing to the next round. As the ball was squared to Christian Maggio, amid a typical amount of chaos in the Chelsea defence, Cole stood in his own goal, and a few feet behind the line. As Maggio fired the ball goalwards from only six yards out, and with the goal at his mercy, Cole launched himself at the ball and managed to hook it clear as it kissed the goal line. The game ended and it seemed that Chelsea's Champions League dream was punctured for another year, leaving The Bottle to gather another few layers of dust. But effectively, whereas Lavezzi's goal had signalled the beginning of the end for André Villas-Boas' tenure, Cole's superhuman clearance had left the way clear for his team to set in motion a chain of events that few would have thought possible.

Ten days after defeat in Naples, on Saturday 3rd March 2012, Gareth McAuley sealed Villas-Boas' fate by scoring the only goal of the game for West Bromwich Albion. Defeat left Chelsea sitting fifth in the Premier League table and contemplating a whole season without Champions League football and all that that would entail; reduced revenue, the risk of players leaving, and the risk of new players not wanting to join. There was also the additional danger that if, in prophesising that the world really would end in December 2012, it turned out that the Mayans were right all along, I, nor anyone else, would ever get to see Chelsea become champions of Europe.

*

We all remember where we were when Kennedy was shot, except that these days, at least half the population don't because we weren't alive on that fateful day in Dallas. For my generation, the equivalent might be the murder of John Lennon; news of which I first learned of in a classroom at Bexhill High School. I heard the news of Villas-Boas' dismissal via a text message from Stuart whilst Vanessa and I were browsing the kitchenware in the Epsom branch of Lakeland. I can remember receiving the news more clearly than that of any other managerial sacking; perhaps because my subconscious felt the full weight of its significance or, more plausibly, because it pleased me more than any other. I did feel sorry for Villas-Boas. He clearly had some innovative ideas and had proved that he had it in him to be a successful manager whilst at FC Porto, but, from day one, it was just as clear that the Chelsea job had arrived too early in his career. Chelsea had a team full of experienced internationals with strong personalities, and the core players – Lampard, Drogba, Terry, Čech and Cole – represented an inner sanctum that must have seemed impenetrable. Roberto Di Matteo was immediately appointed caretaker manager for the rest of the season, and from the outset, he took the view that it was better to use those key players and to keep them on side. His first game in charge was the FA Cup replay at Birmingham City, two days after his appointment, and it was more than a comfort to see him sat on the bench as the new boss. Before long, he was joined by another Chelsea FA Cup hero, Eddie Newton, who had been bought in to assist the new manager, and it was then that everything turned around.

The 2-0 win at Birmingham began an extraordinarily successful period for the new management team, as Chelsea lost only once in the League in the next nine fixtures, and that one defeat came at Manchester City – who were second in the table and heading for their first Premier League title – and then only thanks to two late goals from Sergio Agüero and Samir Nasri. In the FA Cup, the team overcame their fifth round jitters to beat Leicester City 5-2 in the quarter-final and, more thrillingly, Tottenham Hotspur 5-1 in the semi-final at Wembley. But it is in the Champions League that I am hoping that the duo will be able to truly inspire the miraculous.

Just 10 days after his appointment, Di Matteo is about to oversee his first European game as a manager as Napoli arrive at the Bridge with their 3-1 lead for the return leg of their last 16 tie. The match comes a full three weeks after the first leg; a period in which, unfortunately for the Italians, Chelsea have become a different proposition, with a renewed sense of stability and purpose. Di Matteo has named a starting line-up that includes Lampard, Drogba, Terry, Čech and Cole – the five core players, or "Blue Bloods", who've started so few fixtures together this season – and it's a decision that is applauded by every armchair Chelsea manager in the land.

My own experience of the game would be somewhat fragmented. In our capacity as members of the Campaign for Real Ale, myself and a friend have chosen tonight to go to Croydon to pass judgement on two of the pubs shortlisted for the 2012 Sutton and Croydon Pub of the Year award. We witness Didier Drogba's superb 28th minute headed goal whilst in the Cricketers in Addiscombe, and for Chelsea, it is game on. Having determined that we'll score the decor and the service highly, at half-time, we embark upon what we think will be a short walk around the corner to The Claret. By the time we arrive, some 10 to 15 minutes later, the second half is already under way and we've missed John Terry's header; a goal that not only puts his side 2-0 up on the night, but, with the aggregate score level at 3-3, puts Chelsea ahead in the tie, courtesy of the away goal scored in Naples. By the time we've ordered our drinks and settled down, Napoli have scored an away goal of their own; Gökhan Inler having pounced on a loose ball to fire past Petr Čech and put Napoli ahead once more. For all Chelsea's determination, they now need luck to go their way. Had Branislav Ivanović's header hit the arm of a Barcelona defender in the semi-final second leg in 2009, it's highly likely that Chelsea would not have been awarded a penalty. But this is 2012, and as the ball hits the arm of a Napoli defender in the 75th minute, the referee has no hesitation in awarding a penalty kick, which Frank Lampard duly dispatches to take the game into extra-time. I'm too nervous to watch anymore, so we leave The Claret at full-time and head home. I learn, via my phone, that Ivanović has scored as I am walking back from the station. I watch the remainder of extra-time from the front room doorway and, as the final whistle blows and Di Matteo runs onto the pitch to share his joy with the players – just as Mourinho had done seven years before, following victory over Barcelona – it starts to feel as though our luck has changed in the most dramatic and wonderful way.

The sense that destiny might be on Chelsea's side continues as the draw for the quarter-final is made two days later and they are drawn to play Benfica, with the second leg to be played at Stamford Bridge. Like Napoli, Benfica are hardly whipping boys, but when faced with the alternative prospect of having to play Bayern Munich, Real Madrid, AC Milan or the mighty Barcelona at that stage of the competition, facing the Portuguese side gives me a glimmer of hope that, with luck like that on our side, we might go all the way. Fernando Torres inspires a 1-0 win in Portugal and, with Chelsea now having a precious away goal, it seems that they can already look forward to the semi-final.

Having missed that first leg, I sit down to watch the return leg with a naïve level of confidence. In the first half, it seems that the script was being followed to the letter. First, Frank Lampard puts Chelsea 2-0 up on aggregate from the penalty spot, following a foul on Ashley Cole, and then Benfica are reduced to 10 men before the half is out, as Maxi Pereira is sent off for a foul on John Obi Mikel. Despite their lead and numerical advantage, the Blues seem nervous, and when Ramires misses an open goal that would surely have killed the tie-off early in the second half, I fear that something bad is about to happen. As Benfica try to force their way back into the game, I become increasingly certain that, if I stop watching, Chelsea will see the game out without any problems. For the last 10 minutes, I make only fleeting glimpses at the TV, and during one of these, Javi García scores for Benfica. During another, with the away side piling on the pressure and destiny seeming to have left the ground early, Nélson Oliveira steadies himself to score the away goal that will see Benfica progress to the semi-final, but his effort flies wide. The whistles of the crowd that signal that the game is in injury time lure me back to the screen again, just in time to see Raul Meireles break free and hammer home Chelsea's second, decisive goal. They are now one small step closer to the Final.

As small steps go, none could be larger than a two-legged semi-final against Barcelona. It had already been determined that, should they overcome Benfica, Chelsea would be facing the winners of the tie between AC Milan and the reigning European Champions. With the two sides having drawn 0-0 in the first leg in Milan, I was hoping that Chelsea's luck might extend to Milan scoring an unlikely victory in the return. Remarkably, for nine whole minutes, it looked as though they might. In the 32nd minute, Antonio Nocerino cancelled out Lionel Messi's early penalty by scoring the precious away goal that would secure their place in the semi-final. But it was all in vain, and Messi scored another penalty before half-time. Barcelona had proved that to prevent them from scoring more than one goal at home was unthinkable. The Catalans won the game 3-1 to set up a meeting with Chelsea that the Blues will see as the perfect opportunity to exact their revenge for defeat at the same stage of the competition three years ago. The difference is that, this time around, Barcelona are as clear a favourite to win as it is possible to be, whilst Chelsea are still recovering from a state of considerable disarray.

It wouldn't be too much of an exaggeration to say that Barcelona lay siege to Chelsea in the first leg, with the Blues scoring a goal on the break, thanks to the tireless running of Ramires, who crosses for Didier Drogba to wrong-foot Victor Valdés. Chelsea hold on without conceding to complete a smash and grab raid in their own back yard. The 1-0 home win leaves the tie finely balanced, but few could expect the drama that the return leg at Camp Nou would provide. This Barcelona side are regarded by some to be the best team ever to have played the game. If you bear that in mind when considering how poor Chelsea's season has generally been up to this point, then the enormity of their task should become apparent. Just to prevent Barcelona from scoring is difficult enough with a full-strength side, but when Gary Cahill is forced off with a pulled hamstring after only 12 minutes, that task becomes even tougher. That they manage to hold out for 35 minutes is to their credit, but once Sergio Busquets opens the scoring for the home side, it seems that the onslaught will now begin in earnest.

Of all Chelsea's players, you'd have to assume that the captain, John Terry, would've wanted to win the Champions League more than anyone, given the heartache he'd suffered in the competition in years past, so his actions two minutes after Busquets' goal seem difficult to fathom. He appears to blatantly knee Alexis Sánchez in the back of the leg, and the Barca player subsequently collapses as though he's been knocked unconscious. Terry's actions don't go unnoticed by the officials, and the referee has little choice but to send him off.

With Chelsea now playing with 10 men against the world's greatest team, and within six minutes, Barcelona score a second through Andrés Iniesta, odds don't get much more desperate than this. Two minutes later, Ramires is shown a yellow card and the commentator points out that, due to having picked up three bookings in this season's competition, he will now miss the Final, should Chelsea progress. That barely seems relevant in the Blues' current predicament, and limiting Barcelona to five goals or less seems a far more realistic target than to actually score one themselves or get any sort of positive result. But Ramires has other ideas. As half-time beckons, Frank Lampard wins the ball just inside the Barcelona half and Ramires – by this point playing at right back to help bolster Chelsea's depleted defence – makes a darting run forward. Lampard picks him out perfectly and, all of a sudden, the Brazilian is through on goal. He coolly chips the ball over Valdés. Now, with a crucial away goal, the 2-2 aggregate score line means that, as things stand, Chelsea are heading for the Final. They only have to hold out for another 45 minutes. Against a team who have recently put seven goals past one who'd beaten Chelsea just a few months earlier. With 10 players.

They make the worst possible start to the second half, as Didier Drogba is adjudged to have tripped Cesc Fàbregas, just inside the penalty area, giving Lionel Messi, the world's best footballer, the chance to score his first ever goal against Chelsea. As the ball rebounds off the bar with a healthy thwack, it seems that if it hasn't already been happening, something is definitely happening now. There follows 40 plus minutes of defending that is both heroic and desperate, but Barcelona just can't find a way past Petr Čech and his band of merry men. Just as Wayne Bridge had done eight years earlier, Fernando Torres then provides a moment that, in terms of his short Chelsea career, will define him forever. As Ashley Cole wellies the ball clear in the 92nd minute – or should I say picks out an unmarked Torres just inside his own half with a sublime lofted pass – Victor Valdés could be forgiven for being caught cold, having spent the previous 47 minutes with nothing to do. Like the scene in which Omar Sharif appears on the desert horizon and makes his long and languorous entrance in *Lawrence of Arabia*, Torres must seem a mile away to Victor when he begins his run, but within seconds, he is diving at the Chelsea striker's feet in a vain attempt to halt his progress, and then he is watching Torres roll the ball into an empty net.

At last, a game with a proper ending. It is a game like no other, and it has everything. There are twists in abundance, stars who are paid millions, a plot that is inconceivable, yet gripping, a Hollywood aggregate score line, *and* a last gasp goal, scored by a blond hero. My team were underdogs on a massive scale; the brave but depleted troop of Royal Engineers, holed out at Rorke's Drift and besieged by the Zulu masses. But against such overwhelmingly unfavourable odds, the heroes survive and emerge victorious. Football really is a proper entertainment after all. Now I get it.

But this isn't the ending; if only it had been. This is just a teaser before the final act itself. As with all such narratives, there have been the inevitable casualties along the way, and my delight at the result is tempered slightly by my concern that Ivanović and Meireles have played the roles of doomed extras by picking up their third bookings of the competition during the game and, along with Ramires and Terry, will miss the Final. With Gary Cahill now joining David Luiz on the list of the injured, it's looking likely that Chelsea might have to play the Final with only two fully fit and eligible defenders, and without their captain. To add to the pressure, the team's league form has left them lying in sixth place in the Premier League, meaning that winning the Final is now their only chance of qualifying for the Champions League next season. I spend the next few weeks trying to work out what team Di Matteo might choose, and whether we'll have enough players left to put up a fight. This is going to be another Wembley '94.

The following evening, Bayern Munich beat José Mourinho's Real Madrid on penalties to book their own place in the Final, which, ironically, is to be played in their own stadium, the Allianz Arena. If fortune really is on Chelsea's side, it's got a funny way of showing it.

*

On May 5th, 11 days after the semi-final triumph, Chelsea are back at Wembley. In 2002, Di Matteo's Chelsea career was ended by injury and he had been allowed to lead the Chelsea players out for that year's Cup Final as a gesture of recognition and goodwill. He didn't prove lucky on that occasion, but now, 10 years on, he is again leading the team out for a Cup Final, but this time as manager. A 5-1 victory over Tottenham had got them here; a result that I could only have dreamed of prior to kick-off.

Again, they had some luck, with Juan Mata's goal appearing not to have crossed the line, and Petr Čech might've considered himself lucky to have stayed on the pitch after bringing down Emmanuel Adebayor. I watch the Final, hoping that we'll win but inwardly trading defeat to Liverpool this afternoon for some sort of miracle in Munich in a fortnight's time. The game ends 2-1 and, thanks to goals from Ramires and the irrepressible Didier Drogba, this afternoon, Di Matteo has won his first trophy as a manager and Chelsea's fourth FA Cup in six seasons; a feat that had seemed highly unlikely at the turn of the year. Perhaps, as had been the case during the glory years of 1997 to 2000, Di Matteo is once again proving himself to be a living, breathing lucky charm.

The End

"It all comes down to this. One kick of the ball, by Didier Drogba." – Clive Tyldesley, Allianz Arena, Munich, 19th May 2012

As had been written long ago, possibly in the few moments immediately preceding the dawn of time, Didier Drogba makes the long, lonely walk of destiny from the centre circle to the penalty spot. One hundred and twenty minutes couldn't separate the teams, and now, with one kick of a ball, Didier has the opportunity to win the Champions League. For four long years, he has waited for this moment. The goal has never seemed so distant but, like Sisyphus pushing a boulder up a hill for all eternity, he has bought his team this far and now he must break the cycle and fulfil the prophecy. Silence descends. He composes himself, takes three steps back, waits for the whistle, and calmly strokes the ball home. Pandemonium.

Cue 1812 Overture. Roman Abramovich punches the air. It's the perfect climax to an epic film, and this is where I make my entrance. From the opposite end of the stadium, I brush aside one Chelsea fan after another, am briefly knocked off balance by a man wearing nothing but a pair of brown shorts, and regain my composure to launch myself onto the Munich pitch, point my arms to the sky and run, powered by the realisation that, at last, we have won the Champions League.

*

That would have made for a great ending, but it didn't quite happen that way. I was nowhere near Munich on 19th May 2012, although I wish I had been. With that one penalty kick by Didier Drogba, the previous 38 years suddenly made sense. It was meant to happen this way. If they'd been favourites to win the Final, or had even been tipped to win the trophy at any stage of the competition, or even had anywhere near a full-strength team on the night, as an ending, it wouldn't have worked. Drogba's penalty is the denouement to Chelsea's recent story, if not to their history as a whole, and it explains everything; not only why we had to lose in Moscow in 2008 and why Iniesta had to score at the death in 2009, but also why we had to get walloped at Wembley in 1994, and why we had to lose to Scarborough, Scunthorpe, Tranmere, and any number of lower league teams over the years. It had all been leading to this.

Not only was I not in Munich, but I hadn't even watched the match. But the moment I learned the result, there was little doubt in my mind that I could, and should, celebrate with a clear conscience because I contributed to the team's success by not watching them. I'd watched the second leg against Benfica on the TV and Chelsea scraped through against 10 men. I then missed the first leg of the semi-final against Barcelona because we were out with friends, celebrating Vanessa's birthday. Knowing that once I checked the score the first time, I would then need to keep checking throughout the course of the evening, I exercised supreme restraint and refrained from checking the result until we were leaving the restaurant, and I achieved this through a combination of focus and overeating. Chelsea won that night and kept a clean sheet. Having recently overcome my belief that recording a Chelsea match would spell certain doom, I was able to watch the whole game when we got home.

Chelsea were under so much pressure from Barcelona for the majority of the game that I half expected them to finally succumb to fatigue and their opponent's total dominance by conceding during playback. A new superstition was born.

So, that first leg of the semi-final, and my (non) experience of it, handed me the perfect opportunity to avoid the second leg too, whilst, again, not checking the score until the 90 minutes were up. Given how that particular game played out, I had no alternative but to completely avoid the Final as well. As Chelsea's unfeasible run in the competition developed, it was becoming obvious that there was something supernatural at work, and it wasn't just me who thought this; Gary Neville did too. My memories of the season will always be accompanied by his voice, which, whilst working as a commentator for Sky TV, provided so many perfect sound bites during the latter stages of the Blues' Champions League campaign, including; "incredible, absolutely, incredible" as a reaction to Drogba's equaliser in Munich; "OOOOOOOOOOOooooooohhh unbelievable"; his tribute to Mexican commentary and Kate Bush, following Torres' goal in Barcelona and, the most appropriate of all, "*something's happening*", prompted by Chelsea's improbable display against such overwhelmingly unfavourable odds. Something clearly was happening, and I didn't want to be the one who made it stop.

Prior to the Final, I went to ridiculous lengths so as not to cause a single ruffle in the fabric of destiny that had materialised in 2012. The May edition of the *Chelsea FC* magazine remained unmoved for weeks, while every other magazine and newspaper on the magazine chair had been thrown out or filed away. Any Chelsea-related footage I'd recorded on the TV remained untouched while all around it was deleted. Procrastination and laziness took a back seat, as whenever I ignored an empty mug in the bedroom, or the pile of recyclable rubbish that needed taking out, I would stop in my tracks seconds later and go back upstairs for the mug, or back in the house for the rubbish. I did none of this begrudgingly because I knew that, when I did these things, I was doing them for the greater good, because I knew what would happen if I didn't. I was also fully aware that my behaviour was bordering on the insane. Dave Brailsford, head of the British Cycling team, has spoken of the concept of marginal gains; how it's given the cycling team the edge in major competitions and been responsible for the flurry of gold medals in the last two Olympics. It works on the premise that small things – such as always sleeping with the same pillow, washing your hands properly, or wearing kit made from a more streamlined fabric – that alone don't provide a great advantage, when combined, can be the difference between winning and losing. And so it was with the mugs, the rubbish and the *Chelsea FC* magazine. Once the Final was over, the relief at being released from these compulsive shackles was immense and lasted a week, or until we ran out of clean mugs; whichever came sooner.

*

By watching both legs of the semi-final and the Final itself after the event, each game had become the latest quick-fire instalment in an epic footballing trilogy, and the sport itself had at last become an entertainment in the traditional sense of the word.

I have watched the Bayern Munich game more than any other. That might not seem at all surprising, and was helped by my having some time off work to recover from a hernia operation a few days after the match. Chelsea TV replayed the game constantly, and once a day for two weeks, I dutifully watched it from start to finish as I might watch a favourite film, remembering every pass, every tackle, every penalty, until I could replay everything in my mind, exactly as it happened. Though I hadn't watched the game live, I could now bathe in its glory with the confidence of one who knows it has a proper ending and will never let me down. In this picture, the good guys will always win, no matter how outrageous and improbable it might seem. Bayern Munich play in red, but I know it won't matter. When, before kick-off, the camera reveals a huge banner at one end of the stadium that reads "UNSERE STADT, UNSER STADION, UNSER POKAL", which translates as "Our city, our stadium, our cup", I smile wryly at the Bayern fans' ill-informed arrogance. When it's then announced before kick-off that Ryan Bertrand – aged 22, with very few first team appearances to his name, and making his European debut – is in the starting line-up, I'm not anxious at all because I know that he's about to have the game of his life. As Ashley Cole gives away a free kick with a clumsy tackle in the first minute, I stay calm because I know that he won't be booked for it and will hardly put a foot wrong for the rest of the game. When, a minute later, Bastian Schweinsteiger is shown a yellow card for a deliberate handball, I know it's a sign that it just won't be his night. When Franck Ribéry completely misses the ball when attempting a cross and Arjen Robben skies the ball over the bar early on, it means that two of the most feared attacking players in the world won't have the best of nights either. Even as it becomes clear that Chelsea will rarely threaten the Bayern goal and will spend most of the game under constant pressure, I stay in my seat. And when Thomas Müller scores for Bayern in the 82nd minute and the screen cuts to the face of a young Chelsea fan in the crowd, his expression one of anguish and resignation, I can sympathise with him because I've felt the way he does so many times before. But I don't feel that way now because I know that Fernando Torres is about to come on and, with two minutes of normal time remaining, win the corner from which Didier Drogba will head the ball goalwards, and with such power that Manuel Neuer won't have a hope of saving it. In extra-time, as Drogba the hero becomes Drogba the villain by tripping Ribéry in the penalty area, I stay calm, and even feel a tinge of excitement because I know that this is that one well-conceived twist that will make a good story great. When Petr Čech saves the resultant penalty kick from Arjen Robben, the former Chelsea star, I can reflect that, when Chelsea TV's Ben Andrews cries "Kept out by Čech, name on the trophy!", never has a commentator said a truer word. As the penalty shoot-out commences, I am nerveless, even more so when Juan Mata, Chelsea's player of the year, misses Chelsea's first because I know that, before long, Luiz, Lampard and Cole will score for Chelsea and Čech will save from Olić and Schweinsteiger. I also know that Didier Drogba will then provide the perfect ending to a quest that, for Roman Abramovich's Chelsea, has lasted for nine years, but, for me, has lasted a lifetime.

Whilst the game was being played, and Vanessa and I were watching TV programmes about restaurant inspectors and legends of light entertainment, I knew that, at around the time that 90 minutes should be up, someone had scored. I knew this because, through the wall that divides us, I'd heard Kevin shout "Yes!" I waited a few minutes to allow for any injury time at the end of the 90 minutes and I checked my phone to see that the score was 1-1, and that extra-time was being played. I then heard the same cry again about 40 minutes later. It turned out that the first was a reaction to Drogba's equaliser and the second, to his winning penalty. I was completely humbled by this. Whereas I'd openly admitted to wanting Barcelona to beat Manchester United in the finals of both 2009 and 2011, Kevin had wanted Chelsea to lift the trophy and, thankfully, karma hadn't worked against me. But something unseen and miraculous had certainly been at work. If you compare the official pre-match team photos from the Champions League Finals of 2008 and 2012, you'd be forgiven for assuming that the 2008 version had been the one that won the Cup for Chelsea. In that photograph, the players look invincible, determined, and wholly-focused on the job at hand. In the 2012 shot, they look as though they're about to play a friendly against a local pub team. Some players look relaxed, confident even, almost as if they know exactly what's about to happen over the course of the next two-and-a-half hours. Indeed, it seemed obvious that, with everything that had happened during the season – the improbable comebacks, the even more improbable defensive displays, and all the injuries and suspensions the squad had suffered – any other outcome would have made no sense at all. Drogba had been the real villain in 2008. It was he who should've taken the fifth and decisive penalty but who couldn't step forward to do so because he'd been sent off in extra-time, and it was John Terry who had then stepped up to take his place and take the responsibility. Terry had played a major role in the story but it seemed destined that he should stand aside for Didier to rewrite the wrong with what might prove to be the very last kick of his Chelsea career.

Although I hadn't watched the match, I had switched on the TV in the kitchen just in time to see the letter "C" being engraved on the gigantic trophy, and in plenty of time to see the players, and Roberto Di Matteo, climb the steps to lift it. In truth, perhaps that's all I ever wanted; to see them lift the trophy. When I saw Emlyn Hughes hold the European Cup aloft way back in 1977, it was that one moment that I marvelled at, and it was that moment that I would subsequently yearn for. Back then, I'd watched my team win the FA Cup by beating Liverpool 2-1, but four days later, I'd watched someone else's team beat a team from Germany to win the bigger, shinier one. This time, my team had done both. I cried as I watched the players celebrate. There was no shouting from the rooftops or naked runs down the street; just a genuine and semi-stifled outpouring of emotion, prompted both by relief and the enormity of my team's achievement. Vanessa looked confused by my reaction, and a little embarrassed, and I declined to speak to friends who kindly phoned to offer their congratulations because I was stricken by an inability to form words. And then I remembered The Bottle. I walked over to the cupboard within which it had patiently sat for the past few years, took it out, opened it, and poured myself a glass of its mysterious contents. It undoubtedly looked like red wine but it tasted like a sickly combination of wood and battery acid, whereas I'd always assumed that success would taste quite sweet. It seemed that time hadn't been kind to my old friend, which had probably reached the peak of condition in May 2008, when it was first due to be consumed.

*

It was reported that 200,000 fans filled the streets surrounding Stamford Bridge the following day. I'm not sure of the validity of that figure, but I wouldn't be at all surprised. Fulham Road was full to capacity, with each and every man, woman and child there, waiting for a sight of their heroes and a chance to show their appreciation for the players' exertions the previous evening. Vanessa and I managed to get within a couple of hundred yards of the entrance to the ground, but due to the sheer volume of people, we could get no further. This was the same stretch of road upon which 28 years ago, I had been a part of a crowd that had scattered in fear for its safety, and on that day, a part of my life was to take a surprising diversion. But on this, the circumstances were very different; this was the moment that truly made sense of those intervening years. As the double-decker emerged to a tidal roar, I finally caught a glimpse of that famous trophy, its big ears twinkling in the sunlight. We were so far away that I couldn't tell which player was holding the cup aloft. It could've been be Luiz, it could've been Terry or it could've been Drogba. But then it might just as well have been Nevin, Wise or Gronkjaer, or even Stokes, Sunderland or Greenhoff. In their own way, they had all been a part of the story.

Epilogue

Obviously, if in the summer of 2003, Roman Abramovich hadn't made the decision to invest in a football club, I might have lived out my days having never seen Chelsea win the Champions League. His appearance had been the biggest piece of luck I could ever have hoped for. I spent the few weeks following the Final purchasing various bits of commemorative memorabilia, including an inflatable European Cup, a replica shirt with the gold star on it (to indicate that the Club had won the Champions League), a t-shirt sporting the legend "Your City, Your Stadium, Our Cup", a pair of official CFC deely-boppers (for my niece), and as many magazines as I could find. I even bought four copies of the official match programme, perhaps in the hope that my memory might one day fail me to the extent that I might find one of them in a dusty box in the attic and assume that I had actually been there. I immersed myself in news of Chelsea's proposed move to Battersea Power Station, and the impending transfers of exciting, young players such as Eden Hazard and Oscar. Then it dawned on me that it could never really get any better than this. I'd got everything I ever wanted from the game and I now had a renewed sense of perspective. This much became especially clear to me that summer, as I watched every minute of England's European Championship campaign without feeling at all nervous, and without flinching once. I had the will for them to do well but without the usual naïve expectation that they were actually good enough to win the competition. Whilst those around me dived for cover, I sat through the team's penalty shoot-out with Italy from start to finish and, when the predictable occurred and we were knocked out, rather than suffering the usual disappointment, I felt glad that at least we'd reached the quarter-final.

Three weeks later came the moment the nation had been waiting for since July 2005. It is generally accepted, in Great Britain at least, that the London Olympic and Paralympic Games were a great success, and I for one couldn't agree more. The Games absorbed me like no other event ever has. Obviously, it helped that Great Britain (I still can't get used to the name "Team GB") were phenomenally successful and that I was lucky enough to get tickets for several events over the course of both the Olympics and Paralympics. For two whole months, it seemed as though my phone had no other function but to feed me with the results of the wheelchair tennis, team dressage, boccia, 100-metre butterfly, or whichever event was reaching a conclusion at that time, and to then share and discuss this information via text or email. My tears on the night of May 19th had from then on prompted me to well up upon any occasion deemed worthy, and in particular, at the sound of the national anthem when played in honour of a gold medal for Great Britain, and as such, I must have cried at least once a day.

The Paralympics were even more exhilarating, with the hardships overcome by the athletes adding a dimension to the Games that made me well up more frequently. It seemed that whichever event you watched, and for every athlete, there was a story to be told that could humble and inspire. I ended the summer an emotional wreck. Every sport was fantastic. Every sport that is, but football. The women's games were skilful, entertaining, and the honest desire of the players shone through, but watching the men's competition just left me cold. It didn't inhabit the same universe as all the other events and, as such, it didn't belong. It suddenly became apparent to me that football had become the bloated, farting big brother of world sport, although I'd refuted such accusations for years whenever I heard anyone say that footballers were overpaid and that rugby was a far superior game, which was often. This revelation, and the timing of the Olympic Games themselves, tied in neatly with Chelsea winning the Champions League, as if the planets had aligned to draw a line under my obsession with football once and for all. It really couldn't get any better; Chelsea were the champions of Europe, my inflatable Champions League trophy was fully inflated, and The Bottle was empty at last. This was the perfect ending to a lifelong quest and now I could get on with my life, safe in the knowledge that I would no longer care about Chelsea's results because now I was following Ed McKeever and Shanaze Reade on Twitter, and that was the future.

By mid-August, the new Premier League season had begun but I hardly noticed. I'd already determined that I'd be watching cycling, table tennis, handball, canoe slalom, or any other Olympic sport in preference. But as the year progressed, it soon became obvious that all those sports were losing the battle for screen and airtime and that football, as ever, dominated the schedules. Roberto Di Matteo had been given the manager's job on a two-year contract, Juan Mata had struck up an exciting partnership with the Belgian prodigy, Eden Hazard, the young Brazilian, Oscar, scored a spectacular 25-yarder on his Blues debut against Juventus, and before long, I was drawn back in, just in time to see Chelsea lose 3-2 at home to Manchester United. Within a month, Di Matteo had been sacked and replaced, on a short-term contract, by former Liverpool manager and Blues' nemesis, Rafael Benítez; a decision that was met with derision by the majority of Chelsea supporters, due in large part to Benitez's reported comments about Chelsea and their fans in 2007, whilst manager of Liverpool.

✶

In February 2013, I went to Wembley with Kevin to see England play Brazil. It was the first time I'd been to an England match and, to my surprise, they played well, beating the Brazilians 2-1, with Frank Lampard scoring the winning goal. I then watched them play a World Cup qualifier against Montenegro, with a renewed belief that maybe they were actually good enough to win the trophy this time, but despite Rooney scoring to put them 1-0 up in the first half, in which they looked comfortable, it all went wrong after the break, and they were lucky to escape with a 1-1 draw, and disappointment gave way to resignation once more.

On the morning of Wednesday, May 8th 2013, I was having breakfast in a McDonald's car park in Watford as TalkSport presenter, Alan Brazil, made the announcement that I'd started to think I would never hear. After nearly 27 years in charge, and having just won his 13th Premier League title, Sir Alex Ferguson was to stand down as manager of Manchester United. All across the land, fans paid tribute to a man who had won a staggering 38 trophies for his club, whilst secretly wringing their hands with glee at the prospect that, at last, their team might be in with a chance of winning something, now that the great man was gone. After all that time, it was difficult to imagine a Manchester United without Ferguson at the helm. During his tenure, the Club had become a model of stability.

In contrast, when a week later, Chelsea won the Europa League trophy (a game that I actually watched this time), they had done so under the guidance of their eighth manager in nine years. The policy of manager rotation, whether intentional or not, has been widely criticised, but it's hard to deny that, for a Chelsea fan, it has kept things interesting and, above all, it's hard to argue that it hasn't proved successful. In those nine years, Chelsea won 11 major trophies. It was best to think of it, not as though another manager was leaving, but more like a *Doctor Who*-style regeneration: the same manager, but with a different face. Of course, everyone has their favourite *Doctor*, just like every football fan has their favourite former manager. Although some might hope that Tom Baker will one day return to take the role, they know that, realistically, it's never going to happen. The rules don't allow for that. Under Rafa Benitez, Chelsea won their 11th trophy of the Abramovich era, and, in the process, he helped the Club to make another bit of history by becoming the first to hold both European trophies simultaneously. But, for all his past indiscretions, Benitez was never likely to be completely forgiven by the fans, who already knew who they wanted to replace him. They hoped, and I hoped too; and then, as if by magic, The Special One appeared...

Lightning Source UK Ltd.
Milton Keynes UK
UKOW04f0335241115

263367UK00001B/3/P